TV Shows That Teach

100 TV Moments to Get Teenagers Talking

Eddie James and Tommy Woodard
The Skit Guys

ZONDERVAN®

ZONDERVAN.com/
AUTHORTRACKER
follow your favorite authors

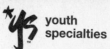
youth specialties

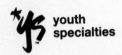
youth specialties

TV Shows That Teach: 100 TV Moments to Get Teenagers Talking
Copyright 2008 by Eddie James and Tommy Woodard

Youth Specialties resources, 300 S. Pierce St., El Cajon, CA 92020 are published by
Zondervan, 5300 Patterson Ave. SE, Grand Rapids, MI 49530.

ISBN-10: 0-310-27365-x
ISBN-13: 978-0-310-27365-3

Cover design by SharpSeven Design
Interior design by David Conn

Printed in the United States of America

08 09 10 11 12 13 • 20 19 18 17 16 15 14 13 12 11 10 9 8 7 6 5 4 3 2

ACKNOWLEDGMENTS

Dedicated to Stephanie James and Angie Woodard, our incredible wives who put up with us hogging the TiVo while we worked on this book.

Special thanks to:
Christi Nalor, Charissa Fishbeck, and Simri Davis.

Cannot forget:
Roni Meek, Jay Howver, and "Urb."
Thanks for making two Skit Guys' dreams come true.

TO THE BUYER OF THIS BOOK:

We've tried to choose TV clips that are downloadable from places such as iTunes, Wal-Mart.com, Amazon.com, and NBC.com—this way you have the fastest, easiest access to the clips as you put together your program. The point being: *There are many "access roads" to these clips aside from renting DVDs or taping programs as they air on TV—use them!*

And have fun with these clips! We sure did.
(Okay, our TiVos need us now...)

Tommy and Eddie
The Skit Guys

Contents

QUICK CLIP LOCATOR—BY TOPIC 6

QUICK CLIP LOCATOR—BY BIBLE REFERENCE 12

THE REASON FOR THIS BOOK 18

How to Use This Book *20* • New Ideas *20* • The Gospel According to Earl *20* • iTunes, Blockbuster, and Best Buy—Oh My! *20* • I Thought You Guys Did Skits…? *21* • Were You Desperate Enough to Use *Desperate Housewives?* *22* • Stuff You May Already Know *23* • What You'll Find in Each Clip Study *24* • By the Way…We Can't Count! *26*

THE TV SHOW CLIP STUDIES (IN ALPHABETICAL ORDER)................27

8 Simple Rules...28

30 Days 40

Alias...52

Desperate Housewives..60

Everybody Loves Raymond...72

Extreme Makeover: Home Edition...82

Frasier 92

Friends..102

Gilmore Girls 112

Grey's Anatomy 120

Heroes 130

Home Improvement...140

House 150

Lost 160

My Name Is Earl..168

The Office 178

Saturday Night Live...188

Seinfeld 202

The Simpsons 212

Survivor: The Australian Outback...222

Ugly Betty 230

Quick Clip Locator by Topic

The 23rd Psalm Lost..........*166*

Abandonment Grey's Anatomy..........*128*

"Abba" Extreme Makeover: Home Edition..........*90*

Abilities Desperate Housewives, Friends, Heroes..........*70, 110, (134, 136)*

Abstinence Desperate Housewives, Gilmore Girls..........*66, 114*

Abundant Life House..........*154*

Abuse Saturday Night Live..........*192*

Abuse of Authority The Office..........*178*

Acceptance Desperate Housewives, The Office, Saturday Night Live..........*66, 182, 188*

Accidents Grey's Anatomy, Survivor: The Australian Outback..........*126, 228*

Achievements Frasier..........*100*

Acting Out for Attention Ugly Betty..........*238*

Addiction 30 Days..........*40*

Admiration My Name Is Earl..........*170*

Adversity Grey's Anatomy, House, Survivor: The Australian Outback..........*124, 152, 222*

Affirmation from Fathers 8 Simple Rules..........*36*

Aging Ugly Betty..........*236*

Alcoholism 30 Days..........*40*

Ambition My Name Is Earl..........*168*

Anger Heroes, The Simpsons..........*130, 214*

Apologizing 30 Days, Everybody Loves Raymond, Friends, Grey's Anatomy, House, My Name Is Earl, Survivor: The Australian Outback..........*44, 72, 108, 126, 156, 174, 224*

Appearance Saturday Night Live, Ugly Betty..........*188, 232*

Apprehension Survivor: The Australian Outback..........*226*

Arguing 8 Simple Rules, 30 Days, Everybody

Loves Raymond, Friends..........*38, 44, (76, 78), 108*

Athletes Grey's Anatomy..........*124*

Attitude Frasier, Friends, The Simpsons..........*96, 104, 214*

Attraction The Office..........*180*

Avoidance The Office, Saturday Night Live..........*178, 196*

Awareness Alias..........*58*

Bearing Others' Burdens Heroes, House..........*138, 150*

Beauty 8 Simple Rules, Ugly Betty..........*36, 236*

Behavior 8 Simple Rules, Gilmore Girls..........*32, 114*

Being Different My Name Is Earl..........*174*

Being Sensitive to Needs Heroes..........*138*

Beliefs 30 Days..........*30*

Bitterness Friends, Lost..........*108, 162*

Blaming Others Everybody Loves Raymond, The Office, The Simpsons..........*76, (178, 186), 216*

Blasphemy My Name Is Earl..........*172*

Blessings Extreme Makeover: Home Edition..........*88*

Body Image Saturday Night Live, Ugly Betty..........*188, 236*

Boundary Lines Desperate Housewives..........*60*

Bullying Frasier, Home Improvement..........*94, 146*

Caring for Others House..........*150*

Carpe Diem Frasier, House, My Name Is Earl..........*100, 154, 176*

Challenges Survivor: The Australian Outback..........*226*

Character Ugly Betty..........*232*

Chauvinism/Feminism Home Improvement..........*144*

Choices 8 Simple Rules, Desperate Housewives, Friends, Grey's Anatomy, Lost, My Name Is Earl, Saturday Night Live, Seinfeld..........*32, 62, 102, 124, (160, 166), 168, 194, (204, 210)*

College Gilmore Girls..........*114*

Communication 8 Simple Rules, 30 Days, Alias, Frasier, Home Improvement, The Simpsons, Ugly Betty..........*36, 44, (54, 56), 92, 140, 212, 238*

Community Extreme Makeover: Home Edition..........*84*

Comparisons Desperate Housewives, Ugly Betty..........*70, 236*

Compassion Alias, House, Survivor: The Australian Outback..........*58, 150, 228*

Compatibility Saturday Night Live..........*198*

Competition Desperate Housewives, My Name Is Earl..........*70, 170*

Condemnation 30 Days, Lost, Survivor: The Australian Outback..........*(44, 50), 166, 224*

Confession Desperate Housewives, Home Improvement, Lost..........*64, 142, 164*

Confidence Saturday Night Live, Seinfeld..........*188, 208*

Confrontation Grey's Anatomy, House, Lost, Seinfeld, Survivor: The Australian Outback..........*128, 156, 160, 204, 224*

Conquering Fear My Name Is Earl, Survivor: The Australian Outback..........*176, 226*

Consequences 8 Simple Rules, Grey's Anatomy, Home Improvement, Saturday Night Live..........*(30, 38), 126, 142, 194*

Courage House, Lost, The Office..........*152, 160, 180*

Crisis Friends..........*104*

Crossing the Line The Office..........*182*

Cruelty The Office..........*182*

Danger Saturday Night Live..........*194*

Dating Gilmore Girls, Home Improvement, The Office, Saturday Night Live..........*114, (140, 144), 180, 198*

Dealing with the Past 8 Simple Rules, Everybody Loves Raymond, Heroes, Lost,

My Name Is Earl, Seinfeld..........*32, 78, 130, 164, 174, 206*

Death Alias, Extreme Makeover: Home Edition, Frasier, Grey's Anatomy, House..........*58, 82, 100, 120, (150, 152, 154)*

Debt 8 Simple Rules..........*28*

Deception Alias, Heroes, My Name Is Earl, Ugly Betty..........*(52, 56), 136, 172, 234*

Decision Making Seinfeld..........*210*

Defeat My Name Is Earl..........*170*

Denial The Office..........*184*

Dependence Ugly Betty..........*230*

Depression Seinfeld..........*204*

Destruction Survivor: The Australian Outback..........*222*

Determination My Name Is Earl..........*170*

Disappointment Grey's Anatomy, Seinfeld..........*124, 204*

Discernment Friends, Heroes..........*108, 138*

Discipline 8 Simple Rules, 30 Days..........*(30, 38), 40*

Divorce Desperate Housewives, Frasier, Grey's Anatomy..........*60, 98, 128*

Does God Make People Sick? House..........*158*

Doing What You "Feel" The Simpsons..........*216*

Doubt Seinfeld..........*200*

Dreams Extreme Makeover: Home Edition, Gilmore Girls, Grey's Anatomy, Heroes, House, My Name Is Earl..........*88, 112, 124, 132, 154, 176*

Drugs and Alcohol Saturday Night Live..........*194, 196*

Duty Heroes, Seinfeld, The Simpsons..........*134, 204, 216*

Eating Saturday Night Live..........*200*

Education Home Improvement, My Name Is Earl..........*148, 168*

Ego The Office..........*186*

Embarrassment Frasier, Ugly Betty..........*94, 232*

Emotions Heroes..........*130*
Empathy Friends..........*110*
Encouragement Seinfeld..........*208*
Entitlement Gilmore Girls..........*116*
Equality Home Improvement..........*144*
Excuses 8 Simple Rules..........*32*
Expectations Everybody Loves Raymond, Saturday Night Live..........*72, 192*
Exploitation Ugly Betty..........*234*
Faith Alias, Extreme Makeover: Home Edition, Frasier, Lost..........*52, 88, 100, 162*
Faith Healers House..........*158*
False Accusations Survivor: The Australian Outback..........*224*
Family Alias, Everybody Loves Raymond, Extreme Makeover: Home Edition, The Simpsons, Ugly Betty..........*56, 76, 90, 212, 230*
Father-Daughter Relationships 8 Simple Rules, Alias..........*36, 54*
Father's Love Extreme Makeover: Home Edition, Grey's Anatomy..........*90, 128*
Favoritism Gilmore Girls..........*116*
Fear Alias, Friends, Lost, Saturday Night Live, Seinfeld..........*58, 104, 166, 192, 206*
Fighting Home Improvement..........*146*
First Impressions Ugly Betty..........*232*
Following the Crowd The Simpsons..........*220*
Food Saturday Night Live..........*200*
Forgiveness Alias, Extreme Makeover: Home Edition, Grey's Anatomy, House, Lost, My Name Is Earl, Survivor: The Australian Outback..........*54, 90, 126, 156, 164, 174, 224*
Friendship Desperate Housewives, Friends, Grey's Anatomy, Heroes, Seinfeld..........*64, 106, 120, 136, 202*
the Future Everybody Loves Raymond, Frasier, My Name Is Earl..........*78, 98, 168*
Generational Sin Ugly Betty..........*230*
Generosity 30 Days, Extreme Makeover: Home Edition..........*42, 84*
Giving Extreme Makeover: Home Edition, The Office, The Simpsons..........*84, 186, 218*
Giving to the Poor 30 Days, Seinfeld..........*42, 202*
Gluttony Saturday Night Live..........*200*
Goals Gilmore Girls, Grey's Anatomy..........*112, 122*
God Everybody Loves Raymond, My Name Is Earl..........*74, 172*
God's Word Desperate Housewives, Heroes..........*62, 134*
Good Versus Evil Alias..........*52*
Gossip Gilmore Girls..........*118*
Grace 8 Simple Rules, Extreme Makeover: Home Edition..........*30, 88*
Greed Friends, Gilmore Girls, Saturday Night Live..........*106, 116, 190*
Grief Extreme Makeover: Home Edition..........*82*
Growing Up Everybody Loves Raymond, Home Improvement..........*80, 140*
Guilt 8 Simple Rules, Desperate Housewives, Grey's Anatomy, Lost..........*38, 62, 126, (162, 164)*
Handling Problems 8 Simple Rules, Desperate Housewives, Friends, Home Improvement..........*28, 62, 104, 146*
Hard Heart House..........*156*
Healing Saturday Night Live..........*196*
Heavenly Father 8 Simple Rules, Extreme Makeover: Home Edition..........*36, 90*
Helping Seinfeld..........*206*
Heroes The Office..........*184*
Homosexuality 30 Days..........*48, 50*
Hope Heroes..........*132*
Human Dignity House..........*150*
Humanity Grey's Anatomy..........*120*
Human Nature Heroes..........*132*
Humiliation Frasier, Home Improvement, The Office, Ugly Betty..........*94, 146, 182, 234*
Humility The Office..........*186*
Hurt Alias, Desperate Housewives, My Name Is Earl..........*(54, 58), 64, 174*
Hurt Feelings Everybody Loves Raymond,

Frasier, Friends..........*78, 94, 108*

Hurtful Words 8 Simple Rules, Everybody Loves Raymond, Frasier, My Name Is Earl..........*38, 72, 96, (174, 176)*

Hypocrisy 8 Simple Rules, Alias..........*32, 52*

Identity Gilmore Girls, Grey's Anatomy, Ugly Betty..........*112, 122, 236*

Image Desperate Housewives, Frasier, Friends..........*64, 94, 106*

Immorality Gilmore Girls..........*114*

Impulsive Actions Seinfeld..........*210*

Infatuation The Office..........*180*

Infidelity Friends..........*102*

Insecurity Desperate Housewives, Friends, My Name Is Earl..........*70, 110, 176*

Integrity Friends..........*102*

Intentions Frasier..........*92*

Interpreting the Bible 30 Days..........*48, 50*

Jealousy Everybody Loves Raymond, Grey's Anatomy..........*78, 122*

Job Interviews Everybody Loves Raymond..........*80*

Judging Others Friends, Saturday Night Live, Survivor: The Australian Outback, Ugly Betty..........*110, 188, 224, 232*

Kindness The Simpsons..........*218*

Leadership My Name Is Earl, The Office..........*170, 178*

Legacy Extreme Makeover: Home Edition, Frasier, The Office, Ugly Betty..........*84, 100, 184, 230*

Letting Go 8 Simple Rules, Alias, Desperate Housewives, Everybody Loves Raymond..........*38, 54, 70, (78, 80)*

Lies Alias, Gilmore Girls, Heroes, Home Improvement, Ugly Betty..........*56, 118, 136, 142, 234*

Lifestyle 30 Days, Saturday Night Live..........*48, 190*

Living Differently Seinfeld..........*202*

Loss Grey's Anatomy, Survivor: The Australian Outback..........*126, 222*

Love Desperate Housewives, The Office, Ugly Betty..........*66, 180, 234*

Loving Others The Simpsons..........*218*

Lust Gilmore Girls, The Office..........*114, 180*

Making a Difference Heroes..........*132*

Manhood Home Improvement..........*140*

Manipulation Frasier..........*98*

Marriage Frasier, Friends, The Simpsons..........*98, 102, 212*

Maturity Desperate Housewives..........*60*

the Meaning of Life Everybody Loves Raymond, Heroes..........*74, 132*

Memories Everybody Loves Raymond, My Name Is Earl..........*78, 174*

Mercy Lost..........*160*

Minding Your Own Business Everybody Loves Raymond, Gilmore Girls..........*80, 118*

Miracles House, Lost..........*158, 162*

Missed Opportunity House..........*154*

Mistakes 8 Simple Rules, Desperate Housewives, Seinfeld.......... *32, 62, (206, 210)*

Misunderstanding Frasier, The Office..........*92, 182*

Money 8 Simple Rules, 30 Days, Friends, Gilmore Girls, Home Improvement, Saturday Night Live..........*28, 42, 106, 116, 148, 190*

Moral Compass 30 Days, Desperate Housewives..........*50, 62*

Morals 8 Simple Rules..........*30*

Motivation Grey's Anatomy, My Name Is Earl..........*122, 168*

Nagging The Simpsons..........*214*

Natural Disaster Survivor: The Australian Outback..........*222*

Neediness The Office..........*184*

Negativity Frasier, The Simpsons..........*96, 214*

Opinions 30 Days, Frasier, Friends..........*48, 96, 108*

Overprotecting 8 Simple Rules, Everybody Loves Raymond..........*38, 80*

Pain Grey's Anatomy, Survivor: The Australian Outback..........*126, 228*

Partying 8 Simple Rules, 30 Days..........*32, 40*

Parent-Child Relationships 8 Simple Rules, Desperate Housewives, Everybody Loves Raymond, Grey's Anatomy..........*28, (60, 66), 72, 128*

Parenting 8 Simple Rules, Desperate Housewives, Frasier, Saturday Night Live, Ugly Betty..........*30, (62, 64), 98, 190, 238*

Parents Alias, Everybody Loves Raymond..........*56, 80*

Peer Influence Seinfeld, Survivor: The Australian Outback..........*202, 226*

Peer Pressure Home Improvement..........*140, 146*

People Pleasing Frasier, The Office..........*92, 178*

Perceptions The Office, Saturday Night Live..........*184, 194*

Permissive Parenting 30 Days..........*40*

Perseverance Survivor: The Australian Outback..........*222*

Personality Traits Friends, My Name Is Earl..........*110, 168*

Plans Frasier, Gilmore Girls, Grey's Anatomy, Seinfeld..........*100, 112, (122, 124), 210*

Power Heroes, My Name Is Earl..........*134, 172*

Practical Jokes The Office..........*182*

Prayer Lost, Survivor: The Australian Outback..........*164, 228*

Prejudice 30 Days, Friends..........*(44, 50), 110*

Pressure Desperate Housewives, Friends..........*64, 104*

Priorities Home Improvement..........*148*

Promises Lost..........*162*

Purpose Everybody Loves Raymond, Frasier, Gilmore Girls, Heroes, My Name Is Earl..........*74, 100, 112, (132, 136), 168*

Questions Everybody Loves Raymond, Heroes..........*74, 132*

Quick Fix Saturday Night Live..........*196*

Quiting Gilmore Girls..........*112*

Rage Heroes..........*130*

Reaching Out Extreme Makeover: Home Edition..........*84, 88*

Reality TV Saturday Night Live..........*192*

Realizations My Name Is Earl..........*168*

Rebellion 30 Days..........*40*

Receiving Correction The Simpsons..........*214*

Redemption Grey's Anatomy, Lost..........*126, 164*

Regrets 8 Simple Rules, House, Lost, My Name Is Earl, Seinfeld..........*154, 164, 166, 168, 210*

Rejection Everybody Loves Raymond, The Office, Seinfeld..........*78, 180, 202*

Relationships Everybody Loves Raymond, Frasier, Gilmore Girls, Home Improvement, The Office, Saturday Night Live..........*78, 96, 114, 144, 184, 198*

Resentment Friends..........*108*

Respect 8 Simple Rules, Desperate Housewives, Frasier, My Name Is Earl, The Office, Survivor: The Australian Outback..........*38, 60, 94, 170, (178, 182, 184), 226*

Responsibility 8 Simple Rules, Home Improvement, Seinfeld, The Simpsons..........*28, (142, 148), (204, 208), 216*

Revenge My Name Is Earl..........*172*

Risk My Name Is Earl, The Office, Survivor: The Australian Outback..........*176, 180, 222*

Role Models 8 Simple Rules, The Office, The Simpsons..........*32, 184, 220*

Roles Desperate Housewives, Home Improvement..........*60, 144*

Sacrifice Extreme Makeover: Home Edition, Grey's Anatomy, Lost..........*90, 120, 160*

Salvation House..........*152*

Sarcasm Friends..........*104*

Saving a Life Grey's Anatomy, Lost..........*120, 160*

Second Chances Extreme Makeover: Home Edition, My Name Is Earl..........*88, 176*

Secrets 8 Simple Rules, Alias, Desperate Housewives, Gilmore Girls, Lost..........*28, (52, 56), 64, 118, 164*

Self-Centered Saturday Night Live..........*198*

Self-Control Heroes, The Simpsons..........*130, 212*

Self-Esteem 8 Simple Rules, Grey's Anatomy, The Office, Saturday Night Live, Ugly Betty..........*36, 128, 186, 188, 236*

Selfishness Desperate Housewives, Friends, House, Saturday Night Live, The Simpsons, Ugly Betty..........*60, 106, 156, 190, 216, 238*

Selflessness Extreme Makeover: Home Edition, Grey's Anatomy, The Simpsons..........*82, 120, 218*

Serving Seinfeld..........*206*

Sex Desperate Housewives, Gilmore Girls, Home Improvement..........*66, 114, 140*

Shame Grey's Anatomy..........*128*

Shirking Responsibility The Office *178*

Sickness Saturday Night Live..........*196*

Significance The Office..........*186*

Sin 30 Days, Alias, Desperate Housewives, Lost, Saturday Night Live..........*48, 52, 62, 166, 194*

Social Status Gilmore Girls..........*116*

Soul Alias, Heroes..........*52, 132*

Spiritual Gifts Heroes..........*136*

Sports Everybody Loves Raymond, Grey's Anatomy..........*72, 124*

Starting Over Extreme Makeover: Home Edition..........*82*

Status Quo The Simpsons..........*220*

Stereotypes 30 Days, The Simpsons..........*44, 220*

Stress Desperate Housewives, Everybody Loves Raymond, The Simpsons..........*64, 76, 214*

Suffering Alias..........*58*

Support Seinfeld..........*208*

Taking Action Grey's Anatomy, Heroes, The Simpsons..........*122, 138, 220*

Taking Care of Each Other Ugly Betty..........*230*

Taking Care of Your Body Saturday Night Live..........*200*

Teasing Home Improvement..........*146*

Temptation Friends, Gilmore Girls, Saturday Night Live..........*102, 114, 194*

Terminal Illness Alias, House..........*58, (150, 152)*

Thankfulness Extreme Makeover: Home Edition..........*84*

Tolerance 30 Days..........*48*

Tragedy Extreme Makeover: Home Edition..........*82*

Trials Lost, Survivor: The Australian Outback..........*166, (222, 228)*

Trust Alias, Friends, Gilmore Girls, Home Improvement..........*52, 118, 102, 142*

Trusting in Conventional Medicine House..........*158*

Turmoil Desperate Housewives..........*64*

Unconditional Love 8 Simple Rules..........*30*

Understanding Others 30 Days, Alias, Heroes, My Name Is Earl..........*44, 54, 138, 174*

Unity The Office..........*186*

Using People The Simpsons, Ugly Betty..........*218, 234*

Values Desperate Housewives, Ugly Betty..........*66, 238*

Virginity Desperate Housewives..........*66*

Vows Friends..........*102*

Wants Versus Needs 30 Days, Frasier..........*42, 98*

Why We're Here Everybody Loves Raymond..........*74*

Working Home Improvement..........*148*

Worry 8 Simple Rules, Friends, Survivor: The Australian Outback..........*38, 104, 222*

Worth 8 Simple Rules, Friends, The Office..........*28, 106, 186*

Yelling Everybody Loves Raymond..........*76*

Quick Clip Locator by Bible Reference

GENESIS
6:6-7......................Seinfeld *210*
7:19.....Survivor: The Australian Outback *222*
25:29-39.......................Seinfeld *210*
27:32-24.......................Seinfeld *210*

EXODUS
2:11-15...........................8 Simple Rules *28*
9:16..............Everybody Loves Raymond *74*
20:12.................30 Days, Ugly Betty *40, 238*
20:17.................................30 Days *42*
23:2............................... The Simpsons *220*

LEVITICUS
18:22......................................30 Days *48, 50*
19:13........................... My Name Is Earl *170*
20:13......................................30 Days *48, 50*
20:26.......................... My Name Is Earl *174*

DEUTERONOMY
4:31............................... Grey's Anatomy *128*
5:16..Ugly Betty *230*
8:5.. 8 Simple Rules *30*
18:22.......................... My Name Is Earl *172*

JOSHUA
1:8.............................Frasier *100*
1:9............................... My Name Is Earl *176*

1 SAMUEL
16:7................. Friends, Saturday Night Live,
Ugly Betty *110, 188, 232*

1 KINGS
11:11............................. The Simpsons *214*

2 CHRONICLES
7:14...30 Days *44*
9:1-8 ....Frasier *100*

ESTHER
4:16...Lost *160*

JOB
4:8...................... Desperate Housewives *70*
5:17.............................. 8 Simple Rules *30*
5:18.......................................House
158
7:11............................. The Simpsons *214*
8:9............................. My Name Is Earl *168*
18:11..................... Saturday Night Live *192*
37:5....................... My Name Is Earl *172*

PSALMS
4:3............................. My Name Is Earl *174*
10:14........Extreme Makeover: Home Edition,
Grey's Anatomy *82, 126*
12:2...Ugly Betty
234
19:14....................... 8 Simple Rules, Frasier,
Gilmore Girls,
The Simpsons *38, 96, 118, 212*
20:4............................ Grey's Anatomy *124*
23............. Extreme Makeover: Home Edition,
Lost *82, 166*
27:14.......................Survivor: The Australian
Outback *226*
29:2-11 .... My Name Is Earl *172*
30:2...House *158*
30:5........................... Grey's Anatomy *126*
32:5..Lost *164*
34:13...........................Frasier, Gilmore Girls,
Home Improvement,
Survivor: The Australian Outback,
Ugly Betty *92, 118, 142, 224, 234*
34:18............................ Grey's Anatomy *126*
37:4............................ Grey's Anatomy *124*
37:21................................. 8 Simple Rules *28*
42:5...Seinfeld *204*
49:3.............Everybody Loves Raymond *72*
55:21............................ The Simpsons *212*
61:7............Everybody Loves Raymond *80*
68:5...Alias *54*
73:26.................. Desperate Housewives *64*
88:18....................................Seinfeld *202*

89:50-51 ....Frasier *94*
103:1-5 .... My Name Is Earl *172*
106:4.....................................Ugly Betty *228*
107:28-31 ....Ugly Betty *228*
111:10................... Saturday Night Live *192*
118:25...Frasier *100*
119:36... The Office, The Simpsons *186, 216*
119:50...Lost *162*
127:3......................................Ugly Betty *230*
139:13-16 .....Everybody Loves Raymond *74*
139:14....................................Ugly Betty *236*
140:1-3 .... My Name Is Earl *174*
147:3...House *158*

PROVERBS
3:5-6 ....Alias *56*
3:5-7 ....Alias *52*
3:12................................ 8 Simple Rules *30*
4:23.......................................Ugly Betty *232*
4:24............ Friends, Survivor: The Australian
Outback *104, 224*
4:26......................Home Improvement *148*
5:22..................... Saturday Night Live *194*
10:16......................... My Name Is Earl *170*
11:2.................................... The Office *186*
11:4.... Survivor: The Australian Outback *223*
11:29.......................................Ugly Betty *230*
12:17.......................Survivor: The Australian
Outback *224*
13:2...Frasier *94*
14:8...Frasier *98*
14:22............Everybody Loves Raymond *80*
14:30............Everybody Loves Raymond *78*
15:13......................................Ugly Betty *232*
15:16..................... Saturday Night Live *190*
15:18...................................Friends *108*
15:21....................... The Simpsons *212*
15:26..Heroes *138*
16:9................Everybody Loves Raymond *80*
17:9...Seinfeld *202*
17:17..............................Seinfeld *202, 208*
18:1................................ The Simpsons *218*
19:21............................. Gilmore Girls *112*
20:1...30 Days *40*
20:19............................. Gilmore Girls *118*
20:25....................................Seinfeld *210*
21:9............................. The Simpsons *214*
22:6..... 30 Days, Everybody Loves Raymond,

Frasier *40, 80, 98*
23:2........................Saturday Night Live *200*
23:4-5 .... Saturday Night Live *190*
23:12....................Home Improvement *148*
23:19............................ Grey's Anatomy *122*
23:20.................... Saturday Night Live *200*
23:29-35 .... Saturday Night *194*
25:15........................... The Simpsons *212*
27:1...House *154*
27:6...Friends *108*
27:10.......................................Seinfeld *202*
27:17.......................................Friends *102*
28:1.................... Saturday Night Live *192*
28:11............................... Gilmore Girls *116*
28:14...House *156*
29:25.......Alias, Saturday Night Live *58, 192*
31:10................................Ugly Betty *236*
31:30....8 Simple Rules, Saturday Night Live,
Ugly Betty *36, 188, 236*

ECCLESIASTES
1:18..Alias *52*
5:2....................................8 Simple Rules *38*
6:12............................. My Name Is Earl *168*
7:26.......................................Ugly Betty *234*

ISAIAH
32:5............................... The Office *182*
40:25-26 ....Everybody Loves Raymond *74*
41:10..........Alias, My Name Is Earl, Survivor:
The Australian Outback *58, 176, 226*
43:7................................. Gilmore Girls *112*
43:18-19 ....Everybody Loves Raymond *78*
53:5...House *158*
54:4..................... My Name Is Earl *176*
55:8-9 ....Heroes *138*
55:9...Lost *162*

JEREMIAH
29:11-13 .... Gilmore Girls *112*
32:18....................................Ugly Betty *230*

LAMENTATIONS
3:18...Seinfeld *204*

EZEKIEL
16:44....................................Ugly Betty *238*

MICAH
7:6...Ugly Betty *238*

HAGGAI
1:9..........................Saturday Night Live *198*

MALACHI
2:16.............................. Grey's Anatomy *128*
4:6.................. Alias, Grey's Anatomy *54, 128*

MATTHEW
5:23-24.........................Frasier, Lost *92, 164*
5:37............................... Grey's Anatomy *122*
6:12...30 Days *44*
6:14...Alias *54*
6:14-15..House *156*
6:19-21.................Survivor: The Australian
Outback *222*
6:24.............................Alias, Friends *52, 106*
6:25...............................8 Simple Rules *28*
6:25-34..30 Days *42*
6:26.....Extreme Makeover: Home Edition *90*
6:33..Seinfeld *210*
6:34...Friends *104*
7:2-5..Friends *110*
7:5.................................8 Simple Rules *32*
7:9-12...............................8 Simple Rules *36*
7:11.....Extreme Makeover: Home Edition *90*
7:12............................. My Name Is Earl *174*
7:13............................... The Simpsons *220*
9:4.. Heroes *138*
9:12.....................Saturday Night Live *196*
10:24...............................The Office *178, 184*
10:39.......................... Grey's Anatomy *120*
15:18-19.......Everybody Loves Raymond *76*
18:21-22...................Frasier, House *94, 156*
19:3-8...............................Frasier *98*
19:3-9..........................Grey's Anatomy *128*
19:23-24......................... Gilmore Girls *116*
19:26...Lost *162*
20:28......................... Grey's Anatomy *120*
21:21...Extreme Makeover: Home Edition *88*
23:27.....................Saturday Night Live *188*
25:14-30..................................... Heroes *136*
25:23................................. The Office *178*
25:34-40.....................................30 Days *42*
25:40...Frasier *94*
26:41..Friends *102*

MARK
7:6..Alias *52*
10:27...................Desperate Housewives *64*
10:45...Extreme Makeover: Home Edition *86*
11:25..House *156*

LUKE
6:29......................Home Improvement *146*
6:30-35.....................................Seinfeld *202*
6:31........................30 Days, Friends *44, 110*
6:37...............Alias, Grey's Anatomy *54, 126*
6:45...............Everybody Loves Raymond *76*
9:62...............Everybody Loves Raymond *78*
12:4-5..House *152*
12:15..........8 Simple Rules, Friends *28, 106*
12:15-21................Saturday Night Live *190*
12:17-20.....................................House *154*
12:23.....................Saturday Night Live *200*
12:48................................... The Office *184*
15:11-32...................... Extreme Makeover:
Home Edition *90*
17:3-4...Alias *54*

JOHN
3:16..Lost *160*
3:36..Lost *166*
6:2..Lost *162*
6:38................................... Heroes *132*
7:24..Friends *110*
10:10.......................... House, Lost *154, 160*
13:15.............................8 Simple Rules *32*
14:21.............................8 Simple Rules *36*
14:27...................... Desperate Housewives,
Saturday Night Live *64, 192*
15:7-9..............................8 Simple Rules *30*
15:13............................. Grey's Anatomy *120*
16:33...Alias *58*
20:23............Everybody Loves Raymond *72*

ACTS
2:44-45.......................................30 Days *42*
3:19....................Desperate Housewives *62*
13:36..................... Frasier, Heroes *100, 132*
19:11-12...Lost *162*
19:18..Lost *164*

ROMANS
1:27......................................30 Days *48, 50*

1:28................... The Simpsons *216*
3:23................... Desperate Housewives *60*
4:4................... My Name Is Earl *170*
5:3-4 .... Survivor: The Australian
Outback *222*
6:11, 18, 22-23 ....Lost *166*
6:12-13 .... Gilmore Girls *114*
6:13-16 .... Desperate Housewives *62*
6:23...................... Saturday Night Live *194*
7:14-25 .... My Name Is Earl *168*
8:1...................Lost, Survivor: The Australian
Outback *166, 224*
8:26..... Extreme Makeover: Home Edition *82*
8:28.................. Everybody Loves Raymond,
Gilmore Girls, Survivor: The Australian
Outback *74, 112, 228*
10:12......................Home Improvement *144*
12:1.................................. Gilmore Girls *114*
12:2.................... Desperate Housewives *70*
12:3....................................... The Office *184*
12:4-6 .... Heroes *136*
12:13... Extreme Makeover: Home Edition *88*
12:18...........................8 Simple Rules *38*
12:19...........................Home Improvement,
My Name Is Earl *146, 172*
13:1....................................... The Office *178*
13:7...................... Friends, My Name Is Earl,
The Office *104, 170, 184*
13:8........................... 8 Simple Rules *28, 38*
14:10...Frasier *96*
15:1...House *150*

1 CORINTHIANS

2:11.. Heroes *138*
6:12.......................... Desperate Housewives,
Saturday Night Live *62, 196*
6:12-20 .... Desperate Housewives *66*
6:18...30 Days *48, 50*
6:18-20 .... Gilmore Girls *114*
6:20...................... Saturday Night Live *200*
7:2-4 .... The Office *180*
10:13...................... Desperate Housewives,
Friends *64, 102*
10:23............................... The Simpsons *216*
10:31............Gilmore Girls, Heroes *112, 132*
12:4..Friends *110*
12:4-11 .... Heroes *136*
13:4-6 ....Frasier *96*

13:4-8 .... The Office, Ugly Betty *180, 234*
13:11.....................Home Improvement *140*
14:33..Frasier *92*
16:13.......... Friends, Survivor: The Australian
Outback *102, 226*

2 CORINTHIANS

1:3-4 ....House *150*
4:8-9 ....Seinfeld *204*
4:15..... Extreme Makeover: Home Edition *88*
4:17............................... Grey's Anatomy *124*
5:9................................. Grey's Anatomy *122*
5:17...Seinfeld *206*
7:9...........................Home Improvement *142*
7:10...House *154*
10:4.. Heroes *134*
10:12...................... Desperate Housewives,
Ugly Betty *70, 236*

GALATIANS

2:6...Ugly Betty *232*
4:6....... Extreme Makeover: Home Edition *90*
5:1........................... Saturday Night Live *196*
5:13......................... Saturday Night Live *196*
5:14..... Extreme Makeover: Home Edition *86*
5:19-21 .... Heroes *130*
5:19-23 ....30 Days *48, 50*
5:22-23 .... The Office *182*
6:1...Seinfeld *204*
6:2...House *150*
6:3................................ Saturday Night Live *198*
6:3-5 .... Desperate Housewives *70*
6:7.......................... Saturday Night Live *194*
6:8...................... Desperate Housewives *70*

EPHESIANS

1:4-14 ....Everybody Loves Raymond *74*
4:2... The Office *180*
4:4-11 .... Heroes *136*
4:22-23 .... The Simpsons *214*
4:28... Heroes *130*
4:29.....................30 Days, Friends *44, 104*
4:31...............................8 Simple Rules *38*
4:32............ The Office, Ugly Betty *182, 232*
5:1-2 ... Extreme Makeover: Home Edition *90*
5:2............................... Grey's Anatomy *120*
5:3...................... Desperate Housewives *66*
5:6................................ The Simpsons *220*

5:18....30 Days, Saturday Night Live *40, 196*
5:22-33 .... The Office *180*
5:28..Friends *102*
5:31...............Everybody Loves Raymond *80*
5:33........................Home Improvement *144*
6:1-2 ....Frasier *98*
6:1-3 .... Desperate Housewives *60*
6:4....................................... 8 Simple Rules,
Everybody Loves Raymond,
Home Improvement *36, (72, 76), 140*
6:7....... Extreme Makeover: Home Edition *86*
6:17... Heroes *134*

PHILIPPIANS
1:6..Alias *56*
1:21........................ Heroes, House *132, 152*
2:3............................. Desperate Housewives,
Extreme Makeover: Home Edition, Frasier,
House, The Office, The Simpsons, Survivor:
The Australian Outback *60, 82, 94, 156,*
(182, 186), (216, 218), 226
2:4...........................Saturday Night Live *198*
2:5-7 ....Home Improvement *144*
2:8...Alias *56*
2:14.........................Frasier, Friends *96, 108*
2:14-16 ....Everybody Loves Raymond *76*
2:21.........................Saturday Night Live *198*
3:7-14 ....Seinfeld *206*
3:13-14 ....Everybody Loves Raymond,
My Name Is Earl *78, 168*
3:14.............................. Grey's Anatomy *122*
3:19........................Saturday Night Live *200*
4:13......................Frasier, Seinfeld *100, 208*

COLOSSIANS
2:8..........................Saturday Night Live *190*
3:8.................................. Heroes *130*
3:9..............................Home Improvement,
Ugly Betty *142, 234*
3:12..... Extreme Makeover: Home Edition *88*
3:13............................ Grey's Anatomy *126*
3:20.....................Frasier, Ugly Betty *98, 238*
3:21..................................... 8 Simple Rules,
Everybody Loves Raymond,
Grey's Anatomy,
Home Improvement *38, 72, 128, 140*
3:23......... Extreme Makeover: Home Edition,
The Office *86, 184*

3:23-24 ....Home Improvement *148*

1 THESSALONIANS
2:8................................... The Simpsons *218*
2:11-12 ....Everybody Loves Raymond *72*
4:3-5 .... Desperate Housewives,
Gilmore Girls *66, 114*
4:11....... The Office, The Simpsons *186, 216*
4:11-12 ....My Name Is Earl *170*
4:13..... Extreme Makeover: Home Edition *82*
4:18...Seinfeld *208*
5:7..30 Days *40*
5:11.......Frasier, Home Improvement, House,
My Name Is Earl *96, 144, 150, 176*
5:12...................................... The Office *182*
5:14...House *150*

2 THESSALONIANS
1:11.. Heroes *132*

1 TIMOTHY
2:5-6 ....Lost *160*
2:8... Heroes *130*
3:4.......................Frasier, Ugly Betty *98, 238*
3:4-5 ....Ugly Betty *230*
4:12....................................... 8 Simple Rules,
Desperate Housewives, Gilmore Girls,
Home Improvement *32, 60, 114, 140*
5:4....................... Desperate Housewives *60*
5:13.................................. Gilmore Girls *118*
6:10...................................30 Days, Friends,
Gilmore Girls *42, 106, 116*
6:17........................Home Improvement *148*
6:18............................... The Simpsons *218*

2 TIMOTHY
1:7.......Alias, House, Survivor: The Australian
Outback *58, 152, 226*
2:23-24 ....Friends *108*
3:1-2 ....Saturday Night Live *190*
3:2-4 ....Saturday Night Live *198*
3:16-17 .... Heroes *134*
4:7...Alias *56*

TITUS
2:6........................ Desperate Housewives *66*
2:6-8 .... 8 Simple Rules *32*
2:11-14 ....Lost *166*

3:10...Seinfeld *204*

HEBREWS
2:17...Lost *166*
2:9-10 ....Lost *160*
3:1.. Heroes *138*
4:12.. Heroes *134*
4:16...................................8 Simple Rules *30*
8:13...Seinfeld *206*
10:14........................... Grey's Anatomy *120*
10:25.......................................Seinfeld *208*
11:25..................... Saturday Night Live *194*
12:1-2 .... Everybody Loves Raymond,
Seinfeld *78, 206*
12:9-10 ....Home Improvement *142*
12:14...Frasier *92*
13:4......................... Desperate Housewives,
The Office *66, 180*
13:5............ Friends, Gilmore Girls *106, 116*
13:6..Alias *58*
13:17..................................... The Office *178*

JAMES
1:2-3 .... Grey's Anatomy, Survivor: The
Australian Outback *124, 228*
1:2-4 ....Survivor: The Australian
Outback *222*
1:19................................. The Simpsons *212*
1:19-20 .... Heroes *130*
1:22-25 .... Grey's Anatomy *122*
1:26.................................. Gilmore Girls *118*
2:1-5 .... Gilmore Girls *116*
2:2-4 ....Saturday Night Live *188*
2:8................................. The Simpsons *218*
3:2...Frasier *92*
3:13-15 .... The Office *186*
3:14...Friends *108*
3:8...................................8 Simple Rules *38*
3:8-10 .... My Name Is Earl *174*
3:9................Everybody Loves Raymond *76*
4:13-14 .... My Name Is Earl *168*
4:13-15 ....House *154*
4:15...House *152*
5:16......................... Desperate Housewives,
House, Lost *(62, 64), 158, 164*

1 PETER
1:6-7 .... Grey's Anatomy, Survivor: The
Australian Outback *124, 228*
2:12.......................Home Improvement *140*
2:13..................................... The Office *178*
2:15.......................Home Improvement *146*
2:16.......................Home Improvement *142*
2:17...................................30 Days *44*
2:19-20 ....Home Improvement *146*
2:24...House *152, 158*
3:3-4 .... Saturday Night Live,
Ugly Betty *188, 236*
3:8-9 .... Friends,
Home Improvement *104, 146*
3:14................................. The Simpsons *220*
3:15-17 ....8 Simple Rules *32*
3:16.... Survivor: The Australian Outback *224*
4:1................................. The Simpsons *214*
4:8...Alias *56*
4:10......... Extreme Makeover: Home Edition,
Heroes, Home Improvement *86, 136, 144*

1 JOHN
1:9.......Desperate Housewives, Lost *62, 164*
2:16.......................Home Improvement *148*
3:1............................. 8 Simple Rules *30, 36*
3:17......... Extreme Makeover: Home Edition,
Friends *88, 106*
4:18.............................My Name Is Earl *176*

JUDE
22...Seinfeld *208*

REVELATION
3:15-16 ....Alias *52*
19:15... Heroes *134*
22:11............................. The Simpsons *220*

The Reason for This Book

Since I'm a child of divorce, I can tell you honestly that my main babysitter was the television. As a kid, when I came home after school, I didn't go outside and play—I watched television. In fact, I knew what time it was by what shows were on! I was fascinated with the flip of a channel (back then we'd have to get up, walk to the TV set, and turn the knob to change the channel) and how I could be transported to a different world. I was in love with everything TV had to offer, from *Hong Kong Phooey* to *Star Trek* to *Mork & Mindy*. I loved to laugh, and I loved the way some shows moved me and made me think. (Okay, I was a weird child.)

I remember after my parents' divorce, my father took me on a ski trip—just the two of us. After a day of skiing, we settled down in our Motel 6 room, and Dad turned on the TV. It was late at night, and whatever show was on was making my dad laugh really hard. Sometimes he'd roll his eyes at the humor, but his laughter is what sticks in my mind, and I'll never forget sitting on that motel-room floor laughing with my dad. For the most part, I was laughing because *he* was, but it made me feel so grown-up even though I had no idea what those short little bits of television comedy were called. Apparently they were called "skits," and what we were watching was a show called *Saturday Night Live*. Thus, at the age of eight, I learned to love skits. Thus, I became a Skit Guy. (Can you tell I just wanted to use the word *thus*?)

Another pivotal moment happened at age 10 while I was watching *Happy Days*. Mom was in class that night working on her degree, and my sister was doing her homework. Tuesday night, seven o'clock (see, I told you!)—me and the television. It was the episode where Richie crashes his motorcycle (season 5, episode 106: "Richie Almost Dies"). I don't remember much about it except the end, but I do remember it was the first time since the divorce that I felt sad. *Richie may die! I've grown up with Richie...he's always been there! Could he really die?* (I had no idea, of course, about contracts and sweeps weeks and ratings.) I clearly remember the scene in the hospital when Fonzie is alone with Richie, talking to God. When the Fonz makes his plea to God, asking him not to let Richie die, it was incredibly powerful for me. At the time it felt *real*, not cheesy or put on—just someone pouring his heart out to God. In some ways, that scene was my introduction to the Creator of the universe. I know Henry Winkler and Ron Howard weren't aiming to make a "touched by an angel" moment, but for me that's what happened.

To this day, when the kids and my wife are asleep, I will curl up with my TiVo and watch shows. I'm still fascinated by TV. If a show moves me, I'm usually on the phone or e-mail talking about it with Tommy, and somewhere down the line—lo and behold—an idea for a skit emerges.

It's a little ironic that these two television shows are pivotal to what Tom and I try to convey onstage when we minister: Skits that make you laugh, make you cry, and hopefully point you to God. I hope with everything I am that these clips—these television shows—and what we say about them provoke "God moments" for you.

Sincerely,
Eddie James
a.k.a., the "bald" Skit Guy
(Now, I'll pass the baton to my buddy Tommy as he gives you the nuts and bolts of this book...)

. . .

T hanks, Ed! I, too, had a life-changing TV moment. However, mine took place when I was a young youth pastor watching *The Simpsons* in the back room of the parsonage where my wife and I lived. (I was in the back room so no one would know I was watching such a tawdry show!) Lisa and Homer are talking and she says, "It's not our fault our generation has short attention spans, Dad. We watch an appalling amount of TV." In his infinite wisdom, Homer replies, "Don't you ever, *ever* talk that way about television!" In that instant, every moment of TV I had watched in my life was justified! (With the exception of the two episodes of *Charles in Charge* I had watched with my sister.)

The whole purpose of this book is not to say that kids watch too much TV. That's just crazy talk—you *can't* watch too much TV! If that were possible, would they make TiVos that can record up to 300 hours of high-definition shows? I think not! The point of this book is summed up by the following quote from one of our great philosophers:

"When will I learn? The answers to life's problems aren't at the bottom of a bottle, they're on TV!"
—Homer *(the guy from Springfield, not the guy from Greece)*

With that in mind, let's look at some ways you can use this book and start teaching your kids valuable lessons from TV!

HOW TO USE THIS BOOK

More than likely you have used or seen the Videos That Teach book series Eddie wrote with Doug Fields. If you're not familiar with these great teaching tools, you can see and purchase them at www.skitguys.com (shameless plug!). This book is similar to those books in terms of look and style, but at the same time it's very different. (Akin to the similarities and differences between Pinky and Leather Tuscadero, if you know what I'm sayin'.)

NEW IDEAS

I was a youth minister for 12 years and constantly used the Videos That Teach books. It was always a great way to find just the right movie clip to help bring home my message; I only wish there had been a tool like *TV Shows That Teach* at the time to help me out. The simple truth is that teenagers and young adults may see one movie a week at the most, but they'll watch around 15 hours of TV each week. This is their world—teenagers are influenced by the style, fashions, words, and actions of the people they see on TV. But I didn't see the value of TV at first; in fact, I was constantly trying to get my kids to watch *less* TV instead of seeing this medium as a great teaching tool.

THE GOSPEL ACCORDING TO EARL

When I'm not a Skit Guy, I'm a teaching pastor at a church that's constantly trying to come up with creative ways to share the truth of the Scriptures. We actually did an entire teaching series using clips from *My Name is Earl*, which is just one of the creative ways you can use this book. Each video clip works well on its own, but you can also do an entire teaching series based on one of the many shows we've researched and fleshed out into studies. In fact, we've made sure every clip from any given show is from the same season. That way you don't have to find a bunch of different seasons to put your clips together. (In other words, if you decide to purchase the series on DVD, then you'll be sure to have five clips you can use from that show.)

iTUNES, BLOCKBUSTER, AND BEST BUY—OH MY!

Speaking of purchasing the series, let's take a look at your options. Just because you're going to show a TV clip doesn't necessarily mean you have to buy the entire series. (But it's a good excuse to use your budget on something you could enjoy for years to come!) Here are some options to consider, along with the pros and cons of each:

DOWNLOADS: You can download most of the shows we've listed in this book from online video providers such as iTunes, Amazon.com, NBC. com, or walmart.com. The best part of downloading the episode is that you don't have to purchase the entire series, and it's possible to get the video at the last minute if you find yourself in a time crunch. The only downside is that downloaded videos can be more difficult to edit. You'll also want to make sure you can play downloaded videos on the TV or projector you'll be using with your group.

RENTALS: Like downloads, most of the TV shows we've listed are available for rent at your local video store. You can also get a subscription through blockbuster.com or netflix.com. The best part of renting the DVDs is that it lets you use the clips without purchasing the entire series, and individual clips are easier to edit if you choose to do so. This is a more practical way to use the DVDs, and it'll save you money, but the downside is that the DVDs may not be available to rent when you need them. You'll want to really plan ahead and make sure the show/episode you're using is available either online or at a local store.

PURCHASES: DVDs of TV shows are available to purchase at any store where you'd find videos for sale—Best Buy, Wal-Mart, Target, Circuit City…you get the idea. You may also have a better selection of DVDs to choose from if you purchase. The best part of purchasing the show is that you own the DVD and can use it as much as you want. Let's emphasize this again: Since we made sure all the clips from any given show included in this book come from the same season, once you purchase that season on DVD, you have at least five clips you can use. You may even find more clips to use than the ones we list. Purchasing the DVD also lends itself to making an entire teaching series out of one show. The downside of purchasing is the cost—the average price of an entire TV show's season is around $30. (Oh yeah, and you might have to explain to your church accountant why you spent budget money to purchase a whole season of *Ugly Betty*!)

I THOUGHT YOU GUYS DID SKITS…?

We *do* do skits. That's why we're called The Skit Guys. And we wouldn't write a book without letting you know about skits you can use. That's why with each TV show clip we break down into studies you'll also find our suggestions for skits that you, your students, or your congregation can perform to further illustrate the message you're trying to communicate. We may also suggest one of our videos to go along with your teaching. All of our skits and videos we suggest can be downloaded from www.skitguys.com or at www. ysunderground.com. (Please overlook the fact that this is a shameless plug for our Web site. And if you're keeping count, that brings the shameless-plug count to two!)

WERE YOU DESPERATE ENOUGH TO USE *DESPERATE HOUSEWIVES?*

Yes…I mean no…I mean yes, we used it, but not out of desperation. The truth is…we may have used several shows that, in their entirety, don't promote the values and beliefs of your church or youth group. That's not the purpose of the shows, and they're not necessarily produced or written by people who share your beliefs and convictions. However, none of the clips in *TV Shows That Teach* contain language or content that's inappropriate for most youth groups.

You see, the purpose of this book isn't to endorse any show or promote any agenda. We're just two guys who see teachable moments all the time while watching TV and thought we'd try to pass along the ideas to others. So we started digging through show after show, looking for the best teachable moments we could find. That's how we came up with the clip breakdowns you'll find in this book.

When the apostle Paul used the idol "to an unknown god" as his visual aid while talking to the meeting of the Areopagus in Acts 17, he wasn't endorsing the worship of idols. He was meeting the Athenians where they were and using an illustration they could follow and understand. We're hoping you'll be able to do the same by using these clips and the studies we've generated to go along with them.

So, if you come across some clips you don't approve of, remember:

• The clip still may produce an amazing teachable moment.
• You can teach good things by pointing out bad things.
• You can still preview the clip and see what you think.
• You can always ask your pastor, supervisor, or a parent about it.
• You don't have to use every clip noted in this book.

Most importantly, you make the call. You're an adult and the leader of your group of teenagers. You'll know if using the clip would be more of a distraction than instruction. Make sure whatever decision you make, you can lay your head on your pillow and feel good about it.

And no…there are no clips from *Arrested Development*. We would've been happy to provide studies from that show, but no one watched it.

STUFF YOU MAY ALREADY KNOW

If you've used video clips to teach before, then you may want to skip reading this part. (You should know, though, that I have written the forthcoming paragraphs using a special encrypted code that brings great happiness to readers...so I'd keep on reading if I were you.)

EDITING: When showing a clip to your audience or small group, you can show it directly from the DVD using the **Start** and **Stop** times we've provided (see "What You'll Find in Each Clip Study" on page 24). However, we suggest that you use some inexpensive editing software and actually "rip" the clip you want and edit it. By doing this you can use a nice fade-in and fade-out at the beginning and end of your clip, and you're also able to make sure you have the right clip that actually starts and stops at the right time. Think about finding students who would be great at the editing process, and consider it a part of their ministry to the church. A word of warning: Make sure whatever you give them to edit is appropriate for them to watch.

SUBTITLES: You may want to use the English version of the subtitles when showing your clips. Not only does it give the clip a cool "foreign film" vibe, but it also helps drive the point home. When the subtitles are on, the audience's eyes are naturally drawn to the words, and they'll read along, really understanding everything that's said. Subtitles can be a very powerful tool. And if you *really* want that foreign-film vibe, use the Spanish or French subtitles.

PREVIEWS: Although these are TV shows and they don't contain the kind of language you'd find in an R-rated movie, some shows use words that you or your audience (or the parents of your audience) may find offensive. We have done our best to make sure there aren't any inappropriate words in the clips we chose, but then again, what we find okay may not be the same as what you find okay for your audience—*so make sure you preview the scene before you show it!* We can't stress that enough. If you find a word you don't approve of but still want to use the clip, consider editing the word out. Get creative with it and have someone with a completely different voice from the actor's put in a different word. It could be fun and could actually make the scene that much more memorable.

COPYRIGHTS: TV shows are fully protected by copyright. Public exhibition, especially when an admission fee is charged, could violate copyright laws. The copyright doctrine of fair use, however, permits certain uses of brief excerpts from copyrighted materials for not-for-profit teaching purposes without permission. If you have specific questions about whether your plans to use TV-show clips or other copyrighted material in your lessons are permissible under these guidelines, consult your church's legal counsel. You may want to consider applying for a blanket licensing agreement from the Motion Picture Licensing Corporation (www.mplc.org) for about $100 per year.

WHAT YOU'LL FIND IN EACH CLIP STUDY

We've tried to make this book as easy to use as possible. In doing so, we labeled everything so you can find your clip quickly and get going. The first thing you'll notice with each clip study is a quippy line about the clip—the **Tag**—to help you get an idea of where we're going with this clip. You can share this line with your audience in some way before you use the clip to get them thinking about what they're going to watch.

Setting up the clip is important for the discussion to come later—if you don't set it up, your audience may enjoy the clip but not get the point you're trying to make with it. Speaking of the point you're trying to make, you'll find a list of topics, Scripture passages, and all the television shows in index form at the front of the book (starting on page 5). *A quick word about the topical and Bible reference indexes (Quick Clip Locators): For entries with multiple clips, we group the TV shows first, then group the corresponding page numbers; just match the order (e.g., second show with second page number) and you're in.*

Here's what else you'll find within each clip study.

TV SHOW: This is the title of the show and lets you know if it's a comedy, drama, or if it's reality-based. Keep in mind that just because a show is a drama doesn't mean the clip will be overtly serious or dramatic. At the same time, a comedy series doesn't always mean the clip is funny. We selected what we thought were the most powerful *teaching* scenes we could find for each show, whether they were funny or not. Therefore, if you aren't familiar with the show, this section helps you know what you're dealing with overall.

SEASON/EPISODE: TV shows are broken into seasons and episodes. The first year a show is on TV is season 1, the next year is season 2, and so on. The first episode of each year is episode 1; the second is episode 2, and so on. Got it yet? So if you're watching a show that was the fifth episode of the third year it was on, you would describe it as "season 3, episode 5." This listing is vital when you're renting or purchasing a show, since you must get the right season and then go to the right episode to find the clip you need. On the front cover of every TV-show DVD, you'll find the season number. Again, make sure you get the right season, or you won't be able to find the clip you need. But if that should happen, turn lemons into lemonade and create your own teachable clips!

EPISODE TITLE: Every episode of a TV show has a title. The point of sharing the title of each episode with you is that some DVDs list the titles of the episodes instead of the episode numbers. Again, we're just trying to make this as easy as pie for you! Speaking of pie, who would make the best pie—Mrs. Garrett, Mrs. Cunningham, or Mrs. Brady? Our money is on Mrs. Garrett. (Don't forget, she was the nanny to Arnold and Willis before she went to that boarding school with all those girls.)

THEMES: Simply put, a list of topics you could address through the clip; choose one for your study…or none at all. (You may have better themes coming to mind!)

THE SERIES/SHOW: If you're not familiar with the TV show, this brief summary will explain things. Even if you do know the show, you can use (or read aloud) the summary to explain the storyline before you show a clip. If you need a more detailed description of the show, go to the all-knowing World Wide Web. We found that www.tv.com and www.imdb.com were great sources of information, especially for shows with complicated storylines and history. You can also go to the network Web site for descriptions of each show (e.g., ABC, NBC, CBS, FOX, etc.). In the end, I'm sure you'll just do like everyone else does and Google it!

THE SCENE: This is a detailed description of the actual clip you'll be using. You'll find **Start** and **Stop** times for your clip here with the first and last lines of the scene to help you know where to cue it up and stop it. We've also included some of the dialogue/script just to show you where the scene is going; it's something we felt was a great tool because although these are TV clips, they still may have some words right before or right after the chosen clip that you wouldn't want to use in your teaching time.

BY THE BOOK: Even though this book is titled *TV Shows That Teach*, we all know that the Bible is where we want to go to find our answers in life. To help you give these clips some biblical perspective, **By the Book** provides a list of Scripture passages that relate to the topics of the clips. You can use them while writing your lesson or as input for small-group discussion.

WHERE TO TAKE IT: This list of discussion questions has been created to clarify the main point of the clip and tie it to the Scripture passages. Some of the questions ask students how the clip made them feel or what they would have done if they had been in a situation similar to the people in the scene. Other questions dig into the Scripture passages or open the door for your small-group participants to go deeper in discussion. Please don't feel like you have to use any or all of these questions—just take what you want and even tailor them to your group if necessary. Use the questions to get a good discussion going, explore the meaning behind the clip, and show teenagers how they can apply what they've learned to their lives.

BY THE WAY...WE CAN'T COUNT!

Yeah, we know this book says it contains 100 TV-clip suggestions. However, when we finished and sent everything to our publisher, they informed us that we'd sent 105. Some people would use this as a moment to tout themselves as "overachievers," but we're going to go ahead and just admit the fact that we can't count. So enjoy the extra five clip ideas—or if there are some clips you don't appreciate, just pretend they're not actually in there!

We hope these TV-show clips can be used to spark deep discussions, create laughs to break down walls so that truth can enter, and take some great moments from Hollywood that can transform a life within the walls of our churches...

Blessings to you!
Tommy Woodard

The TV Show Clip Studies

8 Simple Rules

(COMEDY)

SEASON 1, EPISODE 3: "BRIDGET'S FIRST JOB"

TAG: I *AM* RESPONSIBLE! I JUST WANT THOSE SHOES...

THEMES: Debt, Handling Problems, Money, Parent-Child Relationships, Responsibility, Secrets, Worth

THE SERIES/SHOW: Comedy *8 Simple Rules* demonstrates what can happen when Mom gets a job, Dad stays home, and three kids enter their teenage years. Things are changing at the Hennessy household, and no one is immune when Cate (Katey Sagal) goes back to work as a full-time nurse and Paul (John Ritter) quits his old job as a traveling sportswriter to work at home and keep an eye on the three Hennessy teenagers. Paul gets more than he bargained for, however, dealing with 16-year-old Bridget (Kaley Cuoco), 15-year-old Kerry (Amy Davidson), and 13-year-old son Rory (Martin Spanjers). Facing the facts that his children are growing up and dating is anything but easy; Paul does the only thing a dad can do by creating the "8 Simple Rules for Dating My Teenage Daughter."

THE SCENE: To earn some extra money, Bridget gets a job at the mall at a popular store named Strip Rags. To Paul and Cate's surprise, Bridget takes her job seriously and is a very good salesgirl. Nevertheless, Bridget gets a bit carried away buying clothes with her 40 percent discount and overcharges her account at the store. When her paycheck arrives and she owes $400 more than she has earned, Bridget panics and decides to put the debt on her emergency credit card until she can figure out what to do. But when Cate tries to buy gas, the card is refused because of the new balance, and she can't use the card. Cate arrives home angry and demanding an explanation from the daughter she thought was so responsible.

START: 0:15:43 STOP: 0:17:38 (TOTAL CLIP TIME: 1 MINUTE, 55 SECONDS)

START DIALOGUE: *(Bridget)* I got paid today. *(Puts envelope by Kerry's nose)* Take a whiff. What's that?

(Kerry) The smell of Corporate America.

STOP DIALOGUE: *(Paul)* That's freaky. That's where Bridget works.

BONUS CLIP: Faced with her parents' disappointment, Bridget attempts to explain the choice to cover her debt with the credit card.

START 0:16:26 STOP 0:17:26 (TOTAL CLIP TIME: 1 MINUTE)

START DIALOGUE: *(Paul)* I am so disappointed in you.

(Bridget) Okay, I bought too many clothes, I ran up a huge debt to the store, I forgot about taxes, it would've taken me forever to pay them back.

(Paul) Why didn't you come to us if you got in trouble?

STOP DIALOGUE: *(Bridget)* Because you were proud of me for, like, the first time ever, and I didn't want to disappoint you.

BY THE BOOK: Exodus 2:11-15, Psalm 37:21, Matthew 6:25, Luke 12:15, Romans 13:8

WHERE TO TAKE IT:

1. If money weren't a factor, how would you want to live your life?

2. Is it a sin to want or to have nice things?

3. Why are we so desperate to gain our parents' approval? Why does it hurt so much to disappoint them?

4. Has there ever been a time when people thought you were more responsible than you were? How did it make you feel to know the truth?

5. What's the biggest secret you've ever kept from your parents? What happened when that secret came out?

6. Are secrets ever a good thing?

7. In Exodus 2:11-15, Moses carries a secret of his own. What happens inside our souls when secrets lie dormant?

8. What does the word *debt* mean to you? What do you think of the concept of being in debt? How are we in debt to God?

Visit www.skitguys.com or www.ysunderground.com for additional elements that might add impact to this clip, including "The Mask I Wear" script.

8 Simple Rules
(COMEDY)
SEASON 1, EPISODE 8: "BY THE BOOK"

TAG: TOUGH LOVE IS TOUGH.

THEMES: Consequences, Discipline, Grace, Morals, Parenting, Unconditional Love

THE SERIES/SHOW: Comedy *8 Simple Rules* demonstrates what can happen when Mom gets a job, Dad stays home, and three kids enter their teenage years. Things are changing at the Hennessy household, and no one is immune when Cate (Katey Sagal) goes back to work as a full-time nurse and Paul (John Ritter) quits his old job as a traveling sportswriter to work at home and keep an eye on the three Hennessy teenagers. Paul gets more than he bargained for, however, dealing with 16-year-old Bridget (Kaley Cuoco), 15-year-old Kerry (Amy Davidson), and 13-year-old son Rory (Martin Spanjers). Facing the facts that his children are growing up and dating is anything but easy; Paul does the only thing a dad can do by creating the "8 Simple Rules for Dating My Teenage Daughter."

THE SCENE: Feeling that he's losing control of the girls, Paul resorts to reading a parenting book to get some help. When the girls lie about going to a rock concert, Paul decides to use the suggestions in the book to get them to 'fess up about it, but the girls find out he's been using the book against them and decide to beat him at his own game by tricking Paul into letting them go. Their plan works, and Bridget and Kerry go to the concert, knowing full well that Paul and Cate don't want them there. Paul comes home after looking for the girls at the concert, but soon learns that after the first song was played, the girls felt so guilty that they decided to go home. After a discussion with Cate, Paul goes up to talk with the girls to try to negotiate a cease-fire in the complicated father-child relationship war. As Paul, Bridget, and Kerry share their feelings, they discover that the love between them is as strong as ever.

START: 0:17:55 STOP: 0:20:50 (TOTAL CLIP TIME: 2 MINUTES, 55 SECONDS)

START DIALOGUE: *(Cate)* Without that stupid plan and the book, they would never have gone to that concert. You wouldn't have gone to the concert, and we wouldn't have been worried sick.

STOP DIALOGUE: *(Bridget and Kerry)* I hate you!

(Paul) I love you, too.

(Girls) We really mean it. We totally mean it.

BY THE BOOK: Deuteronomy 8:5, Job 5:17, Proverbs 3:12, John 15:7-9, Hebrews 4:16, 1 John 3:1

WHERE TO TAKE IT:

1. Have you ever felt that discipline from your parents was unfair? Looking back on that situation, has your perspective changed at all?

2. Do you agree with psychiatrists who say that children need and want discipline from their parents? Why or why not?

3. In Deuteronomy 8:5, the Bible states that discipline and love go hand in hand. How hard is it to grasp this concept?

4. How do you feel that God has been "disciplining" you? Does this discipline make you feel more or less loved by God?

5. What does the word *disciple* mean to you? Read John 15:7-9. How does Jesus see the role of his disciples?

6. How much do you associate your relationship with God to your relationship with your dad? Has your earthly father treated you with the unconditional love you read about in the Bible?

7. What would it take to improve the relationship between you and your dad? How willing are you to submit to his discipline and authority?

8. Would you be honest enough to admit that you have a love/hate relationship with your parents, as Bridget and Kerry express? How is it possible to have feelings of hate for someone you love so much?

Visit www.skitguys.com or www.ysunderground.com for additional elements that might add impact to this clip, including Family Conflicts 6.2f, "I Will Ground You…" from Instant Skits.

8 Simple Rules

(COMEDY)

SEASON 1, EPISODE 22: "MOM'S GONE WILD"

TAG: DO AS I SAY, NOT AS I DO.

THEMES: Behavior, Choices, Dealing with the Past, Excuses, Hypocrisy, Mistakes, Partying, Regrets, Role Models

THE SERIES/SHOW: Comedy *8 Simple Rules* demonstrates what can happen when Mom gets a job, Dad stays home, and three kids enter their teenage years. Things are changing at the Hennessy household, and no one is immune when Cate (Katey Sagal) goes back to work as a full-time nurse and Paul (John Ritter) quits his old job as a traveling sportswriter to work at home and keep an eye on the three Hennessy teenagers. Paul gets more than he bargained for, however, dealing with 16-year-old Bridget (Kaley Cuoco), 15-year-old Kerry (Amy Davidson), and 13-year-old son Rory (Martin Spanjers). Facing the facts that his children are growing up and dating is anything but easy; Paul does the only thing a dad can do by creating the "8 Simple Rules for Dating My Teenage Daughter."

THE SCENE: The Hennessy family has gone to Florida for their spring-break vacation, and 16-year-old Bridget and 15-year-old Kerry get caught up in the college-party atmosphere. While the family is watching a news program highlighting the festivities, Bridget and Kerry are shown dancing at a party. When Paul and Cate reprimand the girls for disobeying them, the girls see some archival film footage covering the mayhem of spring break from years past and are surprised to see Cate drinking and flashing the news camera—behavior the girls view as extremely hypocritical. Later, Cate decides to be honest with her daughters about her past behavior, but begins to realize how much that news footage has undermined her authority as a parent.

START: 0:17:21 STOP: 0:18:50 (TOTAL CLIP TIME: 1 MINUTE, 39 SECONDS)

START DIALOGUE: *(Cate)* Oh, girls, come in here.

STOP DIALOGUE: *(Kerry)* Why'd you act like that?

(Cate) I don't know. Back then I was...confused. Maybe unhappy.

BY THE BOOK: Matthew 7:5, John 13:15, 1 Timothy 4:12, Titus 2:6-8, 1 Peter 3:15-17

WHERE TO TAKE IT:

1. When did you first realize that your parents aren't perfect? How did that realization make you feel?

2. Do your parents' past mistakes give you a pass to create your own regrets, as Bridget and Kerry believe in this clip? Would you be willing to learn from their mistakes and avoid choices that might cause you pain?

3. Is a parent being a hypocrite by saying, "Do as I say, not as I do"? What do you think a parent is really trying to accomplish by using such a cliché?

4. Cate confesses to her daughters that her past behavior was motivated by confusion and unhappiness. How often are these the reasons behind most teenagers' poor choices or outrageous actions?

5. With the growing popularity of MySpace and other similar Web sites, is there a difference between the way teenagers behave at church and the way they express themselves on the Internet? What is the reason for that discrepancy? Is it okay to be one person around your Christian friends and someone else online?

6. Have you ever had part of your past that you're none too proud of on tape? How did you feel about seeing yourself on film? Is there any way in today's Internet age to ever get rid of a past that has been filmed?

7. How is it possible to recover from the regrets of the past?

8. Why is it so hard for people to take responsibility for things they're not proud of doing? How often do you see people facing up to the consequences of their actions with honor and honesty?

SCENE TRANSCRIPT:

(Bridget and Kerry come in the front door to Cate's parents' Florida condo.)

(Cate) Oh, girls, come in here.

(Kerry) Mom, what are you doin' here? I thought you'd be at Señor Swanky's for two-for-one tequila slammers.

(Cate) All right—sit. I think it's time we had a little talk. *(The girls enter the bedroom and sit on the bed.)* Okay, look. It's true. When I was a young woman,

there were a few moments where my behavior could have been described as "spirited."

(Bridget) "Spirited"? You flashed a news camera.

(Cate) Fine. I was a little wild.

(Kerry) You're our mother!

(Cate) But my behavior, no matter how immature, does not give you a free pass to behave badly.

(Bridget) Yes, it does.

(Cate) Look, you guys, I did some stupid things that I regret. Maybe you could just learn from my regrets.

(Kerry) Or…we could do them and learn from our own regrets.

(Cate) Does it really look to you like I'm having a good time on that video?

(Both girls) Yeah!

(Cate) Okay…I'm gonna start over. Do as I say, not as I do, or you'll never see daylight again. You got it?

(Both girls) Got it.

(Kerry) Why'd you act like that?

(Cate) I don't know. Back then I was confused. Maybe unhappy.

Visit www.skitguys.com or www.ysunderground.com for additional elements that might add impact to this clip, including Family Conflicts 6.2k, "Monkey See, Monkey Do," from Instant Skits.

8 Simple Rules

(COMEDY)

SEASON 1, EPISODE 1: PILOT

TAG: THERE'S NOTHING MORE POWERFUL THAN A FATHER'S LOVE.

THEMES: Affirmation from Fathers, Beauty, Communication, Father-Daughter Relationships, Heavenly Father, Self-Esteem

THE SERIES/SHOW: Comedy *8 Simple Rules* demonstrates what can happen when Mom gets a job, Dad stays home, and three kids enter their teenage years. Things are changing at the Hennessy household, and no one is immune when Cate (Katey Sagal) goes back to work as a full-time nurse and Paul (John Ritter) quits his old job as a traveling sportswriter to work at home and keep an eye on the three Hennessy teenagers. Paul gets more than he bargained for, however, dealing with 16-year-old Bridget (Kaley Cuoco), 15-year-old Kerry (Amy Davidson), and 13-year-old son Rory (Martin Spanjers). Facing the facts that his children are growing up and dating is anything but easy; Paul does the only thing a dad can do by creating the "8 Simple Rules for Dating My Teenage Daughter."

THE SCENE: Paul punishes his 15-year-old daughter Kerry for her consistently bad attitude by not letting her go to the homecoming dance. Kerry claims that she doesn't care, that it's a stupid dance only idiots would go to. But when Kerry breaks down crying and runs to her bedroom, Paul's older daughter Bridget reveals that Kerry had not been asked to go, helping Paul understand why Kerry has been in such a bad mood all week. Doing his best to be a "good dad," Paul goes to Kerry's room to talk to her, discovering in the process that a high school dance isn't the only thing on his daughter's mind.

START: 0:16:16 STOP: 0:18:25 (TOTAL CLIP TIME: 2 MINUTES, 9 SECONDS)

START DIALOGUE: *(Paul)* Kerry?
(Kerry) Go away!

STOP DIALOGUE: *(Kerry)* What do you know? You're, like, 100. *(Paul walks out of the room feeling dejected.)*

BY THE BOOK: Proverbs 31:30, Matthew 7:9-12, John 14:21, Ephesians 6:4, 1 John 3:1

WHERE TO TAKE IT:

1. How would you describe your relationship with your father?

2. How is the father-daughter relationship different from the father-son relationship? Do girls need different things from their fathers than boys do? What are those things?

3. How does a negative father-daughter relationship affect a young girl's approach to dating?

4. Do most girls you know seek to date a person who is like or unlike their fathers?

5. How is it possible for a young girl without a father to understand God's love for her? What would you say to a girl in that situation?

6. Guys, what kind of father do you want to be? How will you approach the father-daughter relationship?

7. Girls, what's the best thing a father can do for his daughter? What's the worst thing?

8. How important is it for both guys and girls to have their fathers' approval? How does it affect a person's self-esteem if she senses disapproval from her father? How far are you willing to go to make your father proud of you?

Visit www.skitguys.com or www.ysunderground.com for additional elements that might add impact to this clip, including the "Heavenly Daddy" script from Skits That Teach.

8 Simple Rules

(COMEDY)

SEASON 1, EPISODE 4: "WINGS"

TAG: WHY WON'T MOM AND DAD LET ME GROW UP?

THEMES: Arguing, Consequences, Discipline, Guilt, Hurtful Words, Letting Go, Overprotecting, Respect, Worry

THE SERIES/SHOW: Comedy *8 Simple Rules* demonstrates what can happen when Mom gets a job, Dad stays home, and three kids enter their teenage years. Things are changing at the Hennessy household, and no one is immune when Cate (Katey Sagal) goes back to work as a full-time nurse and Paul (John Ritter) quits his old job as a traveling sportswriter to work at home and keep an eye on the three Hennessy teenagers. Paul gets more than he bargained for, however, dealing with 16-year-old Bridget (Kaley Cuoco), 15-year-old Kerry (Amy Davidson), and 13-year-old son Rory (Martin Spanjers). Facing the facts that his children are growing up and dating is anything but easy; Paul does the only thing a dad can do by creating the "8 Simple Rules for Dating My Teenage Daughter."

THE SCENE: Sixteen-year-old Bridget has been asking to get her driver's license for several weeks, but Paul keeps making up excuses as to why she isn't ready. One day she gets upset with him and takes the family car without permission, and no one knows where she has gone. When a police officer brings Bridget home, Paul and Cate are furious at the fact that she disobeyed them. An argument breaks out when Paul won't listen to Bridget, Bridget calls him a jerk, and Cate reprimands her and sends her to her room. Later that night Paul and Cate have a discussion about why Bridget rebelled the way she did, and Cate tells him she thinks it's because he was being so unreasonable about letting Bridget get her license. When Paul confesses that he's just worried about the welfare of his children, Cate tells him he can't keep them from growing up just because he's scared something might happen to them.

START: 0:12:53 STOP: 014:26 (TOTAL CLIP TIME: 1 MINUTE, 33 SECONDS)

START DIALOGUE: *(Cate)* Okay, Bridget's handled. Now, would you try to calm down?

STOP DIALOGUE: *(Paul)* They should tell you that before you bring 'em home from the hospital.

BY THE BOOK: Psalm 19:14, Ecclesiastes 5:2, Romans 12:18, Ephesians 4:31, Colossians 3:21, James 3:8

WHERE TO TAKE IT:

1. Have you ever felt that your parents were standing in the way of your freedom? Looking back at this time, do you still feel that way?

2. What's the one thing your parents do that drives you crazy? Why do you think they do it?

3. What are the rules in your household as far as fighting and arguing? Is name-calling allowed in your house?

4. In Romans 12:18, the Bible states that we are to live at peace with everyone. Would you say there is peace in your household?

5. How does your family handle conflict?

6. Are there any hurtful words spoken by a member of your family that have really stuck with you? What about positive, encouraging words?

7. Have you ever disobeyed a direct order from your parents? What happened in that situation? What do you do when you feel your parents are being completely unreasonable?

8. How do you go about releasing built-up bitterness?

Visit www.skitguys.com or www.ysunderground.com for additional elements that might add impact to this clip, including the "Brady Bunch" script.

30 Days

(REALITY)

SEASON 1, EPISODE 6: "BINGE-DRINKING MOM"

TAG: HI. I'M A MOM, AND I'M AN ALCOHOLIC.

IMPORTANT LEADER NOTE: *Because of the subject matter of this clip, some editing may be required depending on the viewers' needs and maturity level.*

THEMES: Addiction, Alcoholism, Discipline, Partying, Permissive Parenting, Rebellion

THE SERIES/SHOW: *30 Days* is a reality show from filmmaker Morgan Spurlock, best known for the documentary *Super Size Me* in which Spurlock used himself as a guinea pig to investigate the effects of a fast-food diet. Inspired by the results of the documentary and using the same premise for this reality series, Spurlock places individuals in a scenario completely different from their current circumstances for a period of 30 days. During that time participants experience different lifestyles, explore prejudices, and examine cultures foreign to their own.

THE SCENE: Healthy, active, non-drinker Michiel has become very concerned about her daughter Jessica's drinking. In an effort to show college student Jessica the negative effects of drinking, Michiel spends 30 days as a binge drinker. Over the month, Michiel's world falls apart as she spends her nights drunk and her days hungover. Jessica remains unaffected, however, insisting that she can handle the alcohol and won't change. Over lunch one day, Michiel attempts to uncover the depths of Jessica's problem, but as Jessica tells the camera, it may be too late for Michiel to gain control of her wayward daughter.

START 0:14:46 STOP 0:17:48 (TOTAL CLIP TIME: 3 MINUTES, 2 SECONDS)

START DIALOGUE: *(Morgan)* Despite her hangover, Michiel decides to confront Jessica about the previous night of drinking.

STOP DIALOGUE: *(Jessica)* Basically she doesn't enforce a lot of rules with me.

BONUS CLIP:
START 0:31:02 STOP 0:31:53 (TOTAL CLIP TIME: 51 SECONDS)

SCENE TRANSCRIPT:

(Jessica) I appreciate you doing this whole thing, but I'm not gonna change because I'm who I am. And when I was Braden's age, I was like, "I'm never drinking." I had a negative view on all that stuff, and then, of course, I changed. I just feel like, I don't know, like nothing really...it's too late for me to have a different view. I probably will never change my style of drinking per se.

(Michiel) Maybe parents don't keep a line of communication open between your kids and talk about it. Maybe parents don't do enough of that. Maybe I didn't do enough of it with you.

(Jessica) Maybe not, because you sure didn't talk to me about that stuff.

(Michiel) I know.

BY THE BOOK: Exodus 20:12, Proverbs 20:1, Proverbs 22:6, Ephesians 5:18, 1 Thessalonians 5:7

WHERE TO TAKE IT:

1. How have your parents raised you? Have they been strict or permissive with the rules enforcing your behavior?

2. Would you agree with Jessica's statement that your parents have never enforced any rules with you? Is that a good philosophy or a negative one?

3. Do you think if Jessica's mom had enforced rules, Jessica would be in a better situation?

4. What's your view on discipline when it comes to children?

5. What were your thoughts as you watched this clip and the confrontation between mom and daughter? Did you see yourself in any of the conversations?

6. Do you think Michiel got through to her daughter in this situation? If your mom did something like this, would it affect you? Why or why not?

7. Is there a point where it's too late for a parent to begin enforcing rules? Why or why not?

8. Is there an addiction that is tearing your family apart? What would it take for you to seek help for that person or that addiction?

Visit www.skitguys.com or www.ysunderground.com for additional elements that might add impact to this clip, including Family Conflicts 6.2f from Instant Skits.

30 Days

TAG: SEEING HOW THE OTHER SIDE LIVES—THE WORKING POOR.

THEMES: Generosity, Giving to the Poor, Money, Wants Versus Needs

THE SERIES/SHOW: *30 Days* is a reality show from filmmaker Morgan Spurlock, best known for the documentary *Super Size Me* in which Spurlock used himself as a guinea pig to investigate the effects of a fast-food diet. Inspired by the results of the documentary and using the same premise for this reality series, Spurlock places individuals in a scenario completely different from their current circumstances for a period of 30 days. During that time participants experience different lifestyles, explore prejudices, and examine cultures foreign to their own.

THE SCENE: Morgan and his fiancé Alex spend 30 days earning and living on minimum wage. They have no credit card and no resources beyond a week's worth of wage pay. Morgan and Alex have found a cheap apartment and minimum-wage jobs, but no creature comforts. Alex is depressed and just wants to have furniture in the apartment. They learn of an outreach by a local church called The Free Store. Founder Steve Rodgers shares the mission of The Free Store—that there is enough for everyone. Moved by the generosity of people who don't have much, Alex and Morgan are able to furnish their apartment at no cost.

START 0:16:33 STOP 0:18:34 (TOTAL CLIP TIME: 2 MINUTES, 1 SECOND)

START DIALOGUE: *(Alex)* I really, really wish that we could find some furniture.

STOP DIALOGUE: *(Alex)* Who cares if it's rice and beans every night? I've got a table and chair.

BY THE BOOK: Exodus 20:17, Matthew 6:25-34, Matthew 25:34-40, Acts 2:44-45, 1 Timothy 6:10

WHERE TO TAKE IT:

1. How did you feel watching people trying to "make it" in this scene?

2. Have you ever compared your life to someone else's and felt like you fell short? Describe your comparison.

3. What does the Bible say in Exodus 20:17 about wanting what others have? Have you ever been guilty of "coveting"? If so, what did you covet?

4. How much do "creature comforts" help us get through life? Have you ever felt like Alex did, that "rice and beans" were enough?

5. Do you agree with 1 Timothy 6:10, which says that the love of money is the root of all evil? Have you ever had an experience that proved or disproved this verse?

6. The statistics show that the biggest givers are the middle-class "working poor." Why do you think that's true?

7. In Matthew 25:34-40, who do you think Jesus means by "the least of these"?

8. What do you think Jesus would say to you about your giving habits? Do you believe that someone has to be rich in order to give?

Visit www.skitguys.com or www.ysunderground.com for additional elements that might add impact to this clip, including the "Meet the Stewards" script.

30 Days

TAG: SEEING HOW THE OTHER SIDE LIVES—MUSLIMS.

IMPORTANT LEADER NOTE: *Though we have chosen this clip specifically for the purposes of the book format, we believe that this entire episode is thoughtful and appropriate for viewing.*

THEMES: Apologizing, Arguing, Communication, Condemnation, Prejudice, Stereotypes, Understanding Others

THE SERIES/SHOW: *30 Days* is a reality show from filmmaker Morgan Spurlock, best known for the documentary *Super Size Me* in which Spurlock used himself as a guinea pig to investigate the effects of a fast-food diet. Inspired by the results of the documentary and using the same premise for this reality series, Spurlock places individuals in a scenario completely different from their current circumstances for a period of 30 days. During that time participants experience different lifestyles, explore prejudices, and examine cultures foreign to their own.

THE SCENE: Dave Stacy, a West Virginia Christian, spends 30 days living as a Muslim in Dearborn, Michigan, with a Muslim couple, Shamael and Sadia Haque. While he is immersed in this new culture and religion, Dave dresses in traditional Muslim attire, studies the Koran, and takes part in religious practices just as his hosts do. One evening Dave makes dinner for the Haques and their friends, Faisal and Ameena, and the group conversation turns to society's prejudices and stereotypes against Muslims because of terrorist activity committed by Muslim extremists around the world. As the conversation becomes heated, Sadia notices that it's time to pray according to Muslim tradition. In a later interview with Spurlock, Dave describes the dramatic effect the prayer time had on the conversation and atmosphere. In accordance with Dave's realizations, Spurlock conducts several on-the-street interviews, questioning people about their views of the Muslim community.

START: 0:32:24 STOP: 0:35:02 (TOTAL CLIP TIME: 2 MINUTES, 38 SECONDS)

START DIALOGUE: *(Dave)* Have you guys had any problems coming across the border?

STOP DIALOGUE: *(Woman)* If they look scary, then it might bother me a little bit.

BONUS CLIP:

SCENE 2: Dave has just been on a radio program that's highlighting his 30-day journey in the Islam faith and culture. He has answered call-in questions and found himself defending the Islamic community as a whole against the many prejudices and negative stereotypes currently held by Americans. After the radio program, Dave talks with lawyer Harris Ahmed and discusses the need for each culture to apologize for crimes committed by a few extremist radicals.

START 0:38:16 STOP: 0:39:00 (TOTAL CLIP TIME: 1 MINUTE, 24 SECONDS)

SCENE TRANSCRIPT:

(Harris) Hey, you know, I heard you on the radio today. I heard your show. I think you definitely came off genuine and you gave your opinions and stuff, but I was concerned by some of the stuff I heard, because one thing I want to make clear is that on 9/11 we…I mean, I do not think we should have to apologize for that as Muslims…just as Christians shouldn't have to apologize for Eric Rudolf.

(Dave) I, for one, would apologize for people like that.

(Harris) Right. Well, there's a difference between condemnation and apology. Do we condemn what happened on 9/11 and the people that are behind that? Yeah, everybody condemns that…but as far as apologizing for it, it's saying, "Yeah, I was responsible for that in some way." And we're American. So why should we be responsible for something that happened to us?

BY THE BOOK: 2 Chronicles 7:14, Matthew 6:12, Luke 6:31, Ephesians 4:29, 1 Peter 2:17

WHERE TO TAKE IT:

1. What emotions did you experience while watching these clips?

2. How would you have answered Morgan's question about being seated next to a Muslim while on an airplane?

3. What do you know about the Muslim culture? Do you know anyone who follows the Islamic faith?

4. Are we all racists to some degree? Why or why not?

5. In light of the events of September 11, do you think it's fair that Muslims have come under such national scrutiny?

6. In the second clip, Harris explains the difference between condemnation and an apology. Do you agree with his assessment? Do you believe the Muslim community owes America an apology?

7. How do you explain the fact that the perpetrators of the September 11 attacks believed they were serving God?

8. Is there any nation or people to whom the United States owes an apology? Why or why not?

Visit www.skitguys.com or www.ysunderground.com for additional elements that might add impact to this clip, including Taboo Conflicts 6.7a from Instant Skits.

30 Days
(REALITY)
SEASON 1, EPISODE 4: "STRAIGHT MAN IN A GAY WORLD"

TAG: ARE INDIVIDUALS BORN GAY, OR IS IT A CHOICE?

IMPORTANT LEADER NOTE: *Both clips from this episode deal frankly with the gay lifestyle and may require some editing for use with teenagers. Though we believe that the value of discussions from these clips could be incredibly high, we also acknowledge that this is controversial subject matter and should be handled carefully, thoughtfully, and with plenty of discretion according to the viewers' needs and maturity levels.*

THEMES: Homosexuality, Interpreting the Bible, Lifestyle, Opinions, Sin, Tolerance

THE SERIES/SHOW: *30 Days* is a reality show from filmmaker Morgan Spurlock, best known for the documentary *Super Size Me* in which Spurlock used himself as a guinea pig to investigate the effects of a fast-food diet. Inspired by the results of the documentary and using the same premise for this reality series, Spurlock places individuals in a scenario completely different from their current circumstances for a period of 30 days. During that time participants experience different lifestyles, explore prejudices, and examine cultures foreign to their own.

THE SCENE: One of the greatest controversies dividing our nation is whether gays and lesbians are born that way, or whether they choose the lifestyle. In man-on-the-street fashion, Spurlock asks various individuals—some gay, some straight—what they think about homosexuality. The straight individuals claim the Bible says it's a sin and an abomination, while gay people firmly believe they were born into their lifestyles.

START 0:11:25 STOP 0:12:31 (TOTAL CLIP TIME: 1 MINUTE, 6 SECONDS)

START DIALOGUE: *(Spurlock)* So, what does the Bible say about sexual orientation? Although Jesus himself never mentioned it, there are six passages cited against homosexuality, including this—Leviticus, chapter 18, verse 22: "Thou shalt not lie with mankind as with womankind. It is an abomination." No other verse in the Bible has sparked more controversy than that.

STOP SCENE: Two men riding a motorcycle with a rainbow flag.

BONUS CLIP: START: 0:21:32 STOP: 0:21:52 (TOTAL CLIP TIME: 20 SECONDS)

START DIALOGUE: *(Robert Knight—Director of the Culture and Family Institute)* The Bible's got nothing good to say about homosexuality. In fact, from Genesis right through the New Testament, homosexuality is condemned. I don't think gay people are any worse than anyone else, as people. They're sinners. They need Jesus. The only problem is when they say, "No, we don't need Jesus. In fact, we're not even committing a sin." That's when they're deluding themselves.

BY THE BOOK: Leviticus 18:22, Leviticus 20:13, Romans 1:27, 1 Corinthians 6:18, Galatians 5:19-23

WHERE TO TAKE IT:

1. Do you believe that homosexuality is a choice or a genetic predisposition? Why or why not?

2. What examples have you seen that support your opinion?

3. Do you believe that a person's sexual orientation matters to God? Does it matter to you?

4. If you believe that homosexuality is a choice, do you believe that it's a sin?

5. What are some of the dangers of living a homosexual lifestyle in today's society?

6. How have homosexuals been treated by Christians and the church? How could that treatment be changed for the better?

7. Are the media's portrayals of gay characters in movies and TV positive or negative?

8. What can you do to heal some of the wounds between the Christian and gay communities?

Visit www.skitguys.com or www.ysunderground.com for additional elements that might add impact to this clip, including Taboo Conflicts 6.7h from Instant Skits.

30 Days
(REALITY)

SEASON 1, EPISODE 4: "STRAIGHT MAN IN A GAY WORLD"

TAG: SEEING HOW THE OTHER SIDE LIVES—HOMOSEXUALITY.

IMPORTANT LEADER NOTE: *Both clips from this episode deal frankly with the gay lifestyle and may require some editing for use with teenagers. Though we believe that the value of discussions resulting from these clips could be incredibly high, we also acknowledge that this is controversial subject matter and should be handled carefully, thoughtfully, and with plenty of discretion according to the viewers' needs and maturity levels.*

THEMES: Beliefs, Condemnation, Homosexuality, Interpreting the Bible, Moral Compass, Prejudice

THE SERIES/SHOW: *30 Days* is a reality show from filmmaker Morgan Spurlock, best known for the documentary *Super Size Me* in which Spurlock used himself as a guinea pig to investigate the effects of a fast-food diet. Inspired by the results of the documentary and using the same premise for this reality series, Spurlock places individuals in a scenario completely different from their current circumstances for a period of 30 days. During that time participants experience different lifestyles, explore prejudices, and examine cultures foreign to their own.

THE SCENE: Army reservist Ryan Hickmott, 24 and straight, is going to spend 30 days living in San Francisco's Castro area—the largest gay community in the country. Once Ryan moves in with Ed, his gay roommate, he's immediately immersed in gay culture. He attends a gay church and begins a dialog with the Reverend Penny about what the Bible says about homosexuality. During their time together, Reverend Penny hopes to change Ryan's beliefs that homosexuality is a sin, but Ryan refuses to alter his views. In a last-ditch effort, Reverend Penny tries to convince Ryan that his interpretation of the Bible is too literal and therefore unfair.

START: 0:35:04 STOP: 0:37:23 (TOTAL CLIP TIME: 2 MINUTES, 19 SECONDS)

START DIALOGUE: *(Spurlock—voiceover)* Ryan has just a few more days left in the Castro before he heads back home and has one final meeting with Reverend Penny.

(Reverend Penny) Normally, you've been having questions for me. But today I want to have questions for you. What would it take for you to say, "I've changed my mind about homosexuality as a sin"?

STOP DIALOGUE: *(Ed)* Yeah, but it's one belief that is basically one of the most important things in her life.

(Ryan) When she sits down and she straight-up asks me, "The topic of homosexuality—do you think that's sin?" I'm gonna be honest with her and say, "Yeah."

BY THE BOOK: Leviticus 18:22, Leviticus 20:13, Romans 1:27, 1 Corinthians 6:18, Galatians 5:19-23

WHERE TO TAKE IT:

1. What does the word *tolerance* mean to you? How do you think Jesus would define that word?

2. The Bible addresses the issue of homosexuality several times (see the listed verses in **By the Book**). Do you think those verses represent God's views?

3. Read Leviticus 20:13. Do you agree with the idea that this verse is outdated or cultural in nature, as with Old Testament practices of sacrificing animals for atonement? Why or why not?

4. Does the church make homosexuals feel welcome? Should churches accept openly gay people as members?

5. Do you believe it's possible to be Christian and homosexual? Why or why not?

6. Read 1 Corinthians 6:18. How is sexual sin different from other sins?

7. Is there a difference between having homosexual tendencies and living a gay lifestyle?

8. How would you respond if a friend or family member revealed to you that he or she is gay? What would you say to that person?

9. What do you believe Jesus would say to someone like Ed? What about someone like Reverend Penny? Does Ryan accurately represent Jesus in this clip? Why or why not?

Visit www.skitguys.com or www.ysunderground.com for additional elements that might add impact to this clip, including Taboo Conflicts 6.7h from Instant Skits.

Alias

TAG: SO, WHAT'S IT LIKE TO BE A MODERN-DAY PHARISEE?

THEMES: Deception, Faith, Good Versus Evil, Hypocrisy, Lies, Secrets, Sin, Soul, Trust

THE SERIES/SHOW: *Alias* follows the complicated life of Sydney Bristow (Jennifer Garner), a young woman who displays many faces to the world, none of which represent her true identity. Working with "SD-6," a Black Ops division of the CIA, Sydney has been forced to shroud her life in a series of secrets and lies. While those closest to her think she's taking frequent business trips for her job at a prestigious bank, Sydney is actually going on dangerous undercover military operations to maintain the defense and freedom of the United States. For each operation, Sydney must change her identity, taking on new personas and disguises. Sydney's missions sometimes take her across the path of her estranged father Jack Bristow (Victor Garber) on his own mysterious assignments. Father and daughter battle foreign enemies, domestic terrorists, and sometimes each other as they each strive to preserve the freedom of the country they love.

THE SCENE: Sydney has become a double agent working both for SD-6 and undercover for the CIA. Living a double life is becoming more difficult for Sydney, and she's finding it hard to lie to her close colleagues at the agency. She feels burdened that there are so many good people working for SD-6 who don't know they're being deceived, and every time one is killed in the line of duty, Sydney feels as though their blood is on her hands for not telling them the truth. After a difficult mission during which a close friend and colleague was killed, Sydney meets with Michael Vaughn (Michael Vartan), her CIA handler. Sobbing, she confesses her feelings, thankful that someone is there who can understand her personal crisis.

START: 0:32:57 STOP: 0:35:43 (TOTAL CLIP TIME: 2 MINUTES, 46 SECONDS)

START DIALOGUE: *(Sydney)* I feel like I'm losing my mind. Like I don't even know who I am anymore or what I'm doing or why I'm doing it.

STOP DIALOGUE: *(Vaughn)* I've seen you work. I've seen who you are...In this job, you see darkness. You see the worst in people. And though the jobs are different and the missions change and the enemies have a thousand names, the one crucial thing, the one real responsibility you have, is to not let your rage and your resentment and your disgust darken you.

BY THE BOOK: Proverbs 3:5-7, Ecclesiastes 1:18, Matthew 6:24, Mark 7:6, Revelation 3:15-16

WHERE TO TAKE IT:

1. Though most of us aren't literally double agents, sometimes we do live double lives by acting one way with our Christian friends and then changing our language and demeanor when we talk to our non-Christian friends. Describe a time you found yourself in this very situation.

2. Why are we so secretive when it comes to our faith?

3. How hard is it to live in two worlds? Why do we feel like we have to walk that line?

4. Why does sin in our lives put up a barrier between us and God? Have you ever found yourself wishing you could just continue a certain sin and stop feeling bad about it?

5. In the clip, Vaughn talks about seeing darkness but not letting those things darken the soul. Have any of your experiences "darkened" your heart?

6. In Proverbs 3:5-7, what does the Bible say about the heart?

7. In today's world, how hard is it to trust the Lord with all your heart?

8. As you get older, do you find that it's harder or easier to trust God with every situation?

Visit www.skitguys.com or www.ysunderground.com for additional elements that might add impact to this clip, including the "Run in Such a Way" script from Skits That Teach.

Alias

(DRAMA)

SEASON 1, EPISODE 3: "PARITY"

TAG: *SORRY* SEEMS TO BE THE HARDEST WORD.

THEMES: Communication, Father-Daughter Relationships, Forgiveness, Hurt, Letting Go, Understanding Others

THE SERIES/SHOW: *Alias* follows the complicated life of Sydney Bristow (Jennifer Garner), a young woman who displays many faces to the world, none of which represent her true identity. Working with "SD-6," a Black Ops division of the CIA, Sydney has been forced to shroud her life in a series of secrets and lies. While those closest to her think she's taking frequent business trips for her job at a prestigious bank, Sydney is actually going on dangerous undercover military operations to maintain the defense and freedom of the United States. For each operation, Sydney must change her identity, taking on new personas and disguises. Sydney's missions sometimes take her across the path of her estranged father Jack Bristow (Victor Garber) on his own mysterious assignments. Father and daughter battle foreign enemies, domestic terrorists, and sometimes each other as they each strive to preserve the freedom of the country they love.

THE SCENE: Sydney and best friend Francie (Merrin Dungey) discuss their relationships with their fathers. Sydney finds herself jealous of Francie, who has a great relationship with her dad. A lifetime of hurt stands between Sydney and her father Jack, but Francie encourages her to make an effort to forgive him so they can move forward to a better relationship in the future.

START 0:04:59 STOP 0:06:09 (TOTAL CLIP TIME: 1 MINUTE, 10 SECONDS)

START DIALOGUE: *(Sydney)* I can't believe you can call your dad for advice. I just can't imagine.

STOP DIALOGUE: *(Francie)* But hey, if you can find it in your heart to forgive him for being the kind of guy he's been all your life—which I would find impossible and could never do—then you should make a real effort.

BY THE BOOK: Psalm 68:5, Malachi 4:6, Matthew 6:14, Luke 6:37, Luke 17:3-4

WHERE TO TAKE IT:

1. What kind of relationship do you have with your dad?

2. As you watched this clip, did you find yourself wishing you could be honest with your father? What would you say to him if you had the chance?

3. Francie tells Sydney that the only way to begin to heal her relationship with her dad is through forgiveness. Is there someone you need to forgive? If so, whom?

4. When we've been hurt, why do we seem to hold on to pain or anger rather than forgive the offense?

5. Do you think we're supposed to *feel* like forgiving someone before we forgive him or her? What about times when the person who hurt us hasn't asked to be forgiven?

6. Luke 6:37 reads, "Forgive and you will be forgiven." What is this Scripture passage saying?

7. Is there anything in your life that you need to let go of, or surrender, through forgiveness?

8. Is it ever possible to "forgive and forget"?

Visit www.skitguys.com or www.ysunderground.com for additional elements that might add impact to this clip, including the "Baggage" video.

Alias

(DRAMA)

SEASON 1, EPISODE 11: "THE CONFESSION"

TAG: SOMETIMES THE TRUTH IS HARD TO HEAR.

THEMES: Communication, Deception, Family, Lies, Parents, Secrets

THE SERIES/SHOW: *Alias* follows the complicated life of Sydney Bristow (Jennifer Garner), a young woman who displays many faces to the world, none of which represent her true identity. Working with "SD-6," a Black Ops division of the CIA, Sydney has been forced to shroud her life in a series of secrets and lies. While those closest to her think she's taking frequent business trips for her job at a prestigious bank, Sydney is actually going on dangerous undercover military operations to maintain the defense and freedom of the United States. For each operation, Sydney must change her identity, taking on new personas and disguises. Sydney's missions sometimes take her across the path of her estranged father Jack Bristow (Victor Garber) on his own mysterious assignments. Father and daughter battle foreign enemies, domestic terrorists, and sometimes each other as they each strive to preserve the freedom of the country they love.

THE SCENE: Sydney has always believed that her mother was a professor of literature. By accident she finds Russian Cyrillic codes written with invisible ink on the pages of some books her father gave to her mother as wedding gifts. Believing that her father may be a double agent with the KGB, Sydney gives the books to Vaughn to be analyzed by the CIA. The codes reveal the names of CIA agents who were to be murdered by a KGB operative, including Vaughn's father. As Sydney and Vaughn dig deeper into the case, they both find out more than they bargained for—things that change Sydney's image of her mother forever.

START: 0:41:23 STOP: 0:43:57 (TOTAL CLIP TIME: 2 MINUTES, 34 SECONDS)

START DIALOGUE: *(Jack)* This is CIA director Devlin, deputy director Tucker, executive director Gerstner, and these are senior officers Haley, Stafford, and Collum.

STOP DIALOGUE: *(Jack)* But Sydney, I was not that agent…your mother was.

BY THE BOOK: Proverbs 3:5-6, Philippians 1:6, Philippians 2:8, 2 Timothy 4:7, 1 Peter 4:8

WHERE TO TAKE IT:

1. Not many of us have Sydney's traumatic family life, but we all have plenty of drama in our own families. How would you feel if you found out your parents had lied to you about something important?

2. Do you believe you can count on your mom and dad to be who they say they are?

3. How do lies and secrets hurt a family?

4. What can you do to keep the lines of communication open within your family?

5. Who do you identify with the most—your mom or dad? Why?

6. What can you do to become closer to the parent you don't quite see eye-to-eye with?

7. What can you do to help your home life run more smoothly?

Visit www.skitguys.com or www.ysunderground.com for additional elements that might add impact to this clip, including Family Conflicts 6.2e from Instant Skits.

Alias

(DRAMA)

SEASON 1, EPISODE 16: "THE PROPHECY"

TAG: DOES FEAR KEEP YOU FROM FINDING THE ANSWERS?

THEMES: Awareness, Compassion, Death, Fear, Hurt, Suffering, Terminal Illness

THE SERIES/SHOW: *Alias* follows the complicated life of Sydney Bristow (Jennifer Garner), a young woman who displays many faces to the world, none of which represent her true identity. Working with "SD-6," a Black Ops division of the CIA, Sydney has been forced to shroud her life in a series of secrets and lies. While those closest to her think she's taking frequent business trips for her job at a prestigious bank, Sydney is actually going on dangerous undercover military operations to maintain the defense and freedom of the United States. For each operation, Sydney must change her identity, taking on new personas and disguises. Sydney's missions sometimes take her across the path of her estranged father Jack Bristow (Victor Garber) on his own mysterious assignments. Father and daughter battle foreign enemies, domestic terrorists, and sometimes each other as they each strive to preserve the freedom of the country they love.

THE SCENE: Sydney visits cancer-stricken Emily (Amy Irving), the wife of her boss Arvin Sloane (Ron Rifkin). To Sydney's dismay, Emily bluntly discusses her illness and impending death. It hurts Sydney to hear her friend sounding so fatalistic, but Emily is certain that she will die since she waited so long to go to the doctor. Emily explains to Sydney how fear kept her from finding out the truth about her own health.

START: 0:18:17 STOP: 0:19:45 (TOTAL CLIP TIME: 1 MINUTE, 28 SECONDS)

START DIALOGUE: *(Emily)* I know this has been difficult for Arvin. My illness. I look just like everyone else and usually feel that way. Fact is...I won't be alive next Christmas.

STOP DIALOGUE: *(Emily)* Wanting to know the truth, but being too afraid to find the answers.

BY THE BOOK: Proverbs 29:25, Isaiah 41:10, John 16:33, 2 Timothy 1:7, Hebrews 13:6

WHERE TO TAKE IT:

1. Describe a time when you knew something was wrong but chose to ignore it.

2. Do you believe that God is in control of your life no matter what your circumstances may be?

3. Does it build up or tear down your faith to see suffering in the world or in the lives of your loved ones?

4. Have you ever wished you could make a situation better but couldn't bring yourself to do anything for fear of the unknown?

5. How do you think you can ultimately overcome your fears so they don't limit you from moving forward and living a joyful life?

6. When you read 2 Timothy 1:7, how does that verse give you perspective on your present and future problems?

7. Describe a time when you were "paralyzed" with fear, either in a funny or dangerous situation.

8. Do you see yourself as a controlling or trusting type of person?

Visit www.skitguys.com or www.ysunderground.com for additional elements that might add impact to this clip, including the "God is in Control" script.

Desperate Housewives

(COMEDY/DRAMA)

SEASON 1, EPISODE 10: "COME BACK TO ME"

TAG: ARE YOU A "PARENT" TO YOUR MOM OR DAD?

THEMES: Boundary Lines, Divorce, Maturity, Parent-Child Relationships, Respect, Roles, Selfishness

THE SERIES/SHOW: This drama reveals the messy lives of five neighbors living on the charming yet deceptive Wisteria Lane. Flighty divorced mom Susan Mayer (Teri Hatcher), Martha Stewart clone Bree Van De Kamp (Marcia Cross), former professional turned stay-at-home mom Lynette Scavo (Felicity Huffman), spoiled ex-model Gabrielle Solis (Eva Longoria Parker), and sultry real-estate agent Edie Britt (Nicolette Sheridan) trade gossip, secrets, and men under the watchful eye of dearly departed friend Mary Alice Young (Brenda Strong). Having chosen suicide over life in the "perfect" American suburb, Mary Alice now observes the residents of Wisteria Lane with a new and unique perspective, sharing insight with the audience about what truly goes on during the days, and nights, of a "desperate housewife."

THE SCENE: Since his mother's recent suicide, Zach Young (Cody Kasch) has been on the verge of remembering a terrible family secret, and the frustration and anger building up has caused him to be aggressive and act out in strange ways. In order to keep Zach compliant and prevent him from remembering anything significant, Zach's father, Paul (Mark Moses), had been drugging him. To escape his father, Zach goes to his friend Julie (Andrea Bowen) for refuge and help, but when Susan finds Zach hiding in her daughter's room, she immediately sends him back to his father. When Julie demands to know why her mother betrayed her trust, Susan responds that she was attempting to be a responsible mother. Overcome with frustration, Julie lashes out at Susan and tells her who has really been the "mother" around their house.

START: 0:26:02 STOP: 0:27:21 (TOTAL CLIP TIME: 1 MINUTE, 19 SECONDS)

START DIALOGUE: *(Susan)* Here's the candles I borrowed. Thanks.

STOP DIALOGUE: *(Julie)* Well, now Zach's the one who's in trouble. You sent him back to a man who hates him.

BY THE BOOK: Romans 3:23, Ephesians 6:1-3, Philippians 2:3, 1 Timothy 4:12, 1 Timothy 5:4

WHERE TO TAKE IT:

1. Have you ever had to take over the parenting role to help one of your parents during a difficult time?

2. What situation caused your mom or dad to stop parenting (e.g., depression, illness, alcohol or drug abuse, spousal abuse, job stress/long hours, etc.)?

3. In your opinion, is it difficult to reverse the roles of parent to son or daughter?

4. How did you feel about your mom and dad when they couldn't give you the support and attention you needed?

5. Do you think kids lose respect for their parents when they don't act like "mom" or "dad"?

6. Is it important to have your mom or dad as your "best friend"?

7. In the case of a divorce, is the parent-child relationship automatically redefined? In what ways?

8. How is it possible to regain respect for your parents when it has been damaged or lost?

Visit www.skitguys.com or www.ysunderground.com for additional elements that might add impact to this clip, including the "Man to Man" script.

Desperate Housewives
(COMEDY/DRAMA)
SEASON 1, EPISODE 8: "GUILTY"

TAG: MY MORAL COMPASS WILL HAVE TO GO ON THE BACK BURNER FOR THIS ONE.

THEMES: Choices, God's Word, Guilt, Handling Problems, Mistakes, Moral Compass, Parenting, Sin

THE SERIES/SHOW: This drama reveals the messy lives of five neighbors living on the charming yet deceptive Wisteria Lane. Flighty divorced mom Susan Mayer (Teri Hatcher), Martha Stewart clone Bree Van De Kamp (Marcia Cross), former professional turned stay-at-home mom Lynette Scavo (Felicity Huffman), spoiled ex-model Gabrielle Solis (Eva Longoria Parker), and sultry real-estate agent Edie Britt (Nicolette Sheridan) trade gossip, secrets, and men under the watchful eye of dearly departed friend Mary Alice Young (Brenda Strong). Having chosen suicide over life in the "perfect" American suburb, Mary Alice now observes the residents of Wisteria Lane with a new and unique perspective, sharing insight with the audience about what truly goes on during the days, and nights, of a "desperate housewife."

THE SCENE: Caught in a dilemma, Bree mulls over some of her past choices as she and Rex (Steven Culp) try to figure out how to cover up the fact that their son, Andrew (Shawn Pyfrom), hit Mrs. Solis (Lupe Ontiveros) with his car. Andrew was drunk and speeding and left the scene of the crime, and Bree is unable to stand the thought of him going to jail for the rest of his life. She goes to her Bible seeking wisdom, but then devises a plan to have Andrew's car stolen to make it appear as though someone else was the culprit. Bree realizes that rather than gaining guidance from God's Word, she has only made her burden of guilt even heavier than before.

START: 0:00:36 STOP 0:02:42 (TOTAL CLIP TIME: 2 MINUTES, 6 SECONDS)

START DIALOGUE: *(Mary Alice's voice)* There is a widely read book that tells us everyone is a sinner. Of course, not everyone who reads this book feels guilt over the bad things they do. But Bree Van De Kamp did. In fact, Bree had spent most of her life feeling guilty. As a child, she felt guilty about not getting straight As. As a teenager, she felt guilty about letting her boyfriend go to second base. As a newlywed, she felt guilty about taking three weeks to get out her thank-you cards. But she knew the transgressions of her past, and they were nothing compared to the sin she was about to commit.

STOP DIALOGUE: *(Bree)* Well, everybody should go wash up. We're having pancakes for breakfast.

BY THE BOOK: Acts 3:19, Romans 6:13-16, 1 Corinthians 6:12, James 5:16, 1 John 1:9

WHERE TO TAKE IT:

1. What did you think of Rex and Bree's decision?

2. When you watch this clip, would you have done the same thing for a loved one or friend? Why or why not?

3. What do you think your parents would have done if they were in the same situation as the Van De Kamps?

4. Have you ever faced a decision where you went to the Bible and found Scripture to help you through your situation but decided to do things your own way? What was the outcome?

5. Read 1 Corinthians 6:12. What do you think this passage of Scripture is referring to when it comes to your life and decisions?

6. Is it ever good or healthy to get someone out of his mistakes instead of allowing him to face the consequences?

Visit www.skitguys.com or www.ysunderground.com for additional elements that might add impact to this clip, including "Holding Grudges" from Skits That Teach.

Desperate Housewives

(COMEDY/DRAMA)

SEASON 1, EPISODE 8: "GUILTY"

TAG: WE GET BY WITH A LITTLE HELP FROM OUR FRIENDS.

THEMES: Confession, Friendship, Hurt, Image, Parenting, Pressure, Secrets, Stress, Turmoil

THE SERIES/SHOW: This drama reveals the messy lives of five neighbors living on the charming yet deceptive Wisteria Lane. Flighty divorced mom Susan Mayer (Teri Hatcher), Martha Stewart clone Bree Van De Kamp (Marcia Cross), former professional turned stay-at-home mom Lynette Scavo (Felicity Huffman), spoiled ex-model Gabrielle Solis (Eva Longoria Parker), and sultry real-estate agent Edie Britt (Nicolette Sheridan) trade gossip, secrets, and men under the watchful eye of dearly departed friend Mary Alice Young (Brenda Strong). Having chosen suicide over life in the "perfect" American suburb, Mary Alice now observes the residents of Wisteria Lane with a new and unique perspective, sharing insight with the audience about what truly goes on during the days, and nights, of a "desperate housewife."

THE SCENE: Overwhelmed by the stress of motherhood, Lynette has finally had an emotional breakdown and abruptly leaves her children with Susan. Susan passes the children along to Julie (Andrea Bowen) and calls Bree to help her find Lynette. When they finally find her at the school soccer field, depressed and hurting, Lynette tells her friends that she has failed as a mother and can't do it anymore. Susan and Bree relate their own fears about parenting, and all three begin to discuss how hard motherhood really is for each of them. As they talk, Lynette finds herself encouraged that she might not be such a bad mother after all.

START: 0:34:56 STOP: 0:36:37 (TOTAL CLIP TIME: 1 MINUTE, 41 SECONDS)

START DIALOGUE: *(Lynette)* Then I started taking the pills because they gave me energy, but then I couldn't sleep at night and I was so tired in the daytime and it totally messed me up. I love my kids so much. I'm so sorry they have me as a mother.

STOP DIALOGUE: *(Lynette)* Yeah. It really does. *(The women hug her.)*

BY THE BOOK: Psalm 73:26, Mark 10:27, John 14:27, 1 Corinthians 10:13, James 5:16

WHERE TO TAKE IT:

1. Can you share your failures with those closest to you?

2. Why do we try to make it appear as though we have it all together?

3. Is it easier to keep all of your sadness and disappointments to yourself?

4. How do you handle your stress? Are you a "stuffer" or an "exploder"? (Stuffers keep everything inside; exploders release everything in anger.)

5. Why do you suppose it's so hard to admit that we can't handle "the pressure" and need a little help?

6. Does it help you to know that the people you look up to have also failed and know how it feels to be "less than perfect"?

7. Even though this clip refers to parenting issues, what aspects of your life make you feel isolated and alone and struggling just to keep up?

8. Do your parents act like they have it all together? Do you think it's sometimes hard for them to meet the needs of everyone in your family?

9. What were you taught about sharing your problems? Do you think your parents were taught this as well? Why or why not?

Visit www.skitguys.com or www.ysunderground.com for additional elements that might add impact to this clip, including the "Meet the McWraths" script.

TAG: BUT MOM—EVERYONE IS "DOING IT"!

THEMES: Abstinence, Acceptance, Love, Parenting-Child Relationships, Sex, Values, Virginity

THE SERIES/SHOW: This drama reveals the messy lives of five neighbors living on the charming yet deceptive Wisteria Lane. Flighty divorced mom Susan Mayer (Teri Hatcher), Martha Stewart clone Bree Van De Kamp (Marcia Cross), former professional turned stay-at-home mom Lynette Scavo (Felicity Huffman), spoiled ex-model Gabrielle Solis (Eva Longoria Parker), and sultry real-estate agent Edie Britt (Nicolette Sheridan) trade gossip, secrets, and men under the watchful eye of dearly departed friend Mary Alice Young (Brenda Strong). Having chosen suicide over life in the "perfect" American suburb, Mary Alice now observes the residents of Wisteria Lane with a new and unique perspective, sharing insight with the audience about what truly goes on during the days, and nights, of a "desperate housewife."

THE SCENE: Conservative, old-fashioned Bree has been faced with a shock—the discovery of a wrapped condom in the family laundry basket. Even more astounded to find that the condom belongs not to troubled son Andrew (Shawn Pyfrom) but to seemingly perfect daughter Danielle (Joy Lauren), Bree musters up the courage to confront her child about the choices she appears to be making.

START: 0:10:47 STOP: 0:12:23 (TOTAL CLIP TIME: 1 MINUTE, 36 SECONDS)

IMPORTANT LEADER NOTE: *Because of the sensitive nature of this subject, we've included the entire transcript of this scene. We believe you'll find that the show's writers accurately and effectively captured a realistic parent-child conversation about sex that could be an extremely useful discussion starter with your group.*

SCENE TRANSCRIPT:

(Bree) So obviously we need to talk.

(Danielle) I'm still a virgin if that's what you want to know.

(Bree) Good. But why on earth would you need a condom?

(Danielle) 'Cause I'm planning on having sex, and I don't want to get pregnant.

(Bree) Danielle, you are president of the Abstinence Club!

(Danielle) I wasn't planning on running for a second term.

(Bree) Who are you planning on having sex with?

(Danielle) John.

(Bree) John Roland? *(Gabrielle's gardener)* I thought you broke up with him?

(Danielle) No. He broke up with me. And you want to know why? Because I wouldn't do it!

(Bree) Well, if that's the type of boy he is, then good riddance.

(Danielle) Mom, every boy at my school is that type of boy. Besides, it's different with John. I love him.

(Bree) Oh, sweetheart. Just because you give a boy sex doesn't mean you'll get love in return.

(Danielle) So maybe I'm being stupid. So what's the big deal? It's just *sex*.

(Bree) Honey, I am looking out for your happiness. I understand what it's like to be young and feel urges. I waited until I got married, as did your father, and it was so much better.

(Danielle) But Daddy ended up cheating on you. And ever since he moved back, you've been miserable.

(Bree) Why would you say that?

(Danielle) The walls between our bedrooms are paper-thin. I hear more stuff than I probably should. Look, Mom, I love you a lot, but you are the last person to ever give anyone advice about sex and happiness. *(After giving Bree a quick hug and kiss, she leaves.)*

BY THE BOOK: 1 Corinthians 6:12-20, Ephesians 5:3, 1 Thessalonians 4: 3-5, Titus 2:6, Hebrews 13:4

WHERE TO TAKE IT:

1. Would it be difficult for you to talk to your mom or dad about sex?

2. How have you reacted (or would you react) if your mom or dad gave you advice about sex?

3. How do you feel about your parents' relationship when you hear them disagree or argue?

4. As you watch this scene, is Danielle accurately describing a high school relationship? What usually happens when a girl says "no" to a guy?

5. Why do many girls give away their virginity?

6. Why is sex so important in the first place?

7. After Bree says that John may not love Danielle, she retorts, "It's just *sex.*" Is it ever "just sex"? Is it different for guys than it is for girls?

Visit www.skitguys.com or www.ysunderground.com for additional elements that might add impact to this clip, including the "I've Had Sex" script or video.

Desperate Housewives
(COMEDY/DRAMA)
SEASON 1, EPISODE 6: "RUNNING TO STAND STILL"

TAG: ANYTHING THEY CAN DO, I CAN DO BETTER...

THEMES: Abilities, Comparisons, Competition, Insecurity, Letting Go

THE SERIES/SHOW: This drama reveals the messy lives of five neighbors living on the charming yet deceptive Wisteria Lane. Flighty divorced mom Susan Mayer (Teri Hatcher), Martha Stewart clone Bree Van De Kamp (Marcia Cross), former professional turned stay-at-home mom Lynette Scavo (Felicity Huffman), spoiled ex-model Gabrielle Solis (Eva Longoria Parker), and sultry real-estate agent Edie Britt (Nicollette Sheridan) trade gossip, secrets, and men under the watchful eye of dearly departed friend Mary Alice Young (Brenda Strong). Having chosen suicide over life in the "perfect" American suburb, Mary Alice now observes the residents of Wisteria Lane with a new and unique perspective, sharing insight with the audience about what truly goes on during the days, and nights, of a "desperate housewife."

THE SCENE: Lynette and husband Tom (Doug Savant) have just finished a formal dinner party for Tom's boss and coworkers. Knowing that Tom was going to pitch his idea for a new ad campaign, Lynette blurts out Tom's idea, which everyone loves. The focus of the party switches from Tom to Lynette, making Tom feel unimportant. After their guests leave, Tom tells Lynette he didn't appreciate her butting in and accuses her of competing with him. She apologizes, but says that her actual competition is with the "perfect wives" of the neighborhood. Lynette confesses to Tom how hard she tries to keep up with the other moms and how miserably she believes she is failing. Tom reassures Lynette that everyone, especially him, considers her to be a great wife and mother.

START 0:39:12 STOP 0:40:36 (TOTAL CLIP TIME: 1 MINUTE, 14 SECONDS)

START DIALOGUE: *(Lynette)* I was just participating.

STOP DIALOGUE: *(Lynette)* Thanks.

BY THE BOOK: Job 4:8, Romans 12:2, 2 Corinthians 10:12, Galatians 6:3-5, Galatians 6:8

WHERE TO TAKE IT:

1. Why do we compare ourselves to other people?

2. Do you notice families around you trying to "keep up" with each other?

3. In what area do you think you compare yourself or compete with others most often (e.g., grades, looks/fashion, popularity, number of boyfriends/ girlfriends, sports, spirituality, intelligence, etc.)?

4. What does it take to be happy with yourself no matter what the circumstances?

5. If you're not happy with yourself, why do you think that is?

6. What does it mean to have a "competitive spirit"?

7. What does the Bible say about contentment?

8. Take a hard look at yourself when it comes to relationships...do you "one-up" when it comes to conversations and experiences? Does that habit draw people closer to you or push them away?

Visit www.skitguys.com or www.ysunderground.com for additional elements that might add impact to this clip, including the "I Want to be More Like" script.

Everybody Loves Raymond
(COMEDY)
SEASON 6, EPISODE 8: "IT'S SUPPOSED TO BE FUN"

TAG: YOUR DAD SAID YOU LOOK LIKE SCOOBY-DOO.

THEMES: Apologizing, Expectations, Hurtful Words, Parent-Child Relationships, Sports

THE SERIES/SHOW: This situation comedy centers around sportswriter Ray Barone (Ray Romano) and his wife Debra (Patricia Heaton), who deeply regret their decision to move across the street from Ray's parents, Frank and Marie Barone (Peter Boyle and Doris Roberts), who don't know the meaning of the word *boundaries*. Ray's brother Robert (Brad Garrett) is a middle-aged, divorced policeman who has finally moved out of his parents' house and into his own apartment to get on with his life. Though he's the firstborn of the Barone family, Robert suffers from jealousy over Raymond's career and family, as well as low self-esteem because Raymond is the favorite son. Robert's sarcastic motto, hence the title of the show, is, "Everybody loves Raymond!"

THE SCENE: Debra explains to Ray that their son, Geoffrey (Sawyer Sweeten), quit his basketball team after overhearing Ray tell the coach that Geoffrey looked like Scooby-Doo. Ray insists that Geoffrey must have misunderstood what was actually said, provoking a discussion about the importance of parents' words and the power they have on children.

START: 00:08:39 STOP: 00:12:21 (TOTAL CLIP TIME: 3 MINUTES, 42 SECONDS)

START DIALOGUE: *(Debra)* Geoffrey quit basketball.

STOP DIALOGUE: *(Raymond)* I'll talk to him...I'm gonna need a lot of gum.

BY THE BOOK: Psalm 49:3, John 20:23, Ephesians 6:4, Colossians 3:21, 1 Thessalonians 2:11-12

WHERE TO TAKE IT:

1. Do your parents encourage you, comfort you, and urge you to live a righteous life?

2. Are your parents funny? Have they ever hurt you with a joke? Describe what happened.

3. Did you tell your parents that what they said hurt you?

4. Do you think your parents would apologize and make things right if they knew they had hurt you?

5. Since all parents are human and make mistakes, how can we pray for God to help them be the best they can be?

6. Has someone ever heard what you said about him or her and been hurt?

7. What do you think is the best course of action for Ray to take in this situation?

8. Why do you think words are so powerful and can be so hurtful? Why is it that the words of one person can be more hurtful than the words of another?

Visit www.skitguys.com or www.ysunderground.com for additional elements that might add impact to this clip, including the "Catch the Pass" script.

TAG: TELL ME THERE IS A PURPOSE TO IT ALL!

THEMES: God, the Meaning of Life, Purpose, Questions, Why We're Here

THE SERIES/SHOW: This situation comedy centers around sportswriter Ray Barone (Ray Romano) and his wife Debra (Patricia Heaton), who deeply regret their decision to move across the street from Ray's parents, Frank and Marie Barone (Peter Boyle and Doris Roberts), who don't know the meaning of the word *boundaries*. Ray's brother Robert (Brad Garrett) is a middle-aged, divorced policeman who has finally moved out of his parents' house and into his own apartment to get on with his life. Though he's the firstborn of the Barone family, Robert suffers from jealousy over Raymond's career and family, as well as low self-esteem because Raymond is the favorite son. Robert's sarcastic motto, hence the title of the show, is, "Everybody loves Raymond!"

THE SCENE: Ray tells Debra that their daughter Ally (Madylin Sweeten) is wondering about the "meaning of life." During their discussion on how to explain it to her, Frank, Marie, and Robert all come over to watch the "big game" on TV. Debra tries to protest that she and Ray have something important to take care of—Ally and her questions—but Frank and Marie start meddling as usual.

START: 00:11:38 STOP: 00:17:15 (TOTAL CLIP TIME: 4 MINUTES, 37 SECONDS)

START DIALOGUE: *(Debra)* Will you please stop?! It turns out that Ally doesn't want to know *how* we get here; she wants to know *why* we're here—why God put us on earth. And she's waiting for Ray to answer her.

STOP DIALOGUE: *(Raymond)* So, God made us smart enough to know that there's an answer, but not smart enough to figure it out?

BY THE BOOK: Exodus 9:16, Psalm 139:13-16, Isaiah 40:25-26, Romans 8:28, Ephesians 1:4-14

WHERE TO TAKE IT:

1. Can we really know the meaning of life?

2. Does the Bible tell us what the meaning of life really is?

3. How can we find our true purpose in life?

4. Why do you think it was so difficult for Ray and Debra to answer Ally's question?

5. Do you think, like Ray, that "God made us smart enough to know that there's an answer, but not smart enough to figure it out"? If so, why?

6. Though there may be certain things about space and time and the way God created the universe that we'll never understand, answers to questions as important as, "Why did God make me?" are meant to be sought out. How have you tried to answer this question for yourself?

7. What are some resources you could utilize or people you could approach to help in your search for answers?

8. What do you feel like your purpose in life is?

BONUS CLIP: START 00:05:11 STOP 0:07:12 (TOTAL CLIP TIME: 2 MINUTES, 1 SECOND)

SCENE 2: Out of the blue, Ally asks Ray, "Where do babies come from?" catching him unprepared and unable to explain it to her. Debra insists that Ray should be the one to talk with Ally since he's the one she asked, so Ray reads up on the subject to build his confidence. As the scene ends, Ray dutifully goes to Ally's room to talk to his daughter.

Visit www.skitguys.com or www.ysunderground.com for additional elements that might add impact to this clip, including "The Birdcage" script or video.

TAG: LADIES AND GENTLEMEN, I PRESENT TO YOU...THE ANGRY FAMILY!

THEMES: Arguing, Blaming Others, Family, Stress, Yelling

THE SERIES/SHOW: This situation comedy centers around sportswriter Ray Barone (Ray Romano) and his wife Debra (Patricia Heaton), who deeply regret their decision to move across the street from Ray's parents, Frank and Marie Barone (Peter Boyle and Doris Roberts), who don't know the meaning of the word *boundaries*. Ray's brother Robert (Brad Garrett) is a middle-aged, divorced policeman who has finally moved out of his parents' house and into his own apartment to get on with his life. Though he's the firstborn of the Barone family, Robert suffers from jealousy over Raymond's career and family, as well as low self-esteem because Raymond is the favorite son. Robert's sarcastic motto, hence the title of the show, is, "Everybody loves Raymond!"

THE SCENE: Ray and Debra have been at a school open house for twins Michael and Geoffrey (Sullivan and Sawyer Sweeten). While sitting in the classroom, Ray and Debra find themselves watching in horror as Michael reads a story he wrote called "The Angry Family," in front of everyone, including Ray's parents. Back at home, Ray and Debra try to figure out the reason behind Michael's story, point the blame at each other, and end up yelling just like the characters in "The Angry Family."

START: 00:05:21 STOP: 00:06:33 (TOTAL CLIP TIME: 1 MINUTE, 12 SECONDS)

START DIALOGUE: *(Raymond)* Hey—if you were on top of stuff, you could have stopped this story from leaking out!

STOP DIALOGUE: *(Raymond)* Well, you assume that there must be yelling!

BY THE BOOK: Matthew 15:18-19, Luke 6:45, Ephesians 6:4, Philippians 2:14-16, James 3:9

WHERE TO TAKE IT:

1. When Ray says their family is "comparatively normal," what do you think he means?

2. Is yelling normal in your family? If so, when does yelling mostly occur?

3. Tell about a time when your family didn't yell, when a stressful situation was handled more calmly. How did that make you feel?

4. Do you yell at your mom and dad or brothers and sisters? Why?

5. What do you think you could do to deal with stressful situations without yelling?

6. Why do you think we yell at the people we love the most?

7. What can you do the next time you want to yell at someone?

8. How do you feel when someone yells at you about something?

Visit www.skitguys.com or www.ysunderground.com for additional elements that might add impact to this clip, including the "Meet the McWraths" script.

Everybody Loves Raymond
(COMEDY)
SEASON 6, EPISODE 18: "THE BREAK-UP TAPE"

TAG: OH, COME ON, JUST *LET IT GO!*

THEMES: Arguing, Dealing with the Past, the Future, Hurt Feelings, Jealousy, Letting Go, Memories, Rejection, Relationships

THE SERIES/SHOW: This situation comedy centers around sportswriter Ray Barone (Ray Romano) and his wife Debra (Patricia Heaton), who deeply regret their decision to move across the street from Ray's parents, Frank and Marie Barone (Peter Boyle and Doris Roberts), who don't know the meaning of the word *boundaries*. Ray's brother Robert (Brad Garrett) is a middle-aged, divorced policeman who has finally moved out of his parents' house and into his own apartment to get on with his life. Though he's the firstborn of the Barone family, Robert suffers from jealousy over Raymond's career and family, as well as low self-esteem because Raymond is the favorite son. Robert's sarcastic motto, hence the title of the show, is, "Everybody loves Raymond!"

THE SCENE: While cleaning out the basement, Debra finds an old answering-machine tape containing a break-up message from a former girlfriend of Ray's. Discovery of the tape sparks a discussion between Ray and Debra about the boyfriends and girlfriends each dated before they got married. As the conversation progresses, Debra shocks Ray by telling him that there are some things in the house (a pepper grinder, picture frame, lamp, and bird feeder) that were gifts from some of her old boyfriends. Consumed by jealousy, Ray goes out and buys replacements for each item, even writing Debra a poem in hopes that she will throw away the one from her 10th-grade boyfriend. Ray finally blows up and gives Debra an ultimatum to get rid of everything from her past.

START: 00:16:44 STOP: 00:19:25 (TOTAL CLIP TIME: 2 MINUTES, 41 SECONDS)

START DIALOGUE: *(Raymond)* You know what? It's time to clean house.

STOP DIALOGUE: *(Raymond)* See? So what was it? It's like somebody can break up with you at any time for no reason. I just always wanted to know why, you know?

BY THE BOOK: Proverbs 14:30, Isaiah 43:18-19, Luke 9:62, Philippians 3:13-14, Hebrews 12:1-2

WHERE TO TAKE IT:

1. Why do you think we sometimes hold on to the past—especially letters, pictures, and tapes from past relationships?

2. Do you think it's healthy to hold on to memorabilia from past relationships once you have moved on to a committed marriage?

3. How do you really forget those past relationships? Do you really want to? Like Debra said, her past has made her who she is today. How have your past relationships influenced who you are today—positively or negatively?

4. Why do you think Karen's rejection of Ray hurt him so deeply that he held on to the tape for more than a decade?

5. Do you think Ray had a secret fear that Debra might leave him "at any time for no reason"?

6. How do you make peace with past circumstances that you don't understand? Can you let God have that pain and move forward, or do you still harbor hurt feelings or resentment that holds you back?

7. If you've been hurt by someone—a sudden break-up or rejection—how can you begin to heal? Who can you talk with to work through your feelings and begin to let go and move forward with your life?

8. Are there things about your past that you just can't let go? What are they?

Visit www.skitguys.com or www.ysunderground.com for additional elements that might add impact to this clip, including "DTR: Define the Relationship" from Skits That Teach.

Everybody Loves Raymond
(COMEDY)
SEASON 6, EPISODE 16: "THE LUCKY SUIT"

TAG: I JUST GOT A FAX FROM YOUR MOM.

THEMES: Growing Up, Job Interviews, Letting Go, Minding Your Own Business, Overprotecting, Parents

THE SERIES/SHOW: This situation comedy centers around sportswriter Ray Barone (Ray Romano) and his wife Debra (Patricia Heaton), who deeply regret their decision to move across the street from Ray's parents, Frank and Marie Barone (Peter Boyle and Doris Roberts), who don't know the meaning of the word *boundaries*. Ray's brother Robert (Brad Garrett) is a middle-aged, divorced policeman who has finally moved out of his parents' house and into his own apartment to get on with his life. Though he's the firstborn of the Barone family, Robert suffers from jealousy over Raymond's career and family, as well as low self-esteem because Raymond is the favorite son. Robert's sarcastic motto, hence the title of the show, is, "Everybody loves Raymond!"

THE SCENE: Granted an interview for his dream job with the FBI, Robert plans to wear his lucky suit. While Marie is ironing the suit on the morning of the interview, she burns a spot on the back of Robert's jacket, making him unable to wear it. Robert storms from his parents' house to change before the interview, frustrated and upset at his mother's constant meddling in his life. Rather than leaving well enough alone, however, Marie faxes a message to the FBI agent right in the middle of Robert's job interview.

START: 00:09:34 STOP: 00:12:40 (TOTAL CLIP TIME: 3 MINUTES, 6 SECONDS)

START DIALOGUE: *(Frank)* Hey! *(Marie takes the remote and turns off the TV.)*

STOP DIALOGUE: *(Robert)* No, look, enough! Just…just stay out of my life.

BY THE BOOK: Psalm 61:7, Proverbs 14:22, Proverbs 16:9, Proverbs 22:6, Ephesians 5:31

WHERE TO TAKE IT:

1. Why was it wrong for Marie to interfere with Robert's job interview?

2. Why do you think Robert felt like the "peasant" of the family, and that Marie wanted to "keep him down"?

3. Marie claims that her interference was brought on by love for her son and fear for his safety. Does that make it right for her to meddle in his life?

4. Do you ever feel like your parents interfere with your life? If so, why?

5. Have you ever tried to tell your mom or dad how you feel? Why or why not?

6. Do parents have a right or an obligation to do what they can to protect their children? If so, where does that stop?

7. Can you name a time when you wished your parents had interfered in your life about something?

8. Would there have been a proper way for Marie to play a role in Robert's job situation?

BONUS CLIP: START 00:15:13 STOP 0:16:16 (TOTAL CLIP TIME: 1 MINUTE, 3 SECONDS)

SCENE 2: Marie goes to see agent Garfield to talk to him about the FBI position that Robert wants. When Marie pulls out a plate of cookies, agent Garfield starts to see through her "innocent mother act" and confronts her about her behavior.

START DIALOGUE: *(Agent Garfield)* Mrs. Barone, you seem like an intelligent woman.

STOP DIALOGUE: *(Marie)* I can't do it anymore. It's too much.

Visit www.skitguys.com or www.ysunderground.com for additional elements that might add impact to this clip, including Family Conflicts 6.2g from Instant Skits.

Extreme Makeover: Home Edition
(REALITY)
SEASON 1, EPISODE 9: "THE CADIGAN-SCOTT FAMILY"

TAG: LIFE WITHOUT PARENTS.

THEMES: Death, Grief, Selflessness, Starting Over, Tragedy

THE SERIES/SHOW: One of the most positive examples of the reality-TV genre, the team on *Extreme Makeover: Home Edition* is dedicated to renovating the homes of some incredibly worthy families. Nominated by friends or loved ones, each family chosen is sent on a much-deserved vacation while the homes they live in are torn apart and put back together again even better than before. Energetic carpenter Ty Pennington leads a team of design experts, including Constance Ramos (building and planning), Preston Sharp (exteriors and big ideas), Michael Moloney (interiors and glamour), Tracy Hutson (shopping and style), and Paul DiMeo (carpentry), as they plan and design each room of the house to fit the needs, personalities, and wildest dreams of each member of the family—all in seven short days. Emotions run high each week as members of the community join in to donate time, effort, and supplies to a family desperately in need of a blessing.

THE SCENE: The Cadigan-Scotts used to be a big, happy family with eight children—Jennifer, 23, Janice, 21, Daniel, 20, Kelly, 20, Rachel, 18, Jackie, 16, Dolly, 14, and Teresa, 12. But when the kids lose both of their parents to heart attacks within a period of two weeks, eldest daughters Jennifer and Janice leave their own lives behind to come back home and take legal guardianship of the younger children, keeping them together as a family. Rocked by tragedy, these eight siblings need the *Extreme Makeover: Home Edition* team to help them find a new start.

START: 0:04:22 STOP: 0:05:33 (TOTAL CLIP TIME: 1 MINUTE, 11 SECONDS)

START DIALOGUE: *(Ty)* This is your mom and dad's bedroom. No one has slept in here since they passed, right?

(Janice and Jennifer) Right.

(Ty) You have left it literally intact, the way it was.

(Janice and Jennifer) Yeah.

STOP DIALOGUE: *(Michael)* Can you imagine in two weeks, losing both parents?

(Tracy) No, I can't.

(Michael) Nobody and no kid should ever have to deal with that.

BY THE BOOK: Psalm 10:14, Psalm 23, Romans 8:26, Philippians 2:3, 1 Thessalonians 4:13

WHERE TO TAKE IT:

1. What emotions or thoughts went through your mind as you watched this clip?

2. If you lost your parents, would you step in and take care of your family in order to keep it together, as Jennifer and Janice did? What would you have to "give up" in order to assume that role?

3. Read Romans 8:26. Who does the Bible say will come to your aid when you can't even voice your grief?

4. Has a tragedy like this ever occurred in your life? How can the people around you pray for you?

5. Read Psalm 23. How do we survive when walking through the "valley of the shadow of death"?

6. If you were to meet this family, what advice would you give them?

7. What can we learn from this family?

8. How would you make sense of this tragedy? Do you believe that "bad things happen to good people"? Why or why not?

Visit www.skitguys.com or www.ysunderground.com for additional elements that might add impact to this clip, including "The Hurting Helpline" video.

Extreme Makeover: Home Edition

(REALITY)

SEASON 1, EPISODE 5: "THE HARRIS FAMILY"

TAG: ONE PERSON CAN MAKE A DIFFERENCE.

THEMES: Community, Generosity, Giving, Legacy, Reaching Out, Thankfulness

THE SERIES/SHOW: One of the most positive examples of the reality-TV genre, the team on *Extreme Makeover: Home Edition* is dedicated to renovating the homes of some incredibly worthy families. Nominated by friends or loved ones, each family chosen is sent on a much-deserved vacation while the homes they live in are torn apart and put back together again even better than before. Energetic carpenter Ty Pennington leads a team of design experts, including Constance Ramos (building and planning), Preston Sharp (exteriors and big ideas), Michael Moloney (interiors and glamour), Tracy Hutson (shopping and style), and Paul DiMeo (carpentry), as they plan and design each room of the house to fit the needs, personalities, and wildest dreams of each member of the family—all in seven short days. Emotions run high each week as members of the community join in to donate time, effort, and supplies to a family desperately in need of a blessing.

THE SCENE: Alice Harris, known as "Sweet Alice" to her friends and neighbors, has always had a heart for helping others, and her neighbors can't seem to sing her praises enough. She has helped many adults and children in the community of Watts, California, by reaching out and creating numerous programs—including homeless shelters, day cares, after-school programs, and vocational training. She also makes sure every child in the community has a new toy at Christmas. After a flood devastates her neighborhood and destroys her home, however, Sweet Alice finds that she's the one in need of help. Proving that one person's generosity can make a big difference to so many people, Sweet Alice's friends and neighbors pitch in to make sure she comes home to the beautiful new house she deserves.

START: 0:01:29 STOP: 0:03:21 (TOTAL CLIP TIME: 2 MINUTES, 2 SECONDS)

START DIALOGUE: *(Ty)* All right, guys, so welcome to Watts. It's not exactly Pleasantville, guys. And I think a lot of people are quite frightened of it, to be honest with you.

STOP DIALOGUE: *(Reporter)* Sweet Alice Harris—she's been helping thousands of children, but now she's lost everything. All of her possessions are completely contaminated by floodwaters.

(Ty) They had to sleep in their cars for a couple of days until they cleaned out all the water damage and the sewage and all that. Now's the chance for us to give something back to them.

(Tracy) Let's do it.

Additional Scenes: These scenes could be shown throughout your service or edited together as a whole piece depending on your editing software.

SCENE 2: START: 0:31:54 STOP: 0:33:08 (TOTAL CLIP TIME: 2 MINUTES, 14 SECONDS)

START: Sweet Alice looks at her new house in awe.

STOP DIALOGUE: *(Voiceover—Ty)* She never thought somebody would come into Watts and do this, and I think it's awfully cool that we came in where nobody else would come and do something special like that.

SCENE 3: START: 0:38:00 STOP: 0:38:45 (TOTAL CLIP TIME: 45 SECONDS)

START: The *Makeover* cast and Sweet Alice with her family, friends, and church choir stand in front of her new house singing, "This Little Light of Mine."

DIALOGUE: *(Voiceover—Sweet Alice)* I just have to tell the story everywhere I go. You all have done something for me that I couldn't do for myself. It'll make me do more to help people. I'll never stop. I won't forget this. I'm ever so grateful. And my prayer is that you can continue doing what you're doing, and I'm going to continue to do what I'm doing. This is what makes the world a better place. Keep doing what you're doing. God'll bless you. He has blessed me.

SCENE 4: START: 0:38:55 STOP: 0:39:27 (TOTAL CLIP TIME: 32 SECONDS)

DIALOGUE: *(Sweet Alice)* It has changed my whole life. I was tired, and now I'm not tired. I want to do more; I just want to do more. When I came in and opened the door, I couldn't believe it. And I still can't. I just love it. I never understood how you feel when somebody does something out of the ordinary.

I do it all the time for people. Now I know how they feel. They feel good. They're grateful, and they're thankful.

BY THE BOOK: Mark 10:45, Galatians 5:14, Ephesians 6:7, Colossians 3:23, 1 Peter 4:10

WHERE TO TAKE IT:

1. When you watch "Sweet Alice" and learn about her life, what words come to mind about this woman?

2. What kind of an impact do you want to make on the world around you?

3. What does the word *grateful* mean to you?

4. What is the most grateful you have ever been?

5. What would it take to go from "ordinary" to "extraordinary" living?

6. What does the word *legacy* mean to you?

7. What do you hope your legacy will be?

8. What actions are you taking to shape the legacy you will leave?

Visit www.skitguys.com or www.ysunderground.com for additional elements that might add impact to this clip, including "Who's Serving Whom?" from Skits That Teach.

TAG: EVERYONE DESERVES A SECOND CHANCE.

THEMES: Blessings, Dreams, Faith, Grace, Reaching Out, Second Chances

THE SERIES/SHOW: One of the most positive examples of the reality-TV genre, the team on *Extreme Makeover: Home Edition* is dedicated to renovating the homes of some incredibly worthy families. Nominated by friends or loved ones, each family chosen is sent on a much-deserved vacation while the homes they live in are torn apart and put back together again even better than before. Energetic carpenter Ty Pennington leads a team of design experts, including Constance Ramos (building and planning), Preston Sharp (exteriors and big ideas), Michael Moloney (interiors and glamour), Tracy Hutson (shopping and style), and Paul DiMeo (carpentry), as they plan and design each room of the house to fit the needs, personalities, and wildest dreams of each member of the family—all in seven short days. Emotions run high each week as members of the community join in to donate time, effort, and supplies to a family desperately in need of a blessing.

THE SCENE: Contessa Mendoza has overcome many odds in her life. She became an unwed mother at 17 but finished high school with honors and put herself through college, receiving honors there as well. While earning her degree in social work, she raised her seven-year-old daughter Analicia and has helped many other children find safe foster homes and adoptive families of their own. Contessa has even opened up her own home to two boys needing a family, adopting 18-year-old Angel and fostering 13-year-old Tony. The *Extreme Makeover* team designs and builds a beautiful new home for Contessa and her family, but the team goes a step further when they unveil the overhauled car decked out especially for Angel.

START: 0:36:05 STOP: 0:38:29 (TOTAL CLIP TIME: 2 MINUTES 24 SECONDS)

START DIALOGUE: *(Ty)* I guess you remember your old garage with the door you had to post up, right? Check out your new garage.

STOP DIALOGUE: *(Analicia)* I want to tell everybody that this can happen to you, too. You just have to have faith and just wait 'til your time is right. *(Family stands out in front of the house, waving and saying thank you.)*

(Voiceover—Contessa) Your dreams really can come true.

BY THE BOOK: Matthew 21:21, Romans 12:13, 2 Corinthians 4:15, Colossians 3:12, 1 John 3:17

WHERE TO TAKE IT:

1. Describe a time when you reached out to someone in need. What was that like for you?

2. Has there ever been a time in your life when you needed a second chance? What did you do with that opportunity?

3. Have you ever given someone a second chance, even if that person didn't deserve it?

4. What is your definition of the word *grace*?

5. How did the *Extreme Makeover* team show grace to the Mendozas? How did the Mendoza family show grace to others?

6. How has grace been shown to you?

7. The Mendoza family shares about their dreams—what is a dream you have for your life?

8. How could this dream be used to help others and glorify God?

Visit www.skitguys.com or www.ysunderground.com for additional elements that might add impact to this clip, including the "Beenie Weenies" script or video.

Extreme Makeover: Home Edition
(REALITY)
SEASON 1, EPISODE 2: "THE WOSLUM FAMILY"

TAG: DADDY'S HOME.

THEMES: "Abba," Family, Father's Love, Forgiveness, Heavenly Father, Sacrifice

THE SERIES/SHOW: One of the most positive examples of the reality-TV genre, the team on *Extreme Makeover: Home Edition* is dedicated to renovating the homes of some incredibly worthy families. Nominated by friends or loved ones, each family chosen is sent on a much-deserved vacation while the homes they live in are torn apart and put back together again even better than before. Energetic carpenter Ty Pennington leads a team of design experts, including Constance Ramos (building and planning), Preston Sharp (exteriors and big ideas), Michael Moloney (interiors and glamour), Tracy Hutson (shopping and style), and Paul DiMeo (carpentry), as they plan and design each room of the house to fit the needs, personalities, and wildest dreams of each member of the family—all in seven short days. Emotions run high each week as members of the community join in to donate time, effort, and supplies to a family desperately in need of a blessing.

THE SCENE: Trent Woslum, a sergeant in the California National Guard, bought his family a home for Christmas in 2002. Two months later he was deployed to Iraq for 10 months, leaving his wife Dawna with the full responsibility of taking care of their home and raising their three boys, Steven, 12, Nickolas, 7, and Alex, 5. In an effort to surprise Trent with a nice house upon his return, Dawna and the boys sent in a tape to the *Extreme Makeover: Home Edition* producers and were chosen. But the surprise is theirs, because while his wife and sons are vacationing during the renovation, Trent is allowed to come back to the United States—just in time to help Ty and the team finish his family's new home.

START: 0:38:25 STOP: 0:40:34 (TOTAL CLIP TIME: 2 MINUTES, 9 SECONDS)

START DIALOGUE: *(Ty)* All right, there's a big surprise out there. You ready?

STOP DIALOGUE: *(Voiceover—Tracy)* I was blown away. I can't imagine how they felt. That was a better present than their house.

(Voiceover–Paul) This wasn't really about their house. It was about seeing their dad. They forgot about the baseball field, about all the other stuff, and it was just about them having their father back home.

BY THE BOOK: Matthew 6:26, Matthew 7:11, Luke 15:11-32, Galatians 4:6, Ephesians 5:1-2

WHERE TO TAKE IT:

1. What kind of sacrifices has this family made for the freedom of our country?

2. Have you ever made a sacrifice for someone? If so, what was that experience like?

3. What did you feel while watching the Woslum children run to their father in this clip?

4. When we read the parable of the Prodigal Son in Luke 15, we see the son running to his father after going astray. Have you ever found yourself in the position of the prodigal son—in desperate need of grace and forgiveness?

5. The scene gives a great spiritual picture of what it must be like to run into the arms of our heavenly Father. How does that fit in with your view of God? Are you able to picture God with arms open wide for you?

6. In Galatians 4:6, the Hebrew word *Abba* means *Father* or *Daddy*. How does our relationship with our earthly father affect the way we view God?

7. How can you "run" to your heavenly Father?

8. How can you explain God's love to someone who has never had an earthly father?

Visit www.skitguys.com or www.ysunderground.com for additional elements that might add impact to this clip, including "Sam Goody and the Case of the Selfless Father" from Skits That Teach.

Frasier

(COMEDY)

SEASON 7, EPISODE 2: "FATHER OF THE BRIDE"

TAG: WHAT WE'VE GOT HERE IS FAILURE TO COMMUNICATE...

THEMES: Communication, Intentions, Misunderstanding, People Pleasing

THE SERIES/SHOW: The main character of this sitcom—snooty, pretentious Frasier Crane (Kelsey Grammer)—has moved to Seattle to host a radio show after spending many years in Boston on the classic comedy *Cheers*. Needing a fresh start after divorcing his wife, Lilith (Bebe Neuwirth), Frasier now dispenses psychiatric advice by way of his radio show and spends time with his equally pompous brother, Niles (David Hyde Pierce). Frasier's attempt to live a peaceful, orderly life in his luxury high-rise apartment is shattered, however, by the arrival of his father, disabled ex-cop Martin (John Mahoney), with whom Frasier has nothing in common. Constant conflict between Frasier's high-class sensibilities and Martin's practical nature create many *Odd Couple* scenarios, dragging live-in caretaker Daphne (Jane Leeves) and radio-show producer Roz (Peri Gilpin) into the mix on a regular basis.

THE SCENE: Frasier and Martin want to give the engaged Daphne a special wedding present. When she tells them that her overbearing mother is making all the wedding decisions, they decide to pay for her wedding flowers. During the discussion, Martin forces Frasier to eat some spicy beef jerky, giving him a terrible case of the hiccups. While attempting to tell Daphne that he and his father want to pay for her wedding flowers, Frasier's hiccups only allow him to say the word "wedding." Daphne is so thrilled to learn that someone besides her mother is taking responsibility for the wedding—meaning that she can now make her own decisions about the preparations—that Frasier can't bring himself to tell her that she has misunderstood what he was trying to say.

START 0:03:54 STOP 0:06:36 (TOTAL CLIP TIME: 2 MINUTES, 42 SECONDS)

START DIALOGUE: *(Martin)* Oh, Frasier, you're going to love this stuff I got from the farmers market. This guy takes the juiciest cut of filet mignon, slices it real thin, and makes jerky out of it.

STOP DIALOGUE: *(Daphne)* You know what this means, don't you? Now that Mom's not paying, she can't make me have it in England. I can have my wedding how I want it and where I want it, right here! You've answered my prayers. *(She leaves the room again, crying from happiness, and Frasier is left looking a little baffled.)*

BY THE BOOK: Psalm 34:13, Matthew 5:23-24, 1 Corinthians 14:33, Hebrews 12:14, James 3:2

WHERE TO TAKE IT:

1. Describe a time when you had a misunderstanding with another person and felt that you were unable to set things straight.

2. What's the best way to work through a misunderstanding?

3. Why do you think it's so hard to be honest with the people we care about?

4. How could Frasier tell Daphne she misunderstood him without making her feel bad?

5. Describe a time when there was a misunderstanding, and to avoid embarrassment, you followed through with what the other person *thought* you meant. How did that make you feel?

6. Are you a people pleaser?

7. Have you ever lost someone you cared about over a misunderstanding?

Visit www.skitguys.com or www.ysunderground.com for additional elements that might add impact to this clip, including "Sin, Spit, and Sight" from Skits That Teach.

Frasier

(COMEDY)

SEASON 7, EPISODE 3: "RADIO WARS START"

TAG: IT'S ONLY FUNNY 'TIL SOMEONE GETS HURT.

THEMES: Bullying, Embarrassment, Humiliation, Hurt Feelings, Image, Respect

THE SERIES/SHOW: The main character of this sitcom—snooty, pretentious Frasier Crane (Kelsey Grammer)—has moved to Seattle to host a radio show after spending many years in Boston on the classic comedy *Cheers*. Needing a fresh start after divorcing his wife, Lilith (Bebe Neuwirth), Frasier now dispenses psychiatric advice by way of his radio show and spends time with his equally pompous brother, Niles (David Hyde Pierce). Frasier's attempt to live a peaceful, orderly life in his luxury high-rise apartment is shattered, however, by the arrival of his father, disabled ex-cop Martin (John Mahoney), with whom Frasier has nothing in common. Constant conflict between Frasier's high-class sensibilities and Martin's practical nature create many *Odd Couple* scenarios, dragging live-in caretaker Daphne (Jane Leeves) and radio-show producer Roz (Peri Gilpin) into the mix on a regular basis.

THE SCENE: Frasier's radio station KACL has hired a new morning team known as "Carlos and the Chicken," whose show consists of calling unsuspecting individuals to pull pranks on them. Most people think the show is hilarious except Frasier, who has been the victim of one of their pranks. When Frasier and Roz run into Carlos and the Chicken at the coffee shop, Frasier is tempted to tell them how they have made him feel.

START: 0:00:10 STOP: 0:05:32 (TOTAL CLIP TIME: 5 MINUTES, 22 SECONDS)

START DIALOGUE: *(The phone rings several times. Frasier is woken from a sound sleep and answers the phone.)* *(Frasier)* Hello?

STOP DIALOGUE: *(Roz)* Please don't say "shenanigans"!

BY THE BOOK: Psalm 89:50-51, Proverbs 13:2, Matthew 18:21-22, Matthew 25:40, Philippians 2:3
WHERE TO TAKE IT:

1. Why do you think people play pranks and belittle others?

2. Why do people find it humorous to make fun of other people?

3. Have you ever been the target of a bully or humiliating prank? How did you deal with it?

4. With different movies and reality shows, have we taken the humiliation of others to a whole new level? Explain your answer.

5. What does it mean when Jesus says in Matthew 18:21-22 to forgive others "seventy-seven times"?

6. In your opinion, what does Matthew 25:40 mean? Who are "the least of these brothers of mine"?

7. What do you do or say when you see people being bullied or humiliated by others? Do you have a responsibility to help those people?

8. What are some reasons people become bullies? Can they ever change? What would it take for that to happen?

Visit www.skitguys.com or www.ysunderground.com for additional elements that might add impact to this clip, including the "Take Off the Diaper, Put Down the Bottle" script.

Frasier

(COMEDY)

SEASON 7, EPISODE 24: "SOMETHING BORROWED, SOMETHING BLUE"

TAG: I UNDERSTAND WHY YOU DON'T HAVE ANY FRIENDS.

THEMES: Attitude, Hurtful Words, Negativity, Opinions, Relationships

THE SERIES/SHOW: The main character of this sitcom—snooty, pretentious Frasier Crane (Kelsey Grammer)—has moved to Seattle to host a radio show after spending many years in Boston on the classic comedy *Cheers*. Needing a fresh start after divorcing his wife, Lilith (Bebe Neuwirth), Frasier now dispenses psychiatric advice by way of his radio show and spends time with his equally pompous brother, Niles (David Hyde Pierce). Frasier's attempt to live a peaceful, orderly life in his luxury high-rise apartment is shattered, however, by the arrival of his father, disabled ex-cop Martin (John Mahoney), with whom Frasier has nothing in common. Constant conflict between Frasier's high-class sensibilities and Martin's practical nature create many *Odd Couple* scenarios, dragging live-in caretaker Daphne (Jane Leeves) and radio-show producer Roz (Peri Gilpin) into the mix on a regular basis.

THE SCENE: Only 48 hours remain until Daphne's wedding to Donny Douglas (Saul Rubinek). Daphne's mother Gertrude (Millicent Martin) arrives in Seattle and immediately starts insulting everyone with her backhanded compliments and negative comments. The ease with which she complains about everything—hard chairs, bad-smelling tea, and terrible airplane food—renders everyone speechless. No one is safe from Gertrude's sharp tongue, but it becomes obvious that Daphne has learned exactly how to deal with her mother's critical spirit.

START: 0:23:07 STOP: 0:24:31 (TOTAL CLIP TIME: 1 MINUTE, 24 SECONDS)

START DIALOGUE: *(Gertrude)* There's my baby.

STOP DIALOGUE: *(Daphne)* I was worried she'd be in one of her dark moods.

BY THE BOOK: Psalm 19:14, Romans 14:10, 1 Corinthians 13:4-6, Philippians 2:14, 1 Thessalonians 5:11

WHERE TO TAKE IT:

1. Do you know someone who complains about everything?

2. How do you feel when you're around that person?

3. If this person is a family member or coworker, how does his or her negativity affect your family or the group as a whole?

4. What do you think causes this person to be so negative and hurtful?

5. Even though our natural reaction may be to say something hurtful in return, how does God want us to respond to critical or negative people?

6. How can you establish positive boundaries with a negative person when you have to see him or her every day?

7. What do you think this phrase means—"Hurting people hurt people"?

8. How can we determine what type of attitude we're going to have toward experiences and people?

Visit www.skitguys.com or www.ysunderground.com for additional elements that might add impact to this clip, including "Caveman" from Skits That Teach.

Frasier

(COMEDY)

SEASON 7, EPISODE 9: "THE APPARENT TRAP"

TAG: LILITH, IF IT TAKES A WHOLE FLEET OF MINI-BIKES, THIS DIVORCE WILL BE A GOOD ONE FOR FREDERICK.

THEMES: Divorce, the Future, Manipulation, Marriage, Parenting, Wants Versus Needs

THE SERIES/SHOW: The main character of this sitcom—snooty, pretentious Frasier Crane (Kelsey Grammer)—has moved to Seattle to host a radio show after spending many years in Boston on the classic comedy *Cheers*. Needing a fresh start after divorcing his wife, Lilith (Bebe Neuwirth), Frasier now dispenses psychiatric advice by way of his radio show and spends time with his equally pompous brother, Niles (David Hyde Pierce). Frasier's attempt to live a peaceful, orderly life in his luxury high-rise apartment is shattered, however, by the arrival of his father, disabled ex-cop Martin (John Mahoney), with whom Frasier has nothing in common. Constant conflict between Frasier's high-class sensibilities and Martin's practical nature create many *Odd Couple* scenarios, dragging live-in caretaker Daphne (Jane Leeves) and radio-show producer Roz (Peri Gilpin) into the mix on a regular basis.

THE SCENE: Frasier and Lilith spend Thanksgiving together to write a book about helping children through a divorce. While they're working, son Frederick (Trevor Einhorn) takes on the role of matchmaker, attempting to convince his parents through some tricky manipulation that they belong together. After Frasier and Lilith seek advice on how to deal with their son, Lilith begins to suspect that Frederick may actually have a different goal in mind. Lilith convinces Frasier to help her call their son's bluff, with surprising results.

START: 0:15:36 STOP: 0:20:19 (TOTAL CLIP TIME: 4 MINUTES, 43 SECONDS)

START DIALOGUE: *(Lilith)* Frasier, we need to talk.

STOP DIALOGUE: *(Lilith)* Do I know my son, or do I know my son?

BY THE BOOK: Proverbs 14:8, Proverbs 22:6, Matthew 19:3-8, Ephesians 6:1-2, Colossians 3:20, 1 Timothy 3:4

WHERE TO TAKE IT:

1. Are your parents divorced? How has this affected you?

2. Do you ever wish your parents would get back together? Why or why not?

3. Do you think it's harder for divorced parents to discipline their children?

4. Have you ever tried to manipulate your parents' feelings of guilt to get something you wanted?

5. Read Matthew 19:3-8. What does Jesus say in this passage about divorce? Is this Scripture being upheld in today's society?

6. What kind of marriage would you like to have when you're ready? How do you view marriage?

7. Do you believe that God wants people to stay married forever?

8. How can a family heal after a divorce?

Visit www.skitguys.com or www.ysunderground.com for additional elements that might add impact to this clip, including Family Conflicts 6.2a from Instant Skits.

Frasier
(COMEDY)

SEASON 7, EPISODE 8: "THE LATE DR. CRANE"

TAG: WHAT WILL PEOPLE SAY ABOUT ME WHEN I'M GONE?

THEMES: Achievements, Carpe Diem, Death, Faith, Legacy, Plans, Purpose

THE SERIES/SHOW: The main character of this sitcom—snooty, pretentious Frasier Crane (Kelsey Grammer)—has moved to Seattle to host a radio show after spending many years in Boston on the classic comedy *Cheers*. Needing a fresh start after divorcing his wife, Lilith (Bebe Neuwirth), Frasier now dispenses psychiatric advice by way of his radio show and spends time with his equally pompous brother, Niles (David Hyde Pierce). Frasier's attempt to live a peaceful, orderly life in his luxury high-rise apartment is shattered, however, by the arrival of his father, disabled ex-cop Martin (John Mahoney), with whom Frasier has nothing in common. Constant conflict between Frasier's high-class sensibilities and Martin's practical nature create many *Odd Couple* scenarios, dragging live-in caretaker Daphne (Jane Leeves) and radio-show producer Roz (Peri Gilpin) into the mix on a regular basis.

THE SCENE: Frasier has a fender bender, causing him to hit his nose on the steering wheel. When he goes to the ER to have his nose looked at, a mixup occurs, and Frasier's death is announced on TV. The next morning at the coffee shop, he and Roz read over his obituary in the paper, and Frasier laments all the things he hasn't yet achieved in his life, such as writing a novel, running for public office, or doing his own translation of Freud. Roz reminds him that he can still do those things since he isn't actually dead, so Frasier decides to take the opportunity to approach his life in a different way.

START: 0:11:38 STOP: 0:12:55 (TOTAL CLIP TIME: 1 MINUTE, 17 SECONDS)

START DIALOGUE: *(Roz)* Wow, that's something for your scrapbook—your own obituary.

STOP DIALOGUE: *(Frasier)* That is so nice of you. Thank you. Well, you know you're right. What am I doing frittering away my day here in this coffeehouse? I've got things to do. I've got worlds to conquer. I'm gonna go out there and grab the world by the scruff. Look out, destiny, here I come! *(Light-*

ning strikes outside the coffeehouse, and Frasier quickly comes back inside.) Wow, it's really coming down out there!

BY THE BOOK: Joshua 1:8, 2 Chronicles 9:1-8, Psalm 118:25, Acts 13:36, Philippians 4:13

WHERE TO TAKE IT:

1. What are some things you hope to accomplish in your lifetime?

2. Describe when you accomplished something and it made an impact on your life.

3. What kinds of achievements are important to God?

4. If you had to write a summary of your life, what would it say about you up to this moment?

5. If you died tomorrow, would you be happy with how you've lived your life?

6. When you do leave this earth, how do you want to be remembered? What do you want your tombstone to say?

7. Acts 13:36 states that David "served his purpose for his generation" and then died. What do you think *your* purpose is for *your* generation?

Visit www.skitguys.com or www.ysunderground.com for additional elements that might add impact to this clip, including the "Life After High School" script.

Friends

TAG: THERE, BUT FOR THE GRACE OF GOD, GO I.

THEMES: Choices, Infidelity, Integrity, Marriage, Temptation, Trust, Vows

THE SERIES/SHOW: *Friends* is about six New York City twentysomethings learning to navigate the complexities of life, love, and friendship. Anchoring the group are nerdy paleontologist Ross Geller (David Schwimmer) and his sister Monica (Courteney Cox), a former fat girl yearning to be a professional chef, who shares her trendy apartment with Rachel Green (Jennifer Aniston), the object of Ross' longtime secret crush. Across the hall are Ross' college roommate, Chandler Bing (Matthew Perry) and aspiring actor Joey Tribbiani (Matt LeBlanc), and dropping in from her apartment across town is quirky Phoebe Buffay (Lisa Kudrow). By this point in the ninth season, Ross and Rachel share baby daughter Emma, Monica and Chandler have married and are struggling to endure his job transfer to Oklahoma, Phoebe has found the love of her life in Mike (Paul Rudd) and wants to get married, and Joey—back at work at *Days of Our Lives*—is dealing with romantic feelings for Rachel.

THE SCENE: Chandler is commuting back and forth from his home in New York City to his job in Tulsa, Oklahoma. Forced to spend Christmas in Tulsa working on a project, Chandler has mercy on his colleagues and lets them go home. However, female colleague Wendy (Selma Blair) chooses to stay and help Chandler finish the work. When Monica and the gang call to wish him a merry Christmas, Chandler confesses that he and Wendy are the only ones still working. Monica becomes extremely jealous and tells Chandler that she doesn't like the thought of his being alone at the office with a very attractive woman. Though Chandler assures Monica that she has nothing to worry about, he is shocked when Wendy does make a pass at him. Chandler realizes that he has put himself in a very bad situation.

START: 0:11:40 STOP: 0:13:32 (TOTAL CLIP TIME: 2 MINUTES, 52 SECONDS)

START DIALOGUE: *(Joey)* Wait—is Wendy the runner-up Miss Oklahoma?

STOP DIALOGUE: *(Wendy)* Seriously? Happily married? So that phone call before was happy?

(Chandler) Well, look, it's not easy to spend this much time apart. She's entitled to be a little paranoid. Or in this case, right on the money.

BY THE BOOK: Proverbs 27:17, Matthew 26:41, 1 Corinthians 10:13, 1 Corinthians 16:13, Ephesians 5:28

WHERE TO TAKE IT:

1. Do you think Monica was right to be jealous, knowing that her husband was alone with a beautiful woman? Why or why not?

2. What do you think Chandler should have done to keep himself from being put in that situation in the first place?

3. Have you ever been tempted to do something you knew was wrong?

4. Has God ever provided you a way of escape?

5. How can you be prepared to make the right decision the next time temptation comes your way?

6. How do you employ accountability in your life so temptations don't get the best of you?

7. If you were in Chandler's shoes, how hard would it have been to walk away from a "Wendy"?

8. Have you ever seen the result of infidelity in a marriage? What happened as a result of that choice?

Visit www.skitguys.com or www.ysunderground.com for additional elements that might add impact to this clip, including "The Hormone Shuffle" script.

Friends

(COMEDY)

SEASON 9, EPISODE 197: "THE ONE WITH PHOEBE'S BIRTHDAY DINNER"

TAG: WHEN LIFE GIVES YOU LEMONS—MAKE A JOKE OUT OF IT.

THEMES: Attitude, Crisis, Fear, Handling Problems, Pressure, Sarcasm, Worry

THE SERIES/SHOW: *Friends* is about six New York City twentysomethings learning to navigate the complexities of life, love, and friendship. Anchoring the group are nerdy paleontologist Ross Geller (David Schwimmer) and his sister Monica (Courteney Cox), a former fat girl yearning to be a professional chef, who shares her trendy apartment with Rachel Green (Jennifer Aniston), the object of Ross' longtime secret crush. Across the hall are Ross' college roommate, Chandler Bing (Matthew Perry) and aspiring actor Joey Tribbiani (Matt LeBlanc), and dropping in from her apartment across town is quirky Phoebe Buffay (Lisa Kudrow). By this point in the ninth season, Ross and Rachel share baby daughter Emma, Monica and Chandler have married and are struggling to endure his job transfer to Oklahoma, Phoebe has found the love of her life in Mike (Paul Rudd) and wants to get married, and Joey—back at work at *Days of Our Lives*—is dealing with romantic feelings for Rachel.

THE SCENE: Even though Ross and Rachel live together and care for new-born daughter Emma, they live separate lives, and Rachel has had trouble adjusting to her new role as a mother. These issues are magnified when Ross and Rachel accidentally lock themselves out of their apartment with Emma sleeping inside. Rachel starts to worry about Emma and speculates about all of the bad things that could happen to her. Irritated with Rachel's irrational thinking, Ross makes fun of her by making up a crazy scenario of what might actually be going on inside the apartment.

START: 0:11:04 STOP: 0:12:25 (TOTAL CLIP TIME: 1 MINUTE, 21 SECONDS)

START DIALOGUE: *(Ross)* Okay, well, the super's not home. But my mom is gonna be here in a minute, and she has the key.

STOP DIALOGUE: *(Ross)* A pigeon. No. No, wait, no. An *eagle* flew in! Landed on the stove and caught fire! The baby, seeing this, jumps across the apartment to the mighty bird's aid. The eagle, however, misconstrues this as an act of aggression and grabs the baby in its talons. Meanwhile, the faucet fills the apartment with water. Baby and bird, still ablaze, are locked in a death grip, swirling around the whirlpool that fills the apartment!

(Rachel) Boy, are you gonna be sorry if that's true.

BY THE BOOK: Proverbs 4:24, Matthew 6:34, Romans 13:7, Ephesians 4:29, 1 Peter 3:8-9

WHERE TO TAKE IT:

1. What's the difference between humor and sarcasm?

2. When people irritate you, do you find yourself saying sarcastic things back to them?

3. Why do you think it's so easy to retaliate with "humor" that mocks or ridicules someone?

4. What do you think Ross could have said to Rachel that would have made her feel better about their situation?

5. What would help you to stop using sarcasm and start responding more positively to others?

6. Why do you think we all deal with problems so differently?

7. When you're squeezed, or under pressure, what comes out of you as far as attitude, temperament, and character?

8. Are you offended when people respond to you with sarcasm or humor?

Visit www.skitguys.com or www.ysunderground.com for additional elements that might add impact to this clip, including the "Behind the Laughter: A Skit Guys Documentary" video.

Friends

(COMEDY)

SEASON 9, EPISODE 210: "THE ONE WITH THE LOTTERY"

TAG: IF I HAD $30 MILLION, I'D...

THEMES: Greed, Friendship, Image, Money, Selfishness, Worth

THE SERIES/SHOW: *Friends* is about six New York City twentysomethings learning to navigate the complexities of life, love, and friendship. Anchoring the group are nerdy paleontologist Ross Geller (David Schwimmer) and his sister Monica (Courteney Cox), a former fat girl yearning to be a professional chef, who shares her trendy apartment with Rachel Green (Jennifer Aniston), the object of Ross' longtime secret crush. Across the hall are Ross' college roommate, Chandler Bing (Matthew Perry) and aspiring actor Joey Tribbiani (Matt LeBlanc), and dropping in from her apartment across town is quirky Phoebe Buffay (Lisa Kudrow). By this point in the ninth season, Ross and Rachel share baby daughter Emma, Monica and Chandler have married and are struggling to endure his job transfer to Oklahoma, Phoebe has found the love of her life in Mike (Paul Rudd) and wants to get married, and Joey—back at work at *Days of Our Lives*—is dealing with romantic feelings for Rachel.

THE SCENE: The group has gone in together and purchased lottery tickets, hoping to win a jackpot of $30 million. The thought of winning makes everyone a little greedy, and they begin to fight. Phoebe doesn't want to hear her friends fighting over money, so she takes the bowl of lottery tickets out on the balcony and threatens to throw them to the wind to teach them all a lesson. However, when a pigeon flies past and scares her, she really drops the bowl of tickets. Everyone scrambles to get down to the street to retrieve as many as they can find, but when they only return with half of the tickets, they all realize how silly they were being.

START: 0:09:49 STOP: 0:13:36 (TOTAL CLIP TIME: 3 MINUTES, 47 SECONDS)

START DIALOGUE: *(Monica)* Come on, lottery!

STOP DIALOGUE: *(Phoebe)* You guys were so scared. There was no way I was gonna dump this...*(A pigeon flies by and scares Phoebe, who drops the bowl full of tickets.)* Oh! No! I think I broke your bowl.

(Ross) Go! Go! Go! *(They all run outside to find the lost lottery tickets.)*

BY THE BOOK: Matthew 6:24, Luke 12:15, 1 Timothy 6:10, Hebrews 13:5, 1 John 3:17

WHERE TO TAKE IT:

1. If you had $30 million or even $1 million, what would you do with it?

2. In some ways, the lottery tickets in this clip became a false idol. What "idols" in your life keep you preoccupied?

3. Why do people tend to want more money or possessions than they actually need?

4. How can we be content with what God has given us?

5. Why does God desire that we share our blessings with others? How does giving show others that we love God?

6. When you leave this earth, how do you want to be remembered?

7. Do you believe that money can buy happiness? Why or why not?

8. Is it possible to be truly happy without money?

Visit www.skitguys.com or www.ysunderground.com for additional elements that might add impact to this clip, including "The Most Important Thing" video.

Friends

(COMEDY)

SEASON 9, EPISODE 211: "THE ONE WITH RACHEL'S DREAM"

TAG: IF YOU DO NOT MOVE, IT WILL HIT YOU.

THEMES: Apologizing, Arguing, Bitterness, Discernment, Hurt Feelings, Opinions, Resentment

THE SERIES/SHOW: *Friends* is about six New York City twentysomethings learning to navigate the complexities of life, love, and friendship. Anchoring the group are nerdy paleontologist Ross Geller (David Schwimmer) and his sister Monica (Courteney Cox), a former fat girl yearning to be a professional chef, who shares her trendy apartment with Rachel Green (Jennifer Aniston), the object of Ross' longtime secret crush. Across the hall are Ross' college roommate, Chandler Bing (Matthew Perry) and aspiring actor Joey Tribbiani (Matt LeBlanc), and dropping in from her apartment across town is quirky Phoebe Buffay (Lisa Kudrow). By this point in the ninth season, Ross and Rachel share baby daughter Emma, Monica and Chandler have married and are struggling to endure his job transfer to Oklahoma, Phoebe has found the love of her life in Mike (Paul Rudd) and wants to get married, and Joey—back at work at *Days of Our Lives*—is dealing with romantic feelings for Rachel.

THE SCENE: Monica's upscale restaurant, JAVU, is finally drawing a large crowd. When Monica tells Rachel and Phoebe the good news, Phoebe decides to come and entertain the people waiting to get in the restaurant with her infamous music. Monica is worried that Phoebe's out-of-tune singing and eccentric songs will have a negative effect on her restaurant, so she tells Phoebe that JAVU is too high-class for Phoebe's kind of music. Phoebe's hurt feelings cause her to lash out at Monica's cooking, sparking an argument that even includes the restaurant patrons. However, it doesn't take long for both to realize how childish their argument really is.

START: 0:18:58 STOP: 0:21:01 (TOTAL CLIP TIME: 3 MINUTES, 3 SECONDS)

START DIALOGUE: *(Phoebe—singing)* The food here at JAVU, will kill you. The food here at JAVU, will kill you!

STOP DIALOGUE: *(Monica)* I'm sorry.

(Phoebe) I'm sorry, too. *(They hug.)*

BY THE BOOK: Proverbs 15:18, Proverbs 27:6, Philippians 2:14, 2 Timothy 2:23-24, James 3:14

WHERE TO TAKE IT:

1. What causes a silly spat to spiral out of control and turn into a quarrel?

2. Describe a time when someone you care for really hurt your feelings.

3. Has there ever been a time when you felt resentment toward another person? Did you ever let that resentment go, or do you still hold on to it?

4. Why do we try to bring other people into our quarrels?

5. How can you keep yourself from becoming involved in silly spats?

6. On a scale from 1 to 10, how likable are you? What personality traits of yours may keep others "at arm's length"?

7. How do we "let go and let God" when it comes to the hurtful parts of our past?

8. How hard is it for you to apologize when you've said hurtful things to a friend?

Visit www.skitguys.com or www.ysunderground.com for additional elements that might add impact to this clip, including Friendship Conflicts 6.6j, "The Ultimate Sleepover," from Instant Skits.

Friends

TAG: ARE YOU A REAL MAN? NOT THAT I'M JUDGING...

THEMES: Abilities, Empathy, Insecurity, Judging Others, Personality Traits, Prejudice

THE SERIES/SHOW: *Friends* is about six New York City twentysomethings learning to navigate the complexities of life, love, and friendship. Anchoring the group are nerdy paleontologist Ross Geller (David Schwimmer) and his sister Monica (Courteney Cox), a former fat girl yearning to be a professional chef, who shares her trendy apartment with Rachel Green (Jennifer Aniston), the object of Ross' longtime secret crush. Across the hall are Ross' college roommate, Chandler Bing (Matthew Perry) and aspiring actor Joey Tribbiani (Matt LeBlanc), and dropping in from her apartment across town is quirky Phoebe Buffay (Lisa Kudrow). By this point in the ninth season, Ross and Rachel share baby daughter Emma, Monica and Chandler have married and are struggling to endure his job transfer to Oklahoma, Phoebe has found the love of her life in Mike (Paul Rudd) and wants to get married, and Joey—back at work at *Days of Our Lives*—is dealing with romantic feelings for Rachel.

SCENES 1 AND 2: Ross and Rachel have hired a male nanny, Sandy (Freddie Prinze Jr.), to take care of baby Emma. Rachel loves Sandy's sensitivity and the care he gives Emma, but Ross is uncomfortable with Sandy's feminine qualities, such as making French cookies and crying all the time. In Scene 2, Ross decides that he's too uncomfortable with Sandy's sensitivity and can't be around him anymore. After Ross tells Sandy that he's being "let go," Sandy encourages Ross to talk about the reason he's so uncomfortable with sensitive men. In the process of explaining himself, Ross realizes that his discomfort actually comes from his own fear of being too sensitive and not being thought of as a "real man."

SCENE 1: START: 0:17:18 STOP: 0:19:35 (TOTAL CLIP TIME: 2 MINUTES, 17 SECONDS)

START DIALOGUE: *(Ross walks in and sees Rachel and Sandy sitting on the sofa, crying.)* Is everything all right?

STOP DIALOGUE: *(Rachel)* Okay, what is "too sensitive"? *(Ross and Rachel hear the music of a recorder being played in the living room. They both peek out of the*

kitchen door to see Sandy playing a song on his recorder for Emma. Ross feels that his point has been made.)

SCENE 2: START: 0:31:02 STOP: 0:33:29 (TOTAL CLIP TIME: 2 MINUTES, 27 SECONDS)

START DIALOGUE: *(Ross)* Anyway, well, I'm glad there's no hard feelings.

STOP DIALOGUE: *(Rachel walks out of the back carrying baby Emma.)* Emma, one day you're going to grow up and be a big girl, just like your daddy.

BY THE BOOK: 1 Samuel 16:7, Matthew 7:2-5, Luke 6:31, John 7:24, 1 Corinthians 12:4

WHERE TO TAKE IT:

1. Why do you think it's so easy to find fault with other people?

2. Do you tend to judge people on their appearance or their behavior?

3. Have you ever been judgmental toward another person and found that you disliked a particular characteristic or behavior because you secretly saw and disliked those things in yourself?

4. Have you ever had to "take the plank out of your own eye"? How did you go about it?

5. Have you ever been judged by someone? How did it make you feel?

6. Where do we get our judgments and our prejudices? How do we break that pattern?

7. How can you make more of an effort to tolerate people who are very different from you?

8. What is your definition of a "real man"? Does it match our culture's definition? Why or why not?

Visit www.skitguys.com or www.ysunderground.com for additional elements that might add impact to this clip, including the "Abilities" script.

Gilmore Girls
(DRAMA/COMEDY)
SEASON 5, EPISODE 22: "A HOUSE IS NOT A HOME"

TAG: YOU'VE KNOWN WHAT YOU WANTED TO DO SINCE YOU WERE THREE!

THEMES: Dreams, Goals, Identity, Plans, Purpose, Quiting

THE SERIES/SHOW: *Gilmore Girls* is about free-spirited Lorelai (Lauren Graham) and sensible daughter "Rory" (Alexis Bledel) who not only share the same name, but also behave more like sisters than parent and child. Sixteen years ago when Lorelai found herself pregnant and unmarried, she faced a choice—marry the high school boyfriend who got her pregnant or go against the wishes of her high-society parents, Richard and Emily Gilmore (Edward Herrmann and Kelly Bishop), and raise the child on her own. After Rory's birth, Lorelai tried to remain in her parents' home, but their rules, expectations, and goals soon became overwhelming, and now the two "Gilmore girls" are on their own, making a life for themselves in a small Connecticut town called Stars Hollow.

THE SCENE: Lorelai and Rory meet for lunch at a local restaurant so Rory can break the news to Lorelai that she isn't going back to Yale in the fall. Wounded over the fact that top newspaperman Mitchum Huntzberger said she would never fulfill her lifelong dream of being a journalist, Rory finds herself unsure of her future for the first time in her life. After having her purpose and direction snatched away from her, the only thing Rory can think of to do is take a break from Yale and figure out what she really wants to do with her life.

START: 0:25:45 STOP: 0:29:03 (TOTAL CLIP TIME: 3 MINUTES, 18 SECONDS)

START DIALOGUE: *(Lorelai)* So how'd your final go?

STOP DIALOGUE: *(Lorelai)* Message sent. *(Lorelai leaves the table.)*

BY THE BOOK: Proverbs 19:21, Isaiah 43:7, Jeremiah 29:11-13, Romans 8:28, 1 Corinthians 10:31

WHERE TO TAKE IT:

1. Rory's identity has been so intertwined with becoming a journalist that she doesn't know who she is without that goal. Why does she feel she has lost her purpose?

2. Why do you think Rory is willing to risk her relationship with her mother to quit Yale? What does Yale symbolize to Rory?

3. Why do you think Rory is so determined to quit instead of working harder to fulfill her dream? What would you do in the same situation?

4. Though our sense of purpose should come primarily from our relationships with God, we often still gain a sense of purpose from the group of friends we belong to, certain talents we possess, our future professions, our boyfriends/girlfriends, or even from our family names. Be honest with yourself—where does your sense of purpose come from?

5. If our true sense of purpose comes from glorifying God, why is it so easy to associate our purpose with temporal things?

6. What does it mean to "bring glory to God"?

7. What do you dream of doing with your life?

8. Can you think of anything that could keep you from accomplishing that goal? What would you do if you found out it was impossible to achieve your dream?

Visit www.skitguys.com or www.ysunderground.com for additional elements that might add impact to this clip, including the "American Idle" script.

Gilmore Girls
(DRAMA/COMEDY)

SEASON 5, EPISODE 10: "BUT NOT AS CUTE AS PUSHKIN"

TAG: NO RULES, NO CONSEQUENCES.

THEMES: Abstinence, Behavior, College, Dating, Immorality, Lust, Relationships, Sex, Temptation

THE SERIES/SHOW: *Gilmore Girls* is about free-spirited Lorelai (Lauren Graham) and sensible daughter "Rory" (Alexis Bledel) who not only share the same name, but also behave more like sisters than parent and child. Sixteen years ago when Lorelai found herself pregnant and unmarried, she faced a choice—marry the high school boyfriend who got her pregnant or go against the wishes of her high-society parents, Richard and Emily Gilmore (Edward Herrmann and Kelly Bishop), and raise the child on her own. After Rory's birth, Lorelai tried to remain in her parents' home, but their rules, expectations, and goals soon became overwhelming, and now the two "Gilmore girls" are on their own, making a life for themselves in a small Connecticut town called Stars Hollow.

THE SCENE: Now at Yale, Rory has been asked by the headmaster of her former high school to chaperone Anna (Sarah Foret), a 16-year-old Chilton student who wants to visit Yale. Rory takes on the task and shows Anna around the campus—taking her to classes and demonstrating the social aspects of college life—but runs into a surprise as the girls walk in on fellow students Paris (Liza Weil) and Doyle (Danny Strong) having an afternoon of casual sex. Rory is dismayed to realize that instead of being embarrassed by what they've seen, Anna is excited by the freedom the college life seems to offer.

START: 00:30:00 STOP: 00:30:52 (TOTAL CLIP TIME: 52 SECONDS)

START DIALOGUE: *(Anna)* You can do *anything* in college. No rules, no consequences!

STOP DIALOGUE: *(Anna)* Dinner whenever you want, random sex whenever you want. I can't wait to go to college!

BY THE BOOK: Romans 6:12-13, Romans 12:1, 1 Corinthians 6:18-20, 1 Thessalonians 4:3-5, 1 Timothy 4:12

WHERE TO TAKE IT:

1. How do TV shows and movies encourage the belief that as long as two people are consenting adults, it's okay to have sex whenever and with whomever you want?

2. At what age has our society deemed it "normal" to start having sex?

3. Is it okay to have sex if you're in a committed relationship? Why or why not?

4. Why do so many college students stray from the way they were raised?

5. Why does it seem that the college years are an acceptable time to indulge in destructive behavior and make poor decisions?

6. Have your parents talked to you about sex? If so, did they encourage you to wait, or did they say that sex is okay as long as having sex doesn't result in pregnancy?

7. Do you have friends you trust enough to talk to about sex? Do those friends share your standards and beliefs about sex? If you can't talk to your parents, is there a close family member or adult you trust who could answer your questions and give you good advice about sex? Who is that person?

8. How can you better prepare yourself for the temptations that will surround you when you leave home?

Visit www.skitguys.com or www.ysunderground.com for additional elements that might add impact to this clip, including "Here Come the Brides" from Skits That Teach.

Gilmore Girls
(DRAMA/COMEDY)
SEASON 5, EPISODE 13: "WEDDING BELL BLUES"

TAG: MONEY DOESN'T MAKE YOU A JERK!

THEMES: Entitlement, Favoritism, Greed, Money, Social Status

THE SERIES/SHOW: *Gilmore Girls* is about free-spirited Lorelai (Lauren Graham) and sensible daughter "Rory" (Alexis Bledel) who not only share the same name, but also behave more like sisters than parent and child. Sixteen years ago when Lorelai found herself pregnant and unmarried, she faced a choice—marry the high school boyfriend who got her pregnant or go against the wishes of her high-society parents, Richard and Emily Gilmore (Edward Herrmann and Kelly Bishop), and raise the child on her own. After Rory's birth, Lorelai tried to remain in her parents' home, but their rules, expectations, and goals soon became overwhelming, and now the two "Gilmore girls" are on their own, making a life for themselves in a small Connecticut town called Stars Hollow.

THE SCENE: Rory approaches Lorelai as she looks over the seating chart for one of her parents' social events. Lorelai takes the liberty to rearrange the chart to better suit her desires and opinions. As Lorelai switches the chart around, she and Rory discuss the attitudes and behaviors of wealthy people, as well as the fairness of Lorelai's judgment.

START: 0:13:19 STOP: 0:14:58 (TOTAL CLIP TIME: 1 MINUTE, 39 SECONDS)

START DIALOGUE: *(Rory)* What are you doing?

STOP DIALOGUE: *(Lorelai)* I know, I didn't mean it like that.

BY THE BOOK: Proverbs 28:11, Matthew 19:23-24, 1 Timothy 6:10, Hebrews 13:5, James 2:1-5

WHERE TO TAKE IT:

1. Like Lorelai, do you think children who grow up in wealthy families feel "entitled to whatever they want when they want it"? Why or why not?

2. Do you think a person will grow up with better morals and values if she's poor, or if she has money? Why do you think so?

3. For many people, money offers feelings of security. Can you trust God to be your security and to provide you with what you need?

4. Do you know someone who has used his or her fortune unselfishly to do great things? How does this person seem different from other people with great wealth?

5. Do you have good money-managing skills? If not, whom can you ask to teach you to manage your money more wisely?

6. How do you treat people who have more money than you do?

7. How do you treat people who have less money than you do?

Visit www.skitguys.com or www.ysunderground.com for additional elements that might add impact to this clip, including the "Rich Young Ruler" video on You Teach Vol. 2.

Gilmore Girls

(DRAMA/COMEDY)

SEASON 5, EPISODE 3: "WRITTEN IN THE STARS"

TAG: IS IT GOSSIP IF YOU'RE ASKING SOMEONE TO PRAY ABOUT SOMEONE YOU DON'T LIKE?

THEMES: Gossip, Lies, Minding Your Own Business, Secrets, Trust

THE SERIES/SHOW: *Gilmore Girls* is about free-spirited Lorelai (Lauren Graham) and sensible daughter "Rory" (Alexis Bledel) who not only share the same name, but also behave more like sisters than parent and child. Sixteen years ago when Lorelai found herself pregnant and unmarried, she faced a choice—marry the high school boyfriend who got her pregnant or go against the wishes of her high-society parents, Richard and Emily Gilmore (Edward Herrmann and Kelly Bishop), and raise the child on her own. After Rory's birth, Lorelai tried to remain in her parents' home, but their rules, expectations, and goals soon became overwhelming, and now the two "Gilmore girls" are on their own, making a life for themselves in a small Connecticut town called Stars Hollow.

THE SCENE: As Lorelai walks down a street in Stars Hollow, she spies three of the town's most notorious gossips and stops to listen in on the latest scandal.

START: 00:10:37 STOP: 00:11:27 (TOTAL CLIP TIME: 50 SECONDS)

START DIALOGUE: *(Babette)* Are you sure?

(Patty) Jerry found her birth certificate stashed in her bathroom.

STOP DIALOGUE: *(Babette)* I'm not surprised.

BY THE BOOK: Psalm 19:14, Psalm 34:13, Proverbs 20:19, 1 Timothy 5:13, James 1:26

WHERE TO TAKE IT:

1. Have you ever had a trusted friend tell others your secrets? If so, how did you feel when you found out?

2. How hard was it for you to trust that person after that point?

3. Have experiences like those caused you to be more guarded and less open with other people?

4. Do you have any friends you can count on to keep your secrets?

5. Can you keep a secret? How important is it for your friends to trust you with their feelings and information?

6. Why is it sometimes so difficult to keep things to ourselves?

7. How do you respond when someone begins to share gossip?

8. What are some good ways to deal with a conversation that's turning into gossip?

BONUS CLIP: (START 00:29:03 STOP 0:29:42 TOTAL CLIP TIME: 41 SECONDS)

SCENE 2: As Lorelai listens in on the gossipy conversation, she wonders if she and Luke (Scott Patterson) have become part of the rumor mill. When she realizes the ladies aren't talking about her after all, Lorelai is surprised and a bit disappointed.

Visit www.skitguys.com or www.ysunderground.com for additional elements that might add impact to this clip, including "The Barry Springer Show" script.

Grey's Anatomy
(DRAMA)
SEASON 2, EPISODE 6/15: "INTO YOU LIKE A TRAIN"

TAG: THE TOUGHEST CHOICE OF ALL.

THEMES: Death, Friendship, Humanity, Sacrifice, Saving a Life, Selflessness

THE SERIES/SHOW: *Grey's Anatomy* is a medical drama focusing on a handful of interns dealing with the ups and downs of life, both in and out of the hospital. Through no fault of her own, the show's namesake Meredith Grey (Ellen Pompeo) finds herself in the midst of a love triangle with Dr. Derek "McDreamy" Shepherd (Patrick Dempsey) and his wife, Dr. Addison Montgomery-Shepherd (Kate Walsh). Meredith's best friend Cristina Yang (Sandra Oh) is an overachieving, commitment-phobic doctor in love with brilliant surgeon Dr. Preston Burke (Isaiah Washington). George O'Malley (T.R. Knight) is everybody's best friend, while Alex Karev (Justin Chambers) rubs everybody the wrong way. Izzie Stephens (Katherine Heigl) is the eternal optimist, full of emotion, and Dr. Miranda "The Nazi" Bailey (Chandra Wilson) keeps the whole crew running smoothly. Chief of surgery Dr. Richard Webber (James Pickens Jr.) tries to keep the hospital afloat and his staff in line at the expense of his own marriage, proving that almost nobody at Seattle Grace has yet learned how to keep their personal and professional lives separate.

THE SCENE: A horrible train wreck has filled the hospital with wounded passengers, none more dramatic than the terrible injuries sustained by Tom and Bonnie—two people impaled on a single pole. The doctors of Seattle Grace face a difficult decision since only one of the two patients can be saved while the other one must die. Although Bonnie (Monica Keena) is a young lady with a fiancé and her whole life ahead of her, Tom (Bruce A. Young) has fewer injuries and a better chance of survival. As Bonnie begins to realize what saving Tom will mean, she decides to give her life so that someone she barely knows will have a chance to live.

START 0:24:17 STOP 0:27:06 (TOTAL CLIP TIME: 2 MINUTES, 49 SECONDS)

START DIALOGUE: *(Dr. Shepherd)* This is hard because your body is in a certain amount of shock. It's preventing you from feeling pain, feeling the extent of your injuries.

STOP DIALOGUE: *(Bonnie)* Danny wouldn't understand. I've had a couple of hours to process all of this. But if he had to see me and talk to me like this... well, I just think it would be too hard. *(End with close-up on Bonnie.)*

BY THE BOOK: Matthew 10:39, Matthew 20:28, John 15:13, Ephesians 5:2, Hebrews 10:14

WHERE TO TAKE IT:

1. As you watch this scene, what would you be feeling and thinking if you were in Bonnie's shoes?

2. If you were faced with a choice like Bonnie's, what would you want to do or say before you died?

3. How is Bonnie's sacrifice similar to the sacrifice Jesus made for us?

4. How would you feel if you were in Tom's shoes? Would you allow someone to purposely die for you?

5. How do you think Tom should live the rest of his life?

6. Who or what would you give your life for?

7. John 15:13 states that there is no greater love than to lay down your life for a friend. What does this Scripture mean to you in everyday circumstances?

8. What's the most unselfish thing you've ever seen someone do? How did that make you feel? What's the most unselfish thing you've ever done?

Visit www.skitguys.com or www.ysunderground.com for additional elements that might add impact to this clip, including the "Lost and Found: The Prodigal Son" video.

Grey's Anatomy

(DRAMA)

SEASON 2, EPISODE 6/25: "IT'S THE END OF THE WORLD"

TAG: ARE YOU A "DOER" OR A "WATCHER"?

THEMES: Goals, Identity, Jealousy, Motivation, Plans, Taking Action

THE SERIES/SHOW: *Grey's Anatomy* is a medical drama focusing on a handful of interns dealing with the ups and downs of life, both in and out of the hospital. Through no fault of her own, the show's namesake Meredith Grey (Ellen Pompeo) finds herself in the midst of a love triangle with Dr. Derek "McDreamy" Shepherd (Patrick Dempsey) and his wife, Dr. Addison Montgomery-Shepherd (Kate Walsh). Meredith's best friend Cristina Yang (Sandra Oh) is an overachieving, commitment-phobic doctor in love with brilliant surgeon Dr. Preston Burke (Isaiah Washington). George O'Malley (T.R. Knight) is everybody's best friend, while Alex Karev (Justin Chambers) rubs everybody the wrong way. Izzie Stephens (Katherine Heigl) is the eternal optimist, full of emotion, and Dr. Miranda "The Nazi" Bailey (Chandra Wilson) keeps the whole crew running smoothly. Chief of Surgery Dr. Richard Webber (James Pickens Jr.) tries to keep the hospital afloat and his staff in line at the expense of his own marriage, proving that almost nobody at Seattle Grace has yet learned how to keep their personal and professional lives separate.

THE SCENE: The hospital is in chaos, thanks to the arrival of a patient with a live round of World War II ammunition that has pierced his chest. A bomb squad has taken over Seattle Grace, all of the operating rooms have been shut down, and both Cristina and Meredith are right in the middle of the action. Izzie and George, however, are so far away from the danger that they have found a moment to grab a bite to eat. But instead of being relieved, Izzie is frustrated that she and George aren't taking a more active role in the drama, and she impulsively decides that it's time for them to become more than just "watchers."

START 0:30:35 STOP 0:31:43 (TOTAL CLIP TIME: 1 MINUTE, 8 SECONDS)

START SCENE: Izzie sits on the floor, watching the turmoil downstairs.

STOP DIALOGUE: *(George)* Oh, you mean…we're starting right now.

BY THE BOOK: Proverbs 23:19, Matthew 5:37, 2 Corinthians 5:9, Philippians 3:14, James 1:22-25

WHERE TO TAKE IT:

1. Would you consider yourself a "doer" or a "watcher"? Explain your answer.

2. Does the world need both "doers" and "watchers"? Why or why not?

3. Was there ever a time when you should have done something but just sat on the sidelines and watched instead? What was the outcome?

4. What are the top two goals you have for yourself this year? How do you plan to achieve them?

5. Can you recall times when you were motivated by jealousy? What was the outcome?

6. Are you happy with the path your life is on? What would have to happen for you to change the course of your life?

7. What are the pros and cons of being a "doer"?

8. What are the pros and cons of being a "watcher"?

Visit www.skitguys.com or www.ysunderground.com for additional elements that might add impact to this clip, including the "Do Something" script.

Grey's Anatomy

(DRAMA)

SEASON 2, EPISODE 29: "BAND-AID COVERS THE BULLET HOLE"

TAG: WHEN DISAPPOINTMENT HAPPENS, HOW DO YOU RESPOND?

THEMES: Adversity, Athletes, Choices, Disappointment, Dreams, Plans, Sports

THE SERIES/SHOW: *Grey's Anatomy* is a medical drama focusing on a handful of interns dealing with the ups and downs of life, both in and out of the hospital. Through no fault of her own, the show's namesake Meredith Grey (Ellen Pompeo) finds herself in the midst of a love triangle with Dr. Derek "McDreamy" Shepherd (Patrick Dempsey) and his wife, Dr. Addison Montgomery-Shepherd (Kate Walsh). Meredith's best friend Cristina Yang (Sandra Oh) is an overachieving, commitment-phobic doctor in love with brilliant surgeon Dr. Preston Burke (Isaiah Washington). George O'Malley (T.R. Knight) is everybody's best friend, while Alex Karev (Justin Chambers) rubs everybody the wrong way. Izzie Stephens (Katherine Heigl) is the eternal optimist, full of emotion, and Dr. Miranda "The Nazi" Bailey (Chandra Wilson) keeps the whole crew running smoothly. Chief of Surgery Dr. Richard Webber (James Pickens Jr.) tries to keep the hospital afloat and his staff in line at the expense of his own marriage, proving that almost nobody at Seattle Grace has yet learned how to keep their personal and professional lives separate.

THE SCENE: High school hockey player Heath (Teddy Dunn) has fractured his finger in a freak hockey accident. Dr. Torres (Sara Ramirez) and Dr. O'Malley treat Heath's injuries and tell him to go home and take it easy. When Heath states that he has to play in that evening's hockey game, however, both his mother and the doctors protest, informing him that injuring his finger any further would cause irreparable damage. Heath tries to make them understand that college scouts will be at this game and that he actually has a shot at a scholarship. He believes that if he doesn't play in this game, everything he has worked for his entire life will be for nothing.

START: 0:19:24 STOP: 0:20:24 (TOTAL CLIP TIME: 1 MINUTE)

START DIALOGUE: *(Dr. Torres)* I'll schedule the surgery for your son. In the meantime, I'm sending Heath home with a prescription for Hydrocodone to control the pain.

STOP DIALOGUE: *(Heath's mom)* Honey, you can go to community college and get your grades up...*(Heath storms out of the room, angry. She looks at the doctors.)* I'm sorry. I'm sorry. *(She leaves to go after Heath.)*

BY THE BOOK: Psalm 20:4, Psalm 37:4, 2 Corinthians 4:17, James 1:2-3, 1 Peter 1:6-7

WHERE TO TAKE IT:

1. How do you respond when you face disappointment? What do you do when your dreams fall apart?

2. What's the difference between responding to something and reacting to it?

3. Have you ever felt that your life was "over"? What made you feel that way?

4. What lessons have you learned as you look back on your life?

5. In 2 Corinthians 4:17, the Bible speaks of our troubles as being "light" and "momentary." What do you think that means?

6. Why does it feel like our hard times will last forever?

7. How is it possible to avoid the pain of disappointment even when things don't go the way we plan?

8. Are you able to trust that God knows better than you do and that God has a plan for your life? What makes it easier to remember that?

Visit www.skitguys.com or www.ysunderground.com for additional elements that might add impact to this clip, including "The Parable of the Talents 3.29" from Instant Skits.

Grey's Anatomy
(DRAMA)
SEASON 2, EPISODE 33: "DAMAGE CASE"

TAG: I'VE COME TO ASK YOU TO FORGIVE ME.

THEMES: Accidents, Apologizing, Consequences, Forgiveness, Guilt, Loss, Pain, Redemption

THE SERIES/SHOW: *Grey's Anatomy* is a medical drama focusing on a handful of interns dealing with the ups and downs of life, both in and out of the hospital. Through no fault of her own, the show's namesake Meredith Grey (Ellen Pompeo) finds herself in the midst of a love triangle with Dr. Derek "McDreamy" Shepherd (Patrick Dempsey) and his wife, Dr. Addison Montgomery-Shepherd (Kate Walsh). Meredith's best friend Cristina Yang (Sandra Oh) is an overachieving, commitment-phobic doctor in love with brilliant surgeon Dr. Preston Burke (Isaiah Washington). George O'Malley (T.R. Knight) is everybody's best friend, while Alex Karev (Justin Chambers) rubs everybody the wrong way. Izzie Stephens (Katherine Heigl) is the eternal optimist, full of emotion, and Dr. Miranda "The Nazi" Bailey (Chandra Wilson) keeps the whole crew running smoothly. Chief of Surgery Dr. Richard Webber (James Pickens Jr.) tries to keep the hospital afloat and his staff in line at the expense of his own marriage, proving that almost nobody at Seattle Grace has yet learned how to keep their personal and professional lives separate.

THE SCENE: Mercy West surgical intern Marshall Stone (John Cho) works a late shift and drives home drowsy, causing a terrible accident when he falls asleep at the wheel. When the injured people are brought to Seattle Grace, it becomes obvious that 22-year-old expectant mother Melanie Reynolds (Sarah Lafleur) has internal injuries that can't be repaired, although Dr. Karev is able to save her baby through an emergency C-section. While Marshall is in the hospital recovering from his concussion and memory loss, he is horrified to learn that Melanie has died. Marshall wants nothing more than to apologize to Melanie's family and beg for forgiveness, though facing Melanie's father is the hardest thing Marshall has ever had to do.

START: 0:34:15 STOP: 0:36:25 (TOTAL CLIP TIME: 2 MINUTES, 10 SECONDS)

START SCENE: Dr. Bailey stands by Melanie, the car-accident victim who has died in surgery.

STOP SCENE: Melanie's father walks out of Marshall's room.

BY THE BOOK: Psalm 10:14, Psalm 30:5, Psalm 34:18, Luke 6:37, Colossians 3:13

WHERE TO TAKE IT:

1. What did you feel as you watched this scene? Did you sympathize more with Marshall or with Melanie's family?

2. If you had been in Melanie's father's place, would you have been able to forgive?

3. What does it mean to grieve? What have you grieved over?

4. How do we reach out to God in moments of heartache when nothing makes sense?

5. Have you ever felt like God has abandoned you? What does the Bible say in Psalm 34:18?

6. Have you ever caused someone else to grieve? What happened in that situation?

7. How hard is it for you to tell someone, "I'm sorry"?

8. Is it harder to forgive an accident or something done on purpose?

Visit www.skitguys.com or www.ysunderground.com for additional elements that might add impact to this clip, including the "Grace, They Just Don't Get It" script or video.

Grey's Anatomy
(DRAMA)
SEASON 2, EPISODE 27: "YESTERDAY"

TAG: DAD, WHY DID YOU LEAVE?

THEMES: Abandonment, Confrontation, Divorce, Father's Love, Parent-Child Relationships, Self-Esteem, Shame

THE SERIES/SHOW: *Grey's Anatomy* is a medical drama focusing on a handful of interns dealing with the ups and downs of life, both in and out of the hospital. Through no fault of her own, the show's namesake Meredith Grey (Ellen Pompeo) finds herself in the midst of a love triangle with Dr. Derek "McDreamy" Shepherd (Patrick Dempsey) and his wife, Dr. Addison Montgomery-Shepherd (Kate Walsh). Meredith's best friend Cristina Yang (Sandra Oh) is an overachieving, commitment-phobic doctor in love with brilliant surgeon Dr. Preston Burke (Isaiah Washington). George O'Malley (T.R. Knight) is everybody's best friend, while Alex Karev (Justin Chambers) rubs everybody the wrong way. Izzie Stephens (Katherine Heigl) is the eternal optimist, full of emotion, and Dr. Miranda "The Nazi" Bailey (Chandra Wilson) keeps the whole crew running smoothly. Chief of Surgery Dr. Richard Webber (James Pickens Jr.) tries to keep the hospital afloat and his staff in line at the expense of his own marriage, proving that almost nobody at Seattle Grace has yet learned how to keep their personal and professional lives separate.

THE SCENE: After growing up without him, Meredith decides to speak to her absentee father Thatcher (Jeff Perry) for the first time in 20 years. Feeling the need to confront Thatcher about his past actions, Meredith goes to the home he shares with his new wife and family. Though Meredith is willing to admit that life with her mother couldn't have been easy, she needs some answers from her father and gives him the opportunity to explain the choice he made to abandon her and start a new life.

START: 0:31:31 STOP: 0:33:13 (TOTAL CLIP TIME: 1 MINUTE, 42 SECONDS)

START DIALOGUE: *(Meredith)* She had an affair.

STOP DIALOGUE: *(Meredith)* No. I don't need anything from you. *(Meredith walks back to her car.)*

BY THE BOOK: Deuteronomy 4:31, Malachi 2:16, Malachi 4:6, Matthew 19:3-9, Colossians 3:21

WHERE TO TAKE IT:

1. Do you live with both parents or with one? What has that been like for you?

2. Is there more of a special connection between a father and daughter than between a father and son?

3. How important is it for a girl to have her father's love?

4. Have you ever felt abandoned by the people who were supposed to love you the most? Read Deuteronomy 4:31. What does it say about God's commitment to us?

5. How does it affect a young person's self-esteem when he or she is forced to grow up without a father? Does it change the way that person views love?

6. What does the Bible say about divorce in Malachi 2:16 and Matthew 19:3-9?

7. How does divorce affect children?

8. If you were in Meredith's shoes, would you have confronted your father about his choices? What would you say to him?

Visit www.skitguys.com or www.ysunderground.com for additional elements that might add impact to this clip, including "My Hero" from Skits That Teach.

Heroes
(DRAMA)
SEASON 1, EPISODE 14: "DISTRACTIONS"

TAG: I'M SO MAD, I COULD RIP THESE CUFFS OFF AND TASER YOU!

THEMES: Dreams, Hope, Human Nature, Making a Difference, the Meaning of Life, Purpose, Questions, Soul

THE SERIES/SHOW: Though they haven't asked to be special, certain people around the world, including Peter Petrelli (Milo Ventimiglia), Nathan Petrelli (Adrian Pasdar), Isaac Mendez (Santiago Cabrera), Hiro Nakamura (Masi Oka), Niki Sanders (Ali Larter), Micah Sanders (Noah Gray-Cabey), D.L. Hawkins (Leonard Roberts), Matt Parkman (Greg Grunberg), and Claire Bennett (Hayden Panettiere), have suddenly developed superhuman abilities. Following their movements closely is Indian genetics professor Mohinder Suresh (Sendhil Ramamurthy), who pursues them for research purposes. But megalomaniacal Sylar (Zachary Quinto) hunts the mutants for another, more sinister reason—to harvest their DNA, steal their powers, and rule the world. As these extraordinary people learn to understand their abilities and how to use them, they come closer to accepting their destinies.

THE SCENE: Niki Sanders has a split personality—one side of her is a sweet woman who wants nothing more than to take care of her son Micah, but the other side, called "Jessica," is filled with rage and releases her superhuman power. In this scene, Dr. Witherson (Paula Newsome) asks a chained Niki to let her speak with Jessica. As Niki recounts her childhood, Jessica emerges, rips off the chains like they were made of paper, and lunges at Witherson.

START 0:02:40 STOP 0:04:32 (TOTAL CLIP TIME: 1 MINUTE, 52 SECONDS)

START DIALOGUE: *(Tick-tock of a metronome) (Niki)* It sounds like a bomb is about to go off.

STOP DIALOGUE: *(Niki/Jessica)* You should have listened to the little mouse.

BY THE BOOK: Galatians 5:19-21, Ephesians 4:28, Colossians 3:8, 1 Timothy 2:8, James 1:19-20

WHERE TO TAKE IT:

1. Do you ever feel like there are different sides to you? Explain.

2. What are some things that anger you and tend to "set you off"?

3. Would you say you feel good or bad when you're angry?

4. Can you name a time in the past when someone got really angry at you? What happened?

5. What are some ways you work to control your anger?

6. Have you ever experienced real *rage* in your life? How is rage different from regular anger?

7. Galatians 5 includes "fits of rage" as an "act of the sinful nature." Why does that make it even more important to get angry emotions under control?

8. James 1:19-20 is a great passage to memorize for dealing with anger. What do these verses mean to you, and how could they possibly help you deal with anger in the future?

Visit www.skitguys.com or www.ysunderground.com for additional elements that might add impact to this clip, including the "You Cannot Help Me" script.

Heroes
(DRAMA)
SEASON 1, EPISODE 23: "HOW TO STOP AN EXPLODING MAN"

TAG: DOES A DOLPHIN WONDER ABOUT ITS PURPOSE IN LIFE?

THEMES: Hope, Human Nature, Making a Difference, the Mysteries of Life, Purpose

THE SERIES/SHOW: Though they haven't asked to be special, certain people around the world, including Peter Petrelli (Milo Ventimiglia), Nathan Petrelli (Adrian Pasdar), Isaac Mendez (Santiago Cabrera), Hiro Nakamura (Masi Oka), Niki Sanders (Ali Larter), Micah Sanders (Noah Gray-Cabey), D.L. Hawkins (Leonard Roberts), Matt Parkman (Greg Grunberg), and Claire Bennett (Hayden Panettiere), have suddenly developed superhuman abilities. Following their movements closely is Indian genetics professor Mohinder Suresh (Sendhil Ramamurthy), who pursues them for research purposes. But megalomaniacal Sylar (Zachary Quinto) hunts the mutants for another, more sinister reason—to harvest their DNA, steal their powers, and rule the world. As these extraordinary people learn to understand their abilities and how to use them, they come closer to accepting their destinies.

THE SCENE: This scene, the opening to the final episode of season 1, is a montage of different moments from the entire season. Each clip shows the heroes discovering their gifts and struggling to harness them. Throughout the montage, the voice of Mohinder Suresh asks several powerful questions about life, the soul, dreams, and purpose, but the audience is left with more questions than answers.

START 0:00:00 STOP 0:01:31 (TOTAL CLIP TIME: 1 MINUTE, 31 SECONDS)

START DIALOGUE: *(Opening music, Mohinder speaks)* Where does it come from?

STOP DIALOGUE: *(Mohinder)*...touch our hearts and share the pain of trying?

BY THE BOOK: John 6:38, Acts 13:36, 1 Corinthians 10:31, Philippians 1:21, 2 Thessalonians 1:11

WHERE TO TAKE IT:

1. Why do you believe we're here on the earth?

2. What is your definition of the "soul"?

3. Why do you think we dream? What do our dreams accomplish?

4. Where does the quest of our lives come from?

5. Why do we want to matter in the world?

6. What drives us to solve the mysteries of life?

7. Would life be better or easier if we didn't try to figure it out?

8. Who is someone God brought into your life in order to help you, rescue you, or save you?

Visit www.skitguys.com or www.ysunderground.com for additional elements that might add impact to this clip, including the "Ehud, the Left-Handed Man" script.

Heroes

(DRAMA)
SEASON 1, EPISODE 12: "GODSEND"

TAG: YOU WANNA STEAL A SWORD?

THEMES: Abilities, Duty, God's Word, Power

THE SERIES/SHOW: Though they haven't asked to be special, certain people around the world, including Peter Petrelli (Milo Ventimiglia), Nathan Petrelli (Adrian Pasdar), Isaac Mendez (Santiago Cabrera), Hiro Nakamura (Masi Oka), Niki Sanders (Ali Larter), Micah Sanders (Noah Gray-Cabey), D.L. Hawkins (Leonard Roberts), Matt Parkman (Greg Grunberg), and Claire Bennett (Hayden Panettiere), have suddenly developed superhuman abilities. Following their movements closely is Indian genetics professor Mohinder Suresh (Sendhil Ramamurthy), who pursues them for research purposes. But megalomaniacal Sylar (Zachary Quinto) hunts the mutants for another, more sinister reason—to harvest their DNA, steal their powers, and rule the world. As these extraordinary people learn to understand their abilities and how to use them, they come closer to accepting their destinies.

THE SCENE: Hiro Nakamura has the ability to pierce the space-time continuum and travel back and forth in time; however, he hasn't been able to truly control his newfound power. He believes that in order to gain control, he needs to find the ancient sword owned by Japanese legend Takezo Kensai, a wild savage with great powers feared by all of Japan. After a long search, Hiro and his friend Ando Masahashi (James Kyson Lee) have located the sword on a suit of armor once worn by Takezo Kensai. As the two friends realize what they've found, Ando points out a symbol on the sword meaning "great talent...godsend."

START 0:10:43 STOP 0:12:07 (TOTAL CLIP TIME: 1 MINUTE, 24 SECONDS)

START DIALOGUE: *(Hiro, in Japanese)* Takezo Kensai. My father used to tell me…

STOP DIALOGUE: *(Hiro)* I'm saying we take it.

(Ando) We?!

BY THE BOOK: 2 Corinthians 10:4, Ephesians 6:17, 2 Timothy 3:16-17, Hebrews 4:12, Revelation 19:15

WHERE TO TAKE IT:

1. What spiritual parallels can you find in the story of Takezo and the sword?

2. If the sword were to represent God's Word as in Ephesians 6:17, how would you look at this scene differently? What would your "powers" be?

3. How can the sword of the Spirit help you find control in your life?

4. How would you learn to use the sword of the Spirit more effectively?

5. Do you memorize Scripture? Why or why not?

6. Ando points out that the symbol on the sword means "great talent...godsend." What does that mean to you?

7. What does the "great talent" that God gives look like to you? Do you know anyone you believe is a "godsend"?

8. Do you believe God wants to use you? Could you possibly be a "godsend"? Why or why not?

Visit www.skitguys.com or www.ysunderground.com for additional elements that might add impact to this clip, including the "Fully Human, Fully God" script or video.

Heroes
(DRAMA)
SEASON 1, EPISODE 12: "GODSEND"

TAG: YOU CALL THEM GIFTS; I CALL THEM A FREAK SHOW.

THEMES: Abilities, Deception, Friendship, Lies, Purpose, Spiritual Gifts

THE SERIES/SHOW: Though they haven't asked to be special, certain people around the world, including Peter Petrelli (Milo Ventimiglia), Nathan Petrelli (Adrian Pasdar), Isaac Mendez (Santiago Cabrera), Hiro Nakamura (Masi Oka), Niki Sanders (Ali Larter), Micah Sanders (Noah Gray-Cabey), D.L. Hawkins (Leonard Roberts), Matt Parkman (Greg Grunberg), and Claire Bennett (Hayden Panettiere), have suddenly developed superhuman abilities. Following their movements closely is Indian genetics professor Mohinder Suresh (Sendhil Ramamurthy), who pursues them for research purposes. But megalomaniacal Sylar (Zachary Quinto) hunts the mutants for another, more sinister reason—to harvest their DNA, steal their powers, and rule the world. As these extraordinary people learn to understand their abilities and how to use them, they come closer to accepting their destinies.

THE SCENE: Claire has a secret meeting with The Haitian (Jimmy Jean-Louis) and asks to talk to Peter Petrelli. The Haitian warns that if Claire tries to contact Peter, her father will know because Peter is being watched. He admits that the "parents" she met earlier work for her father, as does he. As the conversation continues, The Haitian and Claire discuss their "gifts"—Claire doesn't appreciate or understand her abilities, but the Haitian believes his gift is the work of God.

START 0:24:18 STOP 0:26:16 (TOTAL CLIP TIME: 1 MINUTE, 58 SECONDS)

START DIALOGUE: *(Claire)* Save the cheerleader, save the world. What does that even mean?

STOP DIALOGUE: *(The Haitian)* What you can do, what I can do, that is God. Respect that calling.

BY THE BOOK: Matthew 25:14-30, Romans 12:4-6, 1 Corinthians 12:4-11, Ephesians 4:4-11, 1 Peter 4:10

WHERE TO TAKE IT:

1. Name someone you feel God has gifted. How does that person use those gifts for God?

2. Although none of us has superpowers, we are all gifted in different ways. What do you believe your gifts are?

3. Claire doesn't appreciate her giftedness. Do you look at your gifts as a blessing or a burden?

4. The Haitian tells Claire, "What you can do, what I can do, that is God. Respect that calling." What does that statement mean to you?

5. How can you be better at using your gifts for God?

6. Claire says, "You have to give me something. Nothing in my life has been real." Can you relate to that? Explain.

7. Have you ever felt like you were alone? If so, how did you come out of it?

8. Have you ever had your best friend taken from you? If so, describe.

Visit www.skitguys.com or www.ysunderground.com for additional elements that might add impact to this clip, including the "How Do I Know God's Will?" script.

Heroes
(DRAMA)
SEASON 1, EPISODE 3: "ONE GIANT LEAP"

TAG: I DIDN'T THINK YOU KNEW WHAT I THOUGHT.

THEMES: Bearing Others' Burdens, Being Sensitive to Needs, Discernment, Taking Action, Understanding Others

THE SERIES/SHOW: Though they haven't asked to be special, certain people around the world, including Peter Petrelli (Milo Ventimiglia), Nathan Petrelli (Adrian Pasdar), Isaac Mendez (Santiago Cabrera), Hiro Nakamura (Masi Oka), Niki Sanders (Ali Larter), Micah Sanders (Noah Gray-Cabey), D.L. Hawkins (Leonard Roberts), Matt Parkman (Greg Grunberg), and Claire Bennett (Hayden Panettiere), have suddenly developed superhuman abilities. Following their movements closely is Indian genetics professor Mohinder Suresh (Sendhil Ramamurthy), who pursues them for research purposes. But megalomaniacal Sylar (Zachary Quinto) hunts the mutants for another, more sinister reason—to harvest their DNA, steal their powers, and rule the world. As these extraordinary people learn to understand their abilities and how to use them, they come closer to accepting their destinies.

THE SCENE: Matt Parkman is a police officer who has discovered his ability to hear people's thoughts. This newfound ability has made his life more difficult because he, like the other super humans, hasn't been able to control his power. In this scene, Matt had gone to a bar following a fight with his wife Janice (Elizabeth Lackey). While sitting in the bar, Matt suddenly develops control of his power, gazing around the room and purposely breaking into other people's thoughts.

START 0:38:02 STOP 0:39:19 (TOTAL CLIP TIME: 1 MINUTE, 17 SECONDS)

START DIALOGUE: *(Bartender)* How ya doing?

STOP DIALOGUE: *(Woman at bar)* Would anybody care?

BY THE BOOK: Proverbs 15:26, Isaiah 55:8-9, Matthew 9:4, 1 Corinthians 2:11, Hebrews 3:1

WHERE TO TAKE IT:

1. How would life be different if you could hear other people's thoughts?

2. Do you ever feel like you know what other people are thinking? If so, how does that affect the way you act toward them?

3. What if everyone could hear *your* thoughts? How would that affect your life?

4. How important is your thought life to you?

5. Discuss this statement: "Sow a thought, reap an action. Sow an action, reap a habit. Sow a habit, reap a lifestyle."

6. In Matthew 9:4, we learn that Jesus knows our thoughts. How do you feel about that?

7. According to 1 Corinthians 2:11, what do we know about other people's thoughts?

8. How can you do better at "fixing your thoughts on Jesus," as we're told to do in Hebrews 3:1?

Visit www.skitguys.com or www.ysunderground.com for additional elements that might add impact to this clip, including School Conflicts 6.5c from Instant Skits.

Home Improvement
(COMEDY)
SEASON 6, EPISODE 1: "AT SEA"

TAG: HOW WILL I KNOW WHEN I'M A MAN?

THEMES: Communication, Dating, Growing Up, Manhood, Peer Pressure, Sex

THE SERIES/SHOW: *Home Improvement* is a situation comedy about an accident-prone handyman, Tim "The Tool Man" Taylor (Tim Allen), who hosts his own home-improvement cable show called *Tool Time*. When Tim isn't promoting Binford Tools or classic hot rods on his show with sidekick Al Borland (Richard Karn), he's at home trying to raise the average American family with his wife, Jill (Patricia Richardson). Supermom Jill not only takes care of the house and their three boys, Brad (Zachery Ty Bryan), Randy (Jonathan Taylor Thomas), and Mark (Taran Noah Smith), while working to earn her Ph.D. in psychiatry, but she also gracefully endures Tim's constant attempts to overhaul their house with "more power." Both Tim and Jill rely on eccentric neighbor Wilson (Earl Hindman) for advice and guidance, but the Tool Man usually figures out most family problems in his own unique way.

THE SCENE: After catching Brad making out with his girlfriend on his bed, Jill asks Tim to have a talk with Brad about sex and see how far the two teenagers have taken their relationship. Tim invites Brad to the garage to work on the latest hot rod Tim is restoring—the typical location for a father-son discussion in the Taylor household. Tim finally confesses his true intentions to Brad, and Brad shares his feelings about his girlfriend, sex, and the pressures he's facing. As they talk, Tim tries to share with his son what it really means to "become a man."

START: 0:19:29 STOP: 0:21:40 (TOTAL CLIP TIME: 2 MINUTES, 11 SECONDS)

START DIALOGUE: *(Tim)* I wanna talk about you and Angela.

STOP DIALOGUE: *(Tim)* Your mom and I will tell you.

BY THE BOOK: 1 Corinthians 13:11, Ephesians 6:4, Colossians 3:21, 1 Timothy 4:12, 1 Peter 2:12

WHERE TO TAKE IT:

1. On a scale of 1 to 10, how important is sex to the average teenager? Why do you think so?

2. Have either of your parents ever approached you to have a talk about relationships or sex?

3. How did talking with your parents influence your beliefs about sex and relationships—positively or negatively?

4. Do you think sex makes a boy into a man?

5. What are the qualities of a "real man"?

6. How can a teenage boy stand up to peer pressure and reject the belief that he has to prove his manhood to others?

7. Have you ever felt pressure from friends or society to have sex or be more physical than you think you should be?

8. Apart from what the Bible says, what are some other good reasons to wait until marriage to have sex?

Visit www.skitguys.com or www.ysunderground.com for additional elements that might add impact to this clip, including the "True Love Waits" script.

Home Improvement
(COMEDY)
SEASON 6, EPISODE 20: "MY SON THE DRIVER"

TAG: BACK THE CANOE UP HERE—I NEED THE TRUTH!

THEMES: Confession, Consequences, Lies, Responsibility, Trust

THE SERIES/SHOW: *Home Improvement* is a situation comedy about an accident-prone handyman, Tim "The Tool Man" Taylor (Tim Allen), who hosts his own home-improvement cable show called *Tool Time*. When Tim isn't promoting Binford Tools or classic hot rods on his show with sidekick Al Borland (Richard Karn), he's at home trying to raise the average American family with his wife, Jill (Patricia Richardson). Supermom Jill not only takes care of the house and their three boys, Brad (Zachery Ty Bryan), Randy (Jonathan Taylor Thomas), and Mark (Taran Noah Smith), while working to earn her Ph.D. in psychiatry, but she also gracefully endures Tim's constant attempts to overhaul their house with "more power." Both Tim and Jill rely on eccentric neighbor Wilson (Earl Hindman) for advice and guidance, but the Tool Man usually figures out most family problems in his own unique way.

THE SCENE: The very night Brad passes his driver's test and earns his license, he goes out driving with some of his friends and gets into a fender bender with another car. They strike a deal—the other driver says he'll keep quiet if Brad pays him $400. Fearing his parents will take away his license, Brad pays the man and tells his parents he hit a pole. But when the other driver says he has whiplash and decides to sue the Taylors, Brad must confess his lie and accept his punishment.

START: 0:19:18 STOP: 0:20:50 (TOTAL CLIP TIME: 1 MINUTE, 32 SECONDS)

START DIALOGUE: *(Brad)* Look, I need to talk to you guys about the accident I had. I didn't hit a pole; I hit a car.

STOP DIALOGUE: *(Brad)* Thirty days? *(Tim glares at Brad.)* Sounds fair.

BY THE BOOK: Psalm 34:13, 2 Corinthians 7:9, Colossians 3:9, Hebrews 12:9-10, 1 Peter 2:16

WHERE TO TAKE IT:

1. Why did Brad think it would be easier to lie to his parents about his accident rather than tell the truth?

2. What problems resulted from Brad's lie?

3. In the end, do you think Brad was sorry he had lied to his parents or sorry he got caught?

4. Have you been tempted to lie to your parents to keep from getting punished?

5. Freedom brings responsibility. Did Brad show his parents he was a responsible driver?

6. What do you think Brad would have to do to regain his parents' trust?

7. If you were in Brad's situation, what would you do?

8. Is there ever a time when it's appropriate to lie to someone?

Visit www.skitguys.com or www.ysunderground.com for additional elements that might add impact to this clip, including the "Dad, Give Me My Money Now" script.

Home Improvement
(COMEDY)
SEASON 6, EPISODE 23: "THE FEMININE MISTAKE"

TAG: SO NOW YOU'RE A FEMINIST, TOO?

THEMES: Chauvinism/Feminism, Dating, Equality, Relationships, Roles

THE SERIES/SHOW: *Home Improvement* is a situation comedy about an accident-prone handyman, Tim "The Tool Man" Taylor (Tim Allen), who hosts his own home-improvement cable show called *Tool Time*. When Tim isn't promoting Binford Tools or classic hot rods on his show with sidekick Al Borland (Richard Karn), he's at home trying to raise the average American family with his wife, Jill (Patricia Richardson). Supermom Jill not only takes care of the house and their three boys, Brad (Zachery Ty Bryan), Randy (Jonathan Taylor Thomas), and Mark (Taran Noah Smith), while working to earn her Ph.D. in psychiatry, but she also gracefully endures Tim's constant attempts to overhaul their house with "more power." Both Tim and Jill rely on eccentric neighbor Wilson (Earl Hindman) for advice and guidance, but the Tool Man usually figures out most family problems in his own unique way.

THE SCENE: When Tim and Jill find out that eldest son Brad has been letting his girlfriend Angela (Kristen Clayton) do his laundry, clean his room, and make him snacks, they're shocked at Brad's blatantly sexist attitude. Tim takes Brad out to the garage to have a talk and explains there could be an underlying reason for Angela's willingness to serve Brad. As his son listens, Tim tells Brad everything he knows about men, women, and relationships.

START: 0:16:43 STOP: 0:19:57 (TOTAL CLIP TIME: 3 MINUTES, 14 SECONDS)

START DIALOGUE: *(Brad)* Man, I'm kinda hungry.

STOP DIALOGUE: *(Brad)* Oh, I don't know. About three minutes ago when I was in the garage.

BY THE BOOK: Romans 10:12, Ephesians 5:33, Philippians 2:5-7, 1 Thessalonians 5:11, 1 Peter 4:10

WHERE TO TAKE IT:

1. How has our society contributed to the way you view male and female roles?

2. What does the Bible say about male and female roles?

3. Was it wrong for Brad to take advantage of Angela's kindness by having her do his chores?

4. Have you ever felt like you needed to do things for friends to get them to like you or keep liking you?

5. Are your relationships one-sided or equal? Why?

6. Why is it important for both people to put effort into a relationship?

7. If we're called to serve one another, what does that look like in your relationships?

8. If you could sit down with Angela and talk with her about her relationship with Brad, what would you say?

Visit www.skitguys.com or www.ysunderground.com for additional elements that might add impact to this clip, including "The Psychic" from Skits That Teach.

Home Improvement
(COMEDY)
SEASON 6, EPISODE 14: "THE KARATE KID RETURNS"

TAG: BECAUSE THAT'S WHERE MY FIST HAPPENED TO LAND!

THEMES: Bullying, Fighting, Handling Problems, Humiliation, Peer Pressure, Teasing

THE SERIES/SHOW: *Home Improvement* is a situation comedy about an accident-prone handyman, Tim "The Tool Man" Taylor (Tim Allen), who hosts his own home-improvement cable show called *Tool Time*. When Tim isn't promoting Binford Tools or classic hot rods on his show with sidekick Al Borland (Richard Karn), he's at home trying to raise the average American family with his wife, Jill (Patricia Richardson). Supermom Jill not only takes care of the house and their three boys, Brad (Zachery Ty Bryan), Randy (Jonathan Taylor Thomas), and Mark (Taran Noah Smith), while working to earn her Ph.D. in psychiatry, but she also gracefully endures Tim's constant attempts to overhaul their house with "more power." Both Tim and Jill rely on eccentric neighbor Wilson (Earl Hindman) for advice and guidance, but the Tool Man usually figures out most family problems in his own unique way.

THE SCENE: While Randy and Mark are at the mall, Randy is bullied by an older, bigger kid from his school. Randy's younger brother Mark uses his karate skills to take down the bully, and Randy and Mark both run away. Unbeknownst to Randy, one of his classmates saw the whole incident and writes about it for the next day's school paper. As his fellow students read about how Randy's little brother came to his rescue, Randy is teased and humiliated even worse than before. That evening at home, however, Randy tells his family that even though he was upset earlier, he has made peace with the situation and wants to move on. Tim and Jill are proud of Randy and his display of maturity, but older brother Brad suspects that there may be more to the story.

START: 0:10:01 STOP: 0:12:21 (TOTAL CLIP TIME: 2 MINUTES, 20 SECONDS)

START DIALOGUE: *(Boy #1—Chad)* Hey, Taylor. We need some new loafers. But we're kind of afraid to go to the mall. Think your little brother can come?

STOP DIALOGUE: *(Randy)* Because that's where my fist happened to land.

(Brad) All right! *(High-fives Randy)*

BY THE BOOK: Luke 6:29, Romans 12:19, 1 Peter 2:15, 1 Peter 2:19-20, 1 Peter 3:8-9

WHERE TO TAKE IT:

1. Have you ever had an embarrassing moment spread around school?

2. What would you do if you were in Randy's situation?

3. Do you worry about what other people think about you enough to let a rumor upset you or cause you to act out?

4. Do guys and girls deal with teasing or bullying in different ways?

5. Can you think of some effective and mature ways to handle being teased by others?

6. Can you name a time when you were teased about something? How did you respond?

7. Why do people tease or bully others?

8. How would you apply Luke 6:29 to the situation Randy experienced? Is that realistic? If not, name a realistic solution based on Luke 6:29.

Visit www.skitguys.com or www.ysunderground.com for additional elements that might add impact to this clip, including "Elisha is Jeered 3.13" from Instant Skits.

Home Improvement

(COMEDY)

SEASON 6, EPISODE 11: "WORKIN' MAN BLUES"

TAG: ROB DIDN'T GO TO COLLEGE!

THEMES: Education, Money, Priorities, Responsibility, Working

THE SERIES/SHOW: *Home Improvement* is a situation comedy about an accident-prone handyman, Tim "The Tool Man" Taylor (Tim Allen), who hosts his own home-improvement cable show called *Tool Time*. When Tim isn't promoting Binford Tools or classic hot rods on his show with sidekick Al Borland (Richard Karn), he's at home trying to raise the average American family with his wife, Jill (Patricia Richardson). Supermom Jill not only takes care of the house and their three boys, Brad (Zachery Ty Bryan), Randy (Jonathan Taylor Thomas), and Mark (Taran Noah Smith), while working to earn her Ph.D. in psychiatry, but she also gracefully endures Tim's constant attempts to overhaul their house with "more power." Both Tim and Jill rely on eccentric neighbor Wilson (Earl Hindman) for advice and guidance, but the Tool Man usually figures out most family problems in his own unique way.

THE SCENE: Having gained his parents' permission to get a part-time job, Brad finds a job at a store selling sports and camping equipment that seems to suit him perfectly. He quickly begins to idolize store owner Rob (Mitch Rouse) and works harder each day to impress his boss. Tim and Jill soon become concerned when Brad starts neglecting his friends and family to work more hours at the store, even going so far as to skip his PSAT test to cover for a fellow employee. Believing that Rob must be telling Brad that school isn't important, Tim visits the store to tell Brad to quit. Once he talks to Rob, however, Tim gains a better understanding of the situation.

START: 0:18:37 STOP: 0:20:22 (TOTAL CLIP TIME: 1 MINUTE, 45 SECONDS)

START DIALOGUE: *(Tim)* Hi, I'm Tim Taylor. I'm Brad's dad.

STOP DIALOGUE: *(Rob)* Your dad's right. I wish I had a better one.

BY THE BOOK: Proverbs 4:26, Proverbs 23:12, 23, Colossians 3:23-24, 1 Timothy 6:17, 1 John 2:16

WHERE TO TAKE IT:

1. How important is your education?

2. Have you ever been in a situation similar to Brad's, where working became more important than school?

3. How did Brad's priorities change after he started working?

4. Were his parents right to be concerned? Should they have told him to quit his job?

5. Be completely honest with yourself—what are your priorities? Are they in the right order?

6. Have you let the wrong priorities interfere with your education, friendships, or family relationships? What can you do to change this?

7. How do you deal with situations where your priorities and your parents' aren't the same?

8. If you really followed Colossians 3:23-24, how would that change the way you do things at school, work, and home?

Visit www.skitguys.com or www.ysunderground.com for additional elements that might add impact to this clip, including Work Conflicts 6.3c from Instant Skits.

House
(DRAMA)
SEASON 2, EPISODE 23: "ACCEPTANCE"

TAG: WHEN YOU CARE ENOUGH TO GIVE THE VERY BEST!

THEMES: Bearing Others' Burdens, Caring for Others, Compassion, Death, Human Dignity, Terminal Illness

THE SERIES/SHOW: Dr. Gregory House (Hugh Laurie) is an irreverent, caustic jerk of a guy who belittles his colleagues, insults his patients, and alienates his friends. It just so happens that he's also a brilliant diagnostician specializing in infectious diseases, with a knack for tracking down and treating even the most unusual illnesses while battling his own addictions, chronic pain, and his own worst enemy—himself. On this tense drama series, the doctor known simply as "House" supervises three young doctors, Eric Foreman (Omar Epps), Allison Cameron (Jennifer Morrison), and Robert Chase (Jesse Spencer) at Princeton-Plainsboro Teaching Hospital. His beleaguered supporters include hospital administrator Dr. Lisa Cuddy (Lisa Edelstein) and oncologist Dr. James Wilson (Robert Sean Leonard), who has the dubious distinction of being House's "best friend."

THE SCENE: Dr. Cameron has a patient (Christie Lynn Smith) who is terminal but doesn't know it. True to her nature, Cameron befriends her patient and becomes emotionally involved to the point where she's reluctant to share the diagnosis. Dr. Wilson advises her not to get so involved, stating that an attachment like that isn't worth it. Cameron opens up to Wilson, revealing how the death of her husband has led her to believe that when a person dies, *someone* should care.

START 0:37:02 STOP 0:38:22 (TOTAL CLIP TIME: 1 MINUTE, 20 SECONDS)

START DIALOGUE: *(Dr. Wilson)* Cameron, can I borrow you for a consult?

STOP DIALOGUE: *(Dr. Cameron)* Somebody should be upset.

BY THE BOOK: Romans 15:1, 2 Corinthians 1:3-4, Galatians 6:2, 1 Thessalonians 5:11, 1 Thessalonians 5:14

WHERE TO TAKE IT:

1. What are some burdens that are just too big for one person to carry?

2. Has there been anyone in your life diagnosed with a terminal illness?

3. Were you able to comfort or encourage that person during that time?

4. Have you been on the receiving end of others' care and compassion? How did that impact you?

5. What are some of the physical or practical needs of people who are experiencing a crisis?

6. What are some of the emotional and spiritual needs of those experiencing a crisis? Are any more urgent than others?

7. What aspects of your personality do you need to put aside in order to care for others' needs? Is this an easy thing to do?

8. Read 2 Corinthians 1:3-4. Do these verses inspire you to show compassion?

Visit www.skitguys.com or www.ysunderground.com for additional elements that might add impact to this clip, including the "From Each Other" script.

House
(DRAMA)
SEASON 2, EPISODE 24: "AUTOPSY"

TAG: YOU'RE GOING TO LIVE, BUT WE HAVE TO KILL YOU FIRST.

THEMES: Adversity, Courage, Death, Salvation, Terminal Illness

THE SERIES/SHOW: Dr. Gregory House (Hugh Laurie) is an irreverent, caustic jerk of a guy who belittles his colleagues, insults his patients, and alienates his friends. It just so happens that he's also a brilliant diagnostician specializing in infectious diseases, with a knack for tracking down and treating even the most unusual illnesses while battling his own addictions, chronic pain, and his own worst enemy—himself. On this tense drama series, the doctor known simply as "House" supervises three young doctors, Eric Foreman (Omar Epps), Allison Cameron (Jennifer Morrison), and Robert Chase (Jesse Spencer) at Princeton-Plainsboro Teaching Hospital. His beleaguered supporters include hospital administrator Dr. Lisa Cuddy (Lisa Edelstein) and oncologist Dr. James Wilson (Robert Sean Leonard), who has the dubious distinction of being House's "best friend."

THE SCENE: A young girl, Andie (Sasha Embeth Pieterse), is sick with terminal cancer. She is preparing to undergo a drastic procedure that will "kill" her in order to "reboot" her system, giving the PPTH doctors a very brief window to spot a clot in her brain. Since removing the clot will only prolong Andie's life for another year, Dr. House wants to know how she feels about going through with the procedure and why she's willing to do it.

START 0:29:00 STOP 0:31:28 (TOTAL CLIP TIME: 2 MINUTES, 28 SECONDS)

START DIALOGUE: *(House)* I'm Dr. House.
STOP SCENE: Scene goes black.

BY THE BOOK: Luke 12:4-5, Philippians 1:21, 2 Timothy 1:7, James 4:15, 1 Peter 2:24

WHERE TO TAKE IT:

1. How would you feel if doctors told you they had to take your life in order to heal you?

2. When you think of death, what's the first thing that comes to mind?

3. How does someone dying to "reboot" her system compare to our spiritual lives?

4. Jesus calls us to take up our cross (or "die") daily. What does that mean to you?

5. Do you know anyone who died but was brought back to life? Explain that person's situation.

6. If you know you'll go to heaven when you die, why is death still so terrifying?

7. Do you know anyone who's not afraid of death? Why do you think that person isn't afraid?

8. If you knew you were going to die in six months, would you live differently?

Visit www.skitguys.com or www.ysunderground.com for additional elements that might add impact to this clip, including "The Most Important Thing" video.

House

(DRAMA)

SEASON 2, EPISODE 29: "HUNTING"

TAG: I REGRET...THAT I DON'T HAVE ANY REGRETS.

THEMES: Abundant Life, Carpe Diem, Death, Dreams, Missed Opportunity, Regrets

THE SERIES/SHOW: Dr. Gregory House (Hugh Laurie) is an irreverent, caustic jerk of a guy who belittles his colleagues, insults his patients, and alienates his friends. It just so happens that he's also a brilliant diagnostician specializing in infectious diseases, with a knack for tracking down and treating even the most unusual illnesses while battling his own addictions, chronic pain, and his own worst enemy—himself. On this tense drama series, the doctor known simply as "House" supervises three young doctors, Eric Foreman (Omar Epps), Allison Cameron (Jennifer Morrison), and Robert Chase (Jesse Spencer) at Princeton-Plainsboro Teaching Hospital. His beleaguered supporters include hospital administrator Dr. Lisa Cuddy (Lisa Edelstein) and oncologist Dr. James Wilson (Robert Sean Leonard), who has the dubious distinction of being House's "best friend."

THE SCENE: House and Cameron are discussing Kalvin (Matthew John Armstrong), a patient who has destroyed his body through a life of poor choices. Discovering that he may not have long to live, Kalvin asks to see his father. House is typically irritated by the request, telling Cameron that people should just say what needs to be said and not "save it for a sound bite" before dying. Cameron is more sympathetic, countering that facing regrets is not unusual for a person staring death in the face.

START 0:21:32 STOP 0:22:34 (TOTAL CLIP TIME: 1 MINUTE, 2 SECONDS)

START DIALOGUE: *(House)* So, how's the patient's father?

STOP DIALOGUE: *(Cameron)* Everyone has regrets.

BONUS CLIP: START: 0:30:46 STOP: 0:31:40 (TOTAL CLIP TIME: 56 SECONDS)

(Kalvin) So, I have cancer?

(Dr. Wilson) In all likelihood, yeah. Non-Hodgkin's lymphoma.

(Kalvin) And I am dying.

(Dr. Wilson) We need to biopsy the tumor. It's near your aorta, so getting that sample carries serious risks.

(Kalvin) Is my dad still here?

(Dr. Wilson) He hasn't been in?

(Kalvin) No. *(Kalvin sits sorrowfully, feeling very alone as Dr. Wilson tells him about the procedure. The scene changes to show Kalvin's dad in a waiting room, looking sad and regretful that things have ended this way, with their relationship at odds.)*

BY THE BOOK: Proverbs 27:1, Luke 12:17-20, John 10:10, 2 Corinthians 7:10, James 4:13-15

WHERE TO TAKE IT:

1. Do you have regrets about missed opportunities?

2. Have you known anyone who tried to make up for a lifetime of regrets during a short period of time?

3. Is it possible that regrets are Satan's tool for stealing the joy that we should be experiencing in life?

4. How do you judge your success in life? What brings you joy?

5. How should you live daily in order to prevent future regrets?

6. Do you know anyone who really understands how to "seize the day" (i.e., carpe diem)?

7. If you die today, what would be your greatest regrets? Who would you want by your side?

8. What are some things you would change about your life if you could? What moments would you go back to and live differently?

Visit www.skitguys.com or www.ysunderground.com for additional elements that might add impact to this clip, including the "Last Flight of 206" script.

House

(DRAMA)

SEASON 2, EPISODE 40: "SLEEPING DOGS LIE"

TAG: HEY, HARD HEART—HOW ARE YA?

THEMES: Apologizing, Confrontation, Forgiveness, Hard Heart, Selfishness

THE SERIES/SHOW: Dr. Gregory House (Hugh Laurie) is an irreverent, caustic jerk of a guy who belittles his colleagues, insults his patients, and alienates his friends. It just so happens that he's also a brilliant diagnostician specializing in infectious diseases, with a knack for tracking down and treating even the most unusual illnesses while battling his own addictions, chronic pain, and his own worst enemy—himself. On this tense drama series, the doctor known simply as "House" supervises three young doctors, Eric Foreman (Omar Epps), Allison Cameron (Jennifer Morrison), and Robert Chase (Jesse Spencer) at Princeton-Plainsboro Teaching Hospital. His beleaguered supporters include hospital administrator Dr. Lisa Cuddy (Lisa Edelstein) and oncologist Dr. James Wilson (Robert Sean Leonard), who has the dubious distinction of being House's "best friend."

THE SCENE: Four months ago, Dr. Cameron began writing an article about one of Dr. House's difficult cases and planned to submit it for publishing in a medical journal. Her colleague, Dr. Foreman—knowing she was planning to publish her findings about this particular case—wrote his own article about the case and published it, therefore receiving credit for the idea. Furious, Cameron confronts Foreman about the situation, but he claims he didn't "steal" her article since he wrote about the case from a different point of view. Nevertheless, Cameron still believes what Foreman did was unscrupulous, and their entire team feels the rift between the two doctors. Late one evening, Cameron goes to Foreman to apologize for getting so upset about what he did, acknowledging that they both had the same opportunity to write their own perspective about the case. To keep their friendship from suffering any further, Cameron suggests that they both apologize and move past the incident. But to her surprise, Foreman informs her that they're not really friends, only colleagues. He clearly believes he has done nothing wrong and refuses to give her the apology she thinks she deserves.

START: 0:41:50 STOP: 0:42:55 (TOTAL CLIP TIME: 1 MINUTE, 5 SECONDS)

START DIALOGUE: *(Dr. Cameron)* I don't own House's cases. You had just as much right as I did to write it up. You should have told me, but I should have handled it better, too. If we want this not to get in the way of our friendship, I think we both have to apologize and put it behind us.

STOP DIALOGUE: *(Dr. Foreman)* I like you, really. We have a good time working together. But 10 years from now, we're not going to be hanging out and having dinners. Maybe we'll exchange Christmas cards, say hi, give a hug if we're at the same conference. We're not friends. We're colleagues. And I don't have anything to apologize for. *(Cameron looks shocked.)*

BY THE BOOK: Proverbs 28:14, Matthew 6:14-15, Matthew 18:21-22, Mark 11:25, Philippians 2:3

WHERE TO TAKE IT:

1. Have you ever apologized to someone, but that person refused to accept your apology? How did that make you feel?

2. Have you ever worked very hard on a project, only to find out that someone else had done the same thing? How did that turn out?

3. What does a lack of forgiveness suggest about a person's spiritual condition?

4. When we choose not to forgive, what happens to the individual(s) involved…emotionally? Physically? Spiritually?

5. What does Matthew 6:14-15 say about forgiveness? Can you think of a better reason to offer forgiveness to someone who has hurt you?

6. What does Jesus mean in Matthew 18:21-22 when he says we are to forgive someone "seventy-seven times"?

7. What does it mean to have a "hard heart"?

8. What are you having a difficult time forgiving someone for? What would it take for you to forgive that person?

Visit www.skitguys.com or www.ysunderground.com for additional elements that might add impact to this clip, including "The Good Samaritan 3.22" from Instant Skits.

TAG: CAN I GET AN "AMEN"?

THEMES: Does God Make People Sick? Faith Healers, Miracles, Trusting in Conventional Medicine

THE SERIES/SHOW: Dr. Gregory House (Hugh Laurie) is an irreverent, caustic jerk of a guy who belittles his colleagues, insults his patients, and alienates his friends. It just so happens that he's also a brilliant diagnostician specializing in infectious diseases, with a knack for tracking down and treating even the most unusual illnesses while battling his own addictions, chronic pain, and his own worst enemy—himself. On this tense drama series, the doctor known simply as "House" supervises three young doctors, Eric Foreman (Omar Epps), Allison Cameron (Jennifer Morrison), and Robert Chase (Jesse Spencer), at Princeton-Plainsboro Teaching Hospital. His beleaguered supporters include hospital administrator Dr. Lisa Cuddy (Lisa Edelstein) and oncologist Dr. James Wilson (Robert Sean Leonard), who has the dubious distinction of being House's "best friend."

THE SCENE: Boyd (Thomas Dekker), a 15-year-old faith healer and preacher, is convinced he has the healing power. During a service, Boyd "heals" a paralytic named Agnes (Sandra Marshall), and she is able to walk. But while preaching the word of God's healing, Boyd is suddenly afflicted with terrible pain and asks his father (Will Rogers) for a doctor.

START: 0:00:12 STOP: 0:02:48 (TOTAL CLIP TIME: 2 MINUTES, 36 SECONDS)

START DIALOGUE: *(A church service, people are singing) (Boyd)* Do you feel the Spirit? *(Congregation claps and says a resounding, "Yes!")* And in the 39th year of his reign, Asa was diseased in his feet, until the disease was exceedingly great, yet he didn't seek help from the Lord, but from the physicians. Now, there is nothing wrong with seeing a doctor. But can a doctor heal through the power that Jesus gave his disciples? Men of science can walk through life with blindfolds, never knowing that you or I could not take a single step if we were not uplifted by God.

STOP DIALOGUE: *(Boyd)* No! *(His father realizes that something is wrong and kneels down beside him.)* Daddy, I think I need a doctor.

BY THE BOOK: Job 5:18, Psalm 30:2, Psalm 147:3, Isaiah 53:5, James 5:16, 1 Peter 2:24

WHERE TO TAKE IT:

1. Do you believe people can be healed by faith? What does "by faith" mean in this context?

2. What does the Bible say about healing in the verses provided? In your opinion, who has the authority to heal?

3. Have you ever known anyone who was miraculously healed of a handicap, sickness, or disease?

4. How would you define a "miracle"? Do you believe miracles still happen today?

5. Why do you think Jesus chose to heal the lame, the blind, and the dying?

6. When you see televangelists "healing" people on TV, do you believe that healing is taking place? If yes, why? If no, why not?

7. Why do some people believe in the power of healing?

8. What happens when someone begs for healing but it doesn't come? Why would God choose not to heal someone?

BONUS CLIP:

SCENE 2: When Boyd is brought before House and his team of doctors for diagnosis, they find several small tumors growing in Boyd's brain, causing the hallucinations that Boyd believes are the voice of God. Even after House asks Dr. Wilson to convince Boyd that his life depends on the surgery, Boyd refuses it, believing that God gave him the tumors to make him special. House and Wilson take their case to Boyd's father, but they soon find that he is no more willing to let go of his son's "special power" than Boyd is.

START: 0:21:47 STOP: 0:23:22 (TOTAL CLIP TIME: 1 MINUTE, 45 SECONDS)

START DIALOGUE: *(Dr. Wilson)* Hi. I'm Doctor Wilson.

STOP DIALOGUE: *(Dr. Wilson)* So you believe your son is...a saint? The way I understand it, one of the hallmarks of a saint is humility. Now, someone with true humility would consider the possibility that God hadn't chosen him for that kind of honor. Well, he'd consider the possibility that he just had an illness.

Visit www.skitguys.com or www.ysunderground.com for additional elements that might add impact to this clip, including the "Here I Am, Lord, Send Me" responsive reading.

Lost

(DRAMA)

SEASON 2, EPISODE 23: "LIVE TOGETHER, DIE ALONE"

TAG: MY SACRIFICE.

THEMES: Choices, Confrontation, Courage, Mercy, Sacrifice, Saving a Life

THE SERIES/SHOW: Set on a remote island full of mysteries, *Lost* focuses on the aftermath of a terrible plane crash. Survivors of doomed Flight 815 include beautiful fugitive Kate (Evangeline Lilly), con artist Sawyer (Josh Holloway), former Iraqi militant Sayid (Naveen Andrews), druggie rock star Charlie (Dominic Monaghan), expectant mother Claire (Emilie de Ravin), chubby millionaire Hurley (Jorge Garcia), contractor Michael and son Walt (Harold Perrineau and Malcolm David Kelley), Korean couple Jin and Sun Kwon (Daniel Dae Kim and Yunjin Kim), miraculously cured paralytic John Locke (Terry O'Quinn), and surgeon Jack Shepard (Matthew Fox), who reluctantly assumes leadership of the group. With no hope for rescue in the near future, the survivors must learn to exist on an island populated by secrets, dangerous creatures, and "the Others."

THE SCENE: As part of the mystery of the island, several of the survivors have found an underground hatch containing computer equipment overseen by a shipwrecked man known as Desmond (Henry Ian Cusick). For the last three years, Desmond has been faithfully obeying orders to push a computer button at regular intervals, releasing the electromagnetic pressure of the island which would otherwise build up and explode. Desmond believes that complying with his orders will protect not only the island, but also the rest of the world—including Penny, the woman he loves back home. When the survivors of Flight 815 find him, Desmond attempts to escape the island, placing the responsibility of pushing the button on someone else's shoulders. However, Locke has come to believe that the orders to push the button are unnecessary—a behavioral experiment—and wants to see what would happen if the button isn't pushed at the required time. Unable to escape the island after all, Desmond returns to the hatch just in time to save the day... and give his life for those he loves.

START 1:13:08 STOP 1:17:35 (TOTAL CLIP TIME: 4 MINUTES, 27 SECONDS)

START DIALOGUE: *(Desmond)* Three days before you came down here, before we met, I heard a banging on the hatch door and shouting. But it was you, John, wasn't it? You say there isn't any purpose? No such thing as fate? But you saved my life, brother. So that I could save yours.

STOP DIALOGUE: *(Desmond)* I love you, Penny. *(He turns the key.)*

BY THE BOOK: Esther 4:16, John 3:16, John 10:10, 1 Timothy 2:5-6, Hebrews 2:9-10

WHERE TO TAKE IT:

1. The word *sacrifice* is used in this clip as a verb, meaning "to give up something of value for something or someone else." Have you ever had to sacrifice something of value for a greater cause or to help someone else? What did you learn or gain from this experience?

2. Has anyone ever made a sacrifice for you? How did you feel about that person's actions?

3. Is it important to sacrifice things you want for the people around you? The world around you?

4. Read John 3:16. Do you understand the sacrifice that God, the Father, made for you? What does that sacrifice mean to you?

5. Would you do what Desmond did in this scene?

6. In Esther 4:16, Queen Esther states, "If I perish, I perish." Have you been in a situation where you had to make a choice that could cost you everything?

7. Who do you love so much that you would give your life to save him or her? Who loves you that much?

8. What would it be like to make a sacrifice for someone who didn't know or appreciate it?

Visit www.skitguys.com or www.ysunderground.com for additional elements that might add impact to this clip, including "The Monologue of Peter" script.

Lost

(DRAMA)

SEASON 2, EPISODE 1: "MAN OF SCIENCE, MAN OF FAITH"

TAG: DO YOU BELIEVE IN MIRACLES?

THEMES: Bitterness, Faith, Guilt, Miracles, Promises

THE SERIES/SHOW: Set on a remote island full of mysteries, *Lost* focuses on the aftermath of a terrible plane crash. Survivors of doomed Flight 815 include beautiful fugitive Kate (Evangeline Lilly), con artist Sawyer (Josh Holloway), former Iraqi militant Sayid (Naveen Andrews), druggie rock star Charlie (Dominic Monaghan), expectant mother Claire (Emilie de Ravin), chubby millionaire Hurley (Jorge Garcia), contractor Michael and son Walt (Harold Perrineau and Malcolm David Kelley), Korean couple Jin and Sun Kwon (Daniel Dae Kim and Yunjin Kim), miraculously cured paralytic John Locke (Terry O'Quinn), and surgeon Jack Shepard (Matthew Fox), who reluctantly assumes leadership of the group. With no hope for rescue in the near future, the survivors must learn to exist on an island populated by secrets, dangerous creatures, and "the Others."

THE SCENE: In a flashback to life before the crash, Jack has just performed a surgery on a female patient, Sarah (Julie Bowen), who broke her spine in a car accident. Before the surgery, when Sarah told Jack that she knew she'd never walk again, he promised her he would repair the damage to her spine so she'd be able to dance at her wedding—telling her in no uncertain terms, "I'm going to fix you." After the surgery, Jack goes for a run in a stadium, meeting another runner, Desmond (Henry Ian Cusick).

START: 0:30:14 STOP: 0:34:05 (TOTAL CLIP TIME: 3 MINUTES, 51 SECONDS)

START DIALOGUE: *(Desmond)* All right, brother? *(Note for video-editing purposes: Because of a sprained ankle, Jack curses right before Desmond begins to speak.)*

STOP DIALOGUE: *(Desmond)* Jack, I'm Desmond. *(Shakes Jack's hand)* Well, good luck, brother. See you in another life, yeah? *(Desmond runs off, leaving Jack pondering their conversation.)*

BONUS CLIP:

SCENE 2: After his run, Jack returns to the hospital to sit with Sarah and tell her the bad news that he was unable to repair the damage to her spine. He isn't prepared for what he will discover when Sarah wakes up.

START 0:38:05 STOP 0:41:32 (TOTAL CLIP TIME: 3 MINUTES, 27 SECONDS)

START DIALOGUE: *(Sarah)* Am I alive?

STOP DIALOGUE: *(Sarah)* Yes! *(She cries with joy.)*

BY THE BOOK: Psalm 119:50, Isaiah 55:9, Matthew 19:26, John 6:2, Acts 19:11-12

WHERE TO TAKE IT:

1. Even though we hear about miracles all the time, why is it so hard to believe in them?

2. Why do you think it was so hard for Jack to believe in miracles before he saw that Sarah could move her feet? Why do you think Desmond was able to be so optimistic?

3. Do you believe God can and will perform miracles in this day and age?

4. During Jesus' ministry on earth, he healed anyone who came to him. Today, why do you think God heals some and not others?

5. Describe a time you felt guilty about a promise you didn't keep. What was the outcome of that situation?

6. Jack dealt with his guilt over Sarah's surgery by running in the stadium. How do you deal with disappointment or failure?

7. Have you ever witnessed a miracle? If so, describe it. If not, what do you think a miracle looks like?

8. Is it ever a good idea to make a promise like the one Jack made to Sarah?

Visit www.skitguys.com or www.ysunderground.com for additional elements that might add impact to this clip, including "Jesus Heals a Paralytic 3.17" from Instant Skits.

(DRAMA)

SEASON 2, EPISODE 15: "MATERNITY LEAVE"

TAG: CONFESSION IS GOOD FOR THE SOUL.

THEMES: Confession, Dealing with the Past, Forgiveness, Guilt, Prayer, Redemption, Regrets, Secrets

THE SERIES/SHOW: Set on a remote island full of mysteries, *Lost* focuses on the aftermath of a terrible plane crash. Survivors of doomed Flight 815 include beautiful fugitive Kate (Evangeline Lilly), con artist Sawyer (Josh Holloway), former Iraqi militant Sayid (Naveen Andrews), druggie rock star Charlie (Dominic Monaghan), expectant mother Claire (Emilie de Ravin), chubby millionaire Hurley (Jorge Garcia), contractor Michael and son Walt (Harold Perrineau and Malcolm David Kelley), Korean couple Jin and Sun Kwon (Daniel Dae Kim and Yunjin Kim), miraculously cured paralytic John Locke (Terry O'Quinn), and surgeon Jack Shepard (Matthew Fox), who reluctantly assumes leadership of the group. With no hope for rescue in the near future, the survivors must learn to exist on an island populated by secrets, dangerous creatures, and "the Others."

THE SCENE: The group has found a strange man, Henry Gale (Michael Emerson), whom they believe is one of "the Others." They have locked him in the armory, and Sayid has beaten him, trying to force the man to talk. When Eko (Adewale Akinnuoye-Agbaje) hears that they may have captured one of the Others, he asks to talk with him. The fact that he killed two of the Others is weighing heavily on Eko, and he wants nothing more than to confess his crime and cleanse his soul of guilt.

START 0:38:04 STOP 0:41:13 (TOTAL CLIP TIME: 3 MINUTES, 9 SECONDS)

START DIALOGUE: *(Eko)* Hello. I am Mr. Eko.

STOP DIALOGUE: *(Eko)* Because I needed to tell someone. *(He cuts off part of his beard and leaves the armory.)*

BY THE BOOK: Psalm 32:5, Matthew 5:23-24, Acts 19:18, James 5:16, 1 John 1:9

WHERE TO TAKE IT:

1. Have you ever had to confess something you've done? What was that like? How did the other person respond to you?

2. Why do you think Eko went to Henry to confess his transgression? Wasn't Eko just defending himself when he killed the Others?

3. Do you hold things inside or get things out in the open? Is one personality trait better than the other?

4. If we can confess our sins to God and ask for forgiveness, why do we need to confess our sins to others as well?

5. Can you describe a time you had someone pray for you? Discuss the power of prayer and how it can bring about changed lives.

6. How do secrets tend to come out even though we try to hide them?

7. What are you holding inside that might need to be released?

8. How can confessing a sin or revealing a secret completely change the way you relate to other people?

Visit www.skitguys.com or www.ysunderground.com for additional elements that might add impact to this clip, including "The Way We Pray" video or script.

Lost

(DRAMA)

SEASON 2, EPISODE 10: "THE 23RD PSALM"

TAG: THE GOSPEL ACCORDING TO EKO.

THEMES: The 23rd Psalm, Choices, Condemnation, Fear, Regrets, Sin, Trials

THE SERIES/SHOW: Set on a remote island full of mysteries, *Lost* focuses on the aftermath of a terrible plane crash. Survivors of doomed Flight 815 include beautiful fugitive Kate (Evangeline Lilly), con artist Sawyer (Josh Holloway), former Iraqi militant Sayid (Naveen Andrews), druggie rock star Charlie (Dominic Monaghan), expectant mother Claire (Emilie de Ravin), chubby millionaire Hurley (Jorge Garcia), contractor Michael and son Walt (Harold Perrineau and Malcolm David Kelley), Korean couple Jin and Sun Kwon (Daniel Dae Kim and Yunjin Kim), miraculously cured paralytic John Locke (Terry O'Quinn), and surgeon Jack Shepard (Matthew Fox), who reluctantly assumes leadership of the group. With no hope for rescue in the near future, the survivors must learn to exist on an island populated by secrets, dangerous creatures, and "the Others."

THE SCENE: In a flashback, we discover that Eko (Adewale Akinnuoye-Agbaje) and his fellow gang members tried to smuggle drugs out of Nigeria while masquerading as priests. When Eko's brother Yemi (Adetokumboh M'Cormack) informed the Nigerian military of the gang's intentions, soldiers arrived to stop the gang's plane from leaving. During the battle, Yemi and several other gang members were shot by the soldiers. Though Eko put his wounded brother on the plane, Eko was prevented from boarding by another gang member and was left behind as the plane flew off to crash on the very island where Eko now finds himself as a survivor of Flight 815. While in the jungle, Eko and Charlie come across the gang's wrecked plane, and Eko finds the skeleton of his long-dead brother. Sobbing with grief, Eko begs God to forgive him for allowing Yemi to lose his life as a result of his choices. As Charlie watches, Eko prepares the only funeral he is able to give his brother.

START 0:37:29 STOP 0:39:20 (TOTAL CLIP TIME: 1 MINUTE, 51 SECONDS)

START DIALOGUE: *(Charlie)* So, are you a priest, or aren't you?

STOP DIALOGUE: *(Eko)* Yes. I am. *(Recites the 23rd Psalm)* The Lord is my shepherd. I shall not want. He maketh me to lie down in green pastures. He leadeth me beside the still waters. He restoreth my soul. He leadeth me in the path of righteousness for his name's sake. Yea, though I walk through the shadow of the valley of death, *(Charlie joins in)* I fear no evil, for thou art with me. Thy rod, thy staff, they comfort me. Thou preparest a table before me, in the presence of thine enemies. Thou anointest my head with oil; my cup runneth over. Surely goodness and mercy shall follow me, all the days of my life, and I will dwell in the house of the Lord forever. Amen.

BY THE BOOK: Psalm 23, John 3:36, Romans 6:11, 18, 22-23, Romans 8:1, Titus 2:11-14, Hebrews 2:17

WHERE TO TAKE IT:

1. How do our sinful choices prevent us from honoring God?

2. As you listened to the 23rd Psalm, what are some of the phrases that stick in your mind?

3. What does the phrase, "He maketh me to lie down in green pastures," mean?

4. What about the phrase, "He restoreth my soul"?

5. Do you think there are different degrees of sin? Are some sins just worse than others?

6. Romans 8:1 says, "There is now no condemnation for those who are in Christ Jesus." Do you sometimes feel condemned even though you've asked for forgiveness? If so, what can you do to conquer those feelings?

7. Have your choices or actions ever had a negative effect on a friend or family member? How did that situation make you feel?

8. Do you feel responsible for the well-being of any of your loved ones? What do you do to protect that person?

Visit www.skitguys.com or www.ysunderground.com for additional elements that might add impact to this clip, including Sin Conflicts 6.9b from Instant Skits.

My Name Is Earl

(COMEDY)

SEASON 2, EPISODE 45: "GED"

TAG: HOW DO YOU SPELL GED?

THEMES: Ambition, Choices, Education, the Future, Motivation, Personality Traits, Purpose, Realizations, Regrets

THE SERIES/SHOW: Earl Hickey (Jason Lee) hasn't done a lot he's proud of. But after a winning lottery ticket changes the slacker's life, Earl vows to right every wrong he's ever committed and apologize to everyone he's ever hurt in an effort to repay the "karmic shift" that brought him his windfall. Aided by his less-than-brilliant brother Randy (Ethan Suplee) and their friend Catalina (Nadine Velazquez), and impeded by feisty ex-wife Joy (Jaime Pressly), Earl works his way through a long list of his past sins, crossing them off after doing his best to make things right.

THE SCENE: While applying for credit, Earl is asked numerous questions about his employment, housing, and education. When his application is denied because of his lack of a high school diploma, Earl realizes how much of his life he has wasted and decides to get his GED.

START 0:00:40 STOP 0:02:02 (TOTAL CLIP TIME: 2 MINUTES, 11 SECONDS)

START DIALOGUE: *(Credit-union employee)* Next.

STOP SCENE: Scene ends.

BY THE BOOK: Job 8:9, Ecclesiastes 6:12, Romans 7:14-25, Philippians 3:13-14, James 4:13-14

WHERE TO TAKE IT:

1. Have you ever had a wake-up call about the way your life is going? What was it, and how did it happen for you?

2. Describe a time when you felt small and stupid compared to other people. How did you handle those feelings?

3. When it comes to changing our lives, why does it seem so hard to actually remake ourselves into different people?

4. Read Romans 7:14-25; even Paul found himself doing things he didn't want to do. Could you say the same about some of your choices?

5. Do you know anyone who has been talking about making a change, but hasn't done it yet? What keeps us in a rut?

6. How do you motivate yourself to change your personality traits?

7. What are some things you wish you could change about yourself? What do you think other people would change about you?

8. In Philippians 3:13-14, Paul tells us to forget the things that are behind us. Is there ever a time that you can use your past to motivate yourself to change the future, as Earl did? If so, then why does Paul suggest forgetting the past?

Visit www.skitguys.com or www.ysunderground.com for additional elements that might add impact to this clip, including the "No Purpose Guys" video.

My Name Is Earl
(COMEDY)

SEASON 2, EPISODE 46: "GET A REAL JOB"

TAG: EARL THE LEADER.

THEMES: Admiration, Competition, Defeat, Determination, Leadership, Respect

THE SERIES/SHOW: Earl Hickey (Jason Lee) hasn't done a lot he's proud of. But after a winning lottery ticket changes the slacker's life, Earl vows to right every wrong he's ever committed and apologize to everyone he's ever hurt in an effort to repay the "karmic shift" that brought him his windfall. Aided by his less-than-brilliant brother Randy (Ethan Suplee) and their friend Catalina (Nadine Velazquez), and impeded by feisty ex-wife Joy (Jaime Pressly), Earl works his way through a long list of his past sins, crossing them off after doing his best to make things right.

THE SCENE: Earl and Randy have been hired at an appliance store—Earl as a salesman and Randy in the docks. Earl earnestly tries to be successful in selling appliances, but Rick (Sean Astin), another salesman with junior-college experience, constantly sabotages him. Earl finally gets a sale that will meet his quota, but the dockworkers are unwilling to help him pull all of his stock to fill the order because of tension between them and the salesmen. Earl proceeds to do all of the work himself, earning the dockworkers' respect. When he returns to the store to tell his customer she's all ready to go, he finds out that Rick has stolen his sale. Disappointed and feeling like a failure, Earl goes to the boss' office to resign, but the good will he has built with the dockworkers saves the day.

START 0:20:33 STOP 0:23:45 (TOTAL CLIP TIME: 3 MINUTES, 12 SECONDS)

START DIALOGUE: *(Rick)* Closing time.

STOP DIALOGUE: *(Earl)* I was feeling really good.

BY THE BOOK: Leviticus 19:13, Proverbs 10:16, Romans 4:4, Romans 13:7, 1 Thessalonians 4:11-12

WHERE TO TAKE IT:

1. How do you function in the times when you feel most alone?

2. Earl hustles to make the order, gaining the admiration and the help of the dock crew. Has anyone ever stepped in for you out of respect? How did that make you feel?

3. If you were in Earl's shoes, would you have been able to show the leadership and honesty he showed in a difficult situation? Why or why not?

4. When someone stands up on your behalf and says he or she believes in you, how does that make you feel? Does it change the way you behave?

5. What does the Bible say in these verses about the kind of wages we should be earning?

6. Do you work hard for the money, the character, or the role in society you've been given?

7. What does the word *leader* mean to you? What qualities do you believe a leader possesses?

8. Is competition at work (or school, home, etc.) ever okay?

Visit www.skitguys.com or www.ysunderground.com for additional elements that might add impact to this clip, including the "Agony of Defeat" script.

My Name Is Earl

(COMEDY)

SEASON 2, EPISODE 30: "MADE A LADY THINK I WAS GOD"

TAG: THIS IS GOD, AND YOU OWE ME.

THEMES: Blasphemy, Deception, God, Power, Revenge

THE SERIES/SHOW: Earl Hickey (Jason Lee) hasn't done a lot he's proud of. But after a winning lottery ticket changes the slacker's life, Earl vows to right every wrong he's ever committed and apologize to everyone he's ever hurt in an effort to repay the "karmic shift" that brought him his windfall. Aided by his less-than-brilliant brother Randy (Ethan Suplee) and their friend Catalina (Nadine Velazquez), and impeded by feisty ex-wife Joy (Jaime Pressly), Earl works his way through a long list of his past sins, crossing them off after doing his best to make things right.

THE SCENE: Millie Banks (Roseanne Barr), the manager at Earl's old trailer park, was constantly giving Earl and Joy citations. In an effort to get Millie to stop, Earl pretends to be the voice of God—using her willingness to obey "The Voice" for his own gain. Earl relishes the power and the advantage he has over Millie as he exacts his "holy" revenge.

START 0:04:03 STOP 0:05:08 (TOTAL CLIP TIME: 1 MINUTE, 5 SECONDS)

START DIALOGUE: *(Earl)* Ten-four, Rubber Ducky.

STOP DIALOGUE: *(Earl)* And shake it all about.

BY THE BOOK: Deuteronomy 18:22, Job 37:5, Psalm 29:2-11, Psalm 103:1-5, Romans 12:19

WHERE TO TAKE IT:

1. The scene shows Earl doing funny things to Millie in God's name. What cruel things have been done in God's name?

2. What does it mean to hear God's voice?

3. Read Psalm 29:2-11. What does the Bible say about God's voice?

4. What does the Bible say in Psalm 103:1-5 about God's attributes?

5. We are in essence "walking Bibles" or testaments to God's character. Does your "voice" display God's attributes?

6. Why do so many people do foolish or terrible things, thinking they've heard God's voice?

7. How can we be certain God is speaking to us?

8. Do you believe God has called you to do something? If so, what is that "one thing"?

Visit www.skitguys.com or www.ysunderground.com for additional elements that might add impact to this clip, including the "That's Not My Jesus" script from Best of the Skit Guys Vol. 1.

My Name Is Earl
SEASON 2, EPISODE 27: "STICKS & STONES"

TAG: HEY, BEARDED LADY...I WANTED TO SAY I'M SORRY...

THEMES: Apologizing, Being Different, Dealing with the Past, Forgiveness, Hurtful Words, Memories, Understanding Others

THE SERIES/SHOW: Earl Hickey (Jason Lee) hasn't done a lot he's proud of. But after a winning lottery ticket changes the slacker's life, Earl vows to right every wrong he's ever committed and apologize to everyone he's ever hurt in an effort to repay the "karmic shift" that brought him his windfall. Aided by his less-than-brilliant brother Randy (Ethan Suplee) and their friend Catalina (Nadine Velazquez), and impeded by feisty ex-wife Joy (Jaime Pressly), Earl works his way through a long list of his past sins, crossing them off after doing his best to make things right.

THE SCENE: Earl and Randy seek out Maggie Lester (Judy Greer), a girl Earl teased mercilessly years ago, so Earl can apologize and make amends. After finding Maggie, Earl is surprised to learn that she now travels with a carnival freak show as the "Bearded Lady." As he and Randy spend time with Maggie and her friends, Earl discovers that he really likes the circus freaks and wants to take them out for ice cream. But Maggie refuses, explaining that Earl doesn't understand what it's like to be different.

START 0:10:37 STOP 0:12:31 (TOTAL CLIP TIME: 1 MINUTE, 54 SECONDS)

START DIALOGUE: *(Earl)* What's going on?

STOP SCENE: Earl walks off the diving board.

BY THE BOOK: Leviticus 20:26, Psalm 4:3, Psalm 140:1-3, Matthew 7:12, James 3:8-10

WHERE TO TAKE IT:

1. Earl tries to do the right thing, but it backfires on him. Have you ever tried to make amends, but it didn't turn out the way you wanted?

2. How do you treat people who ask for your forgiveness?

3. Is it difficult to admit mistakes? Why or why not?

4. Do you, like Earl, have memories of being made fun of or teased? How do those memories affect the person you are today?

5. In Leviticus 20:26, God calls us to be "set apart"; what does that mean?

6. How does being set apart make us "freaks" to the rest of the world?

7. What does "holiness" mean?

8. Have you ever teased anyone who was different? Have you ever apologized to that person? Is there anything you can do to understand him or her better?

Visit www.skitguys.com or www.ysunderground.com for additional elements that might add impact to this clip, including "The Breakfast Club" script.

My Name Is Earl
(COMEDY)

SEASON 2, EPISODE 27: "STICKS & STONES"

TAG: CARPE DIEM!

THEMES: Carpe Diem, Conquering Fear, Hurtful Words, Insecurity, Living Your Dreams, Risk, Second Chances

THE SERIES/SHOW: Earl Hickey (Jason Lee) hasn't done a lot he's proud of. But after a winning lottery ticket changes the slacker's life, Earl vows to right every wrong he's ever committed and apologize to everyone he's ever hurt in an effort to repay the "karmic shift" that brought him his windfall. Aided by his less-than-brilliant brother Randy (Ethan Suplee) and their friend Catalina (Nadine Velazquez), and impeded by feisty ex-wife Joy (Jaime Pressly), Earl works his way through a long list of his past sins, crossing them off after doing his best to make things right.

THE SCENE: After encouraging the carnival freaks to "live life," Earl decides to face the fear that has plagued him since his childhood—jumping off the high dive. Earl was never able to jump off the high dive as a kid because of the teasing he endured due to a physical abnormality, but meeting Maggie's friends has given him the courage he always lacked. He climbs up on the board and almost loses his nerve, but a look down reveals all his carnival friends—supporting and encouraging him. When Earl finally takes the leap, his willingness to be vulnerable inspires his friends, and they all take a leap of faith of their own.

START 0:17:33 STOP 0:19:44 (TOTAL CLIP TIME: 2 MINUTES, 11 SECONDS)

START DIALOGUE: *(Earl)* The next morning I went down to the pool.

STOP DIALOGUE: *(Earl)* All Tommy ever wanted was to be a kid.

BY THE BOOK: Joshua 1:9, Isaiah 41:10, Isaiah 54:4, 1 Thessalonians 5:11, 1 John 4:18

WHERE TO TAKE IT:

1. What is your biggest fear?

2. Ralph Waldo Emerson states, "Do the thing you fear, and the death of fear is certain." How does that apply to you? What do you think this means?

3. What does the Bible say in these verses about fear?

4. The saying, "Sticks and stones may break my bones, but words will never hurt me," is probably one of the biggest lies ever told. What words have hurt you the most? Who said those words to you?

5. Have you ever been responsible for hurting someone with words?

6. How can we stare our fears in the face and make them obsolete?

7. When is the last time you did something you were terrified to do? What happened?

8. What were the things Christ was fearful of? How can we model his behavior?

Visit www.skitguys.com or www.ysunderground.com for additional elements that might add impact to this clip, including "The Holiness of God" dramatic reading from Skits That Teach.

The Office

TAG: ARE YOU A LEADER, OR DO YOU JUST LOOK LIKE ONE?

THEMES: Abuse of Authority, Avoidance, Blaming Others, Leadership, People Pleasing, Respect, Shirking Responsibility

THE SERIES/SHOW: This "mockumentary" follows a staff of quirky office workers at the Dunder-Mifflin Paper Supply Company. Regional manager Michael Scott (Steve Carell) may think he's the world's best boss, but behind his back his staff disagrees—considering him obnoxious and unfunny. But though most of the office workers roll their eyes at Michael on a regular basis, each of them has their own set of issues and oddities that make the Dunder-Mifflin office an interesting place to work. Jim (John Krasinski) spends his time pining for perpetually engaged receptionist Pam Beesly (Jenna Fischer) and harassing his cubicle mate, Dwight Schrute (Rainn Wilson), whose title is assistant *to* the regional manager, not assistant regional manager, as he likes to believe. Between Michael's attempts at humor and Dwight's attempts to take over the entire company, the staff of Dunder-Mifflin provides a peek into the funny side of office politics.

THE SCENE: Michael's boss Jan (Melora Hardin) has informed Michael that he needs to find a less expensive health plan for his employees to save the company money. Michael tries to get out of it because he doesn't want to make everyone mad, so he passes the responsibility to Dwight, who immediately becomes crazed with power. Much to everyone's dismay, Dwight slashes benefits left and right, while Michael spends the day hiding in his office, claiming to be "busy." At the end of the day, the Dunder-Mifflin workers corner their boss to complain about both the new health plan and their bossy coworker.

START 0:08:08 STOP 0:09:33 (TOTAL CLIP TIME: 1 MINUTE, 21 SECONDS)

START SCENE: Michael comes out of the restroom.

STOP DIALOGUE: *(Angela)* Nothing, Kevin.

BY THE BOOK: Matthew 10:24, Matthew 25:23, Romans 13:1, Hebrews 13:17, 1 Peter 2:13

WHERE TO TAKE IT:

1. Leadership means taking actions that may make some people mad or upset. Does it scare you to be in that type of position? Why or why not?

2. Have you ever avoided your responsibility and passed the buck like Michael did with Dwight? How did that situation turn out?

3. Why do we avoid confrontation? Is there a way to face confrontation without anger or harsh words?

4. Why do some people have a hard time submitting to authority? Why is it harder to submit to someone you don't respect?

5. What does it mean when someone has no "backbone"? Can that be said about you?

6. Would you rather face up to a difficult situation or have someone take your place?

7. How much are you concerned about others' opinions of you? How far would you go to protect your position or reputation?

8. Would you rather be a leader or a follower? Why?

Visit www.skitguys.com or www.ysunderground.com for additional elements that might add impact to this clip, including the "Larry the Liar" script.

The Office
(COMEDY)
SEASON 1, EPISODE 6: "HOT GIRL"

TAG: SO YOU'RE SAYING THERE MIGHT BE A CHANCE...

THEMES: Attraction, Courage, Dating, Infatuation, Love, Lust, Rejection, Risk

THE SERIES/SHOW: This "mockumentary" follows a staff of quirky office workers at the Dunder-Mifflin Paper Supply Company. Regional manager Michael Scott (Steve Carell) may think he's the world's best boss, but behind his back his staff disagrees—considering him obnoxious and unfunny. But though most of the office workers roll their eyes at Michael on a regular basis, each of them has their own set of issues and oddities that make the Dunder-Mifflin office an interesting place to work. Jim (John Krasinski) spends his time pining for perpetually engaged receptionist Pam Beesly (Jenna Fischer) and harassing his cubicle mate, Dwight Schrute (Rainn Wilson), whose title is assistant *to* the regional manager, not assistant regional manager, as he likes to believe. Between Michael's attempts at humor and Dwight's attempts to take over the entire company, the staff of Dunder-Mifflin provides a peek into the funny side of office politics.

THE SCENE: A traveling purse salesperson, Katy (Amy Adams), has set up shop in the Dunder-Mifflin conference room, causing havoc among the male employees who are all attracted to her. Dwight wants to ask Katy out and goes to Michael for permission, but Michael has already weaseled his way into taking Katy home after the workday is over. Thanks to his own overactive imagination about what lies ahead, Michael refuses to give Dwight permission to ask Katy for a date.

START 0:13:30 STOP 0:14:54 (TOTAL CLIP TIME: 1 MINUTE, 10 SECONDS)

START DIALOGUE: *(Michael)* I should have never let the temp touch this.

STOP SCENE: Dwight looks away from Michael, disappointed.

BONUS CLIP:

SCENE 2: Dwight finally gets up enough nerve to go into the conference room in front of coworker Angela (Angela Kinsey) and ask Katy out. Katy rejects Dwight with no explanation, and he goes back to his chair dejected and miserable.

START 0:16:26 STOP 0:17:26 (TOTAL CLIP TIME: 1 MINUTE)

START DIALOGUE: *(Katy)* You seem to like to touch things. Try the velvet.

STOP DIALOGUE: *(Angela)* Gray, dark gray, charcoal.

BY THE BOOK: 1 Corinthians 7:2-4, 1 Corinthians 13:4-8, Ephesians 4:2, Ephesians 5:22-33, Hebrews 13:4

WHERE TO TAKE IT:

1. Why is physical attraction sometimes so strong that it controls our behavior? Why is it difficult to really "be yourself" around someone you're attracted to?

2. What do you want in a relationship? Do you have a list of things you look for? What's on that list?

3. From past relationships, what have you discovered that you *don't* want?

4. What characteristics do you look for in a boyfriend or girlfriend?

5. Have you ever risked revealing your feelings to someone else, only to be turned down? What did you learn from that experience?

6. What's your definition of the word *love*?

7. Read 1 Corinthians 13:4-8. Are those things important to you in a love relationship? Could you say that any of those words represent the way you treat others?

8. Why does the kind of rejection Dwight faced hurt so much and stay with us so long? How can you avoid rejection like that?

Visit www.skitguys.com or www.ysunderground.com for additional elements that might add impact to this clip, including the "I'm in Love with You" video on You Teach Vol. 1.

The Office
(COMEDY)

SEASON 1, EPISODE 1: "PILOT"

TAG: YOU HAVE NO DISCERNMENT IN YOUR DNA.

THEMES: Acceptance, Crossing the Line, Cruelty, Humiliation, Misunderstanding, Practical Jokes, Respect

THE SERIES/SHOW: This "mockumentary" follows a staff of quirky office workers at the Dunder-Mifflin Paper Supply Company. Regional manager Michael Scott (Steve Carell) may think he's the world's best boss, but behind his back his staff disagrees—considering him obnoxious and unfunny. But though most of the office workers roll their eyes at Michael on a regular basis, each of them has their own set of issues and oddities that make the Dunder-Mifflin office an interesting place to work. Jim (John Krasinski) spends his time pining for perpetually engaged receptionist Pam Beesly (Jenna Fischer) and harassing his cubicle mate, Dwight Schrute (Rainn Wilson), whose title is assistant *to* the regional manager, not assistant regional manager, as he likes to believe. Between Michael's attempts at humor and Dwight's attempts to take over the entire company, the staff of Dunder-Mifflin provides a peek into the funny side of office politics.

THE SCENE: Michael is in his office with new temp Ryan Howard (B.J. Novak), giving Ryan the rundown on Dunder-Mifflin office politics. When Pam enters to give Michael a message, Michael asks her to sit down and begins to talk about the impending layoffs. In another ill-advised attempt at humor, Michael decides to play a joke on Pam, trying to convince her that she is being fired, even going so far as to accuse her of stealing sticky notes. Pam is devastated, claiming she's never stolen so much as a paper clip. Michael finally confesses to his joke, but unfortunately the opportunity for humor has passed him by.

START 0:18:22 STOP 0:20:52 (TOTAL CLIP TIME: 2 MINUTES, 30 SECONDS)

START DIALOGUE: *(Michael)* Oh, hey, do you like *The Jamie Kennedy Experiment*?

STOP SCENE: End before voiceover begins.

BY THE BOOK: Isaiah 32:5, Galatians 5:22-23, Ephesians 4:32, Philippians 2:3, 1 Thessalonians 5:12

WHERE TO TAKE IT:

1. Has a practical joke like Michael's ever landed you in hot water? How did that make you feel?

2. Have you ever been a victim of a practical joke?

3. What does the word *respect* mean to you? How can you tell when someone respects you?

4. In your opinion, what person in your life is most deserving of your respect? What person is the least deserving of respect? (No naming names from the second question!)

5. Has there ever been a time when you were so desperate for approval that you put someone else down to get it? Did your plan work?

6. Do you agree with the statement that people who put others down do so to feel better about themselves? If so, does it really work that way?

7. Read Galatians 5:22-23. Which of these "fruits of the Spirit" are apparent in your life? Which do you need to ask God to grow in you?

8. What was the most embarrassing or humiliating experience of your life? How did you survive that experience?

Visit www.skitguys.com or www.ysunderground.com for additional elements that might add impact to this clip, including "The Fall" from Skits That Teach.

The Office

(COMEDY)

SEASON 1, EPISODE 1: "PILOT"

TAG: MY HEROES ARE BOB HOPE, ABRAHAM LINCOLN, BONO...AND GOD.

THEMES: Denial, Heroes, Legacy, Neediness, Perceptions, Relationships, Respect, Role Models

THE SERIES/SHOW: This "mockumentary" follows a staff of quirky office workers at the Dunder-Mifflin Paper Supply Company. Regional manager Michael Scott (Steve Carell) may think he's the world's best boss, but behind his back his staff disagrees—considering him obnoxious and unfunny. But though most of the office workers roll their eyes at Michael on a regular basis, each of them has their own set of issues and oddities that make the Dunder-Mifflin office an interesting place to work. Jim (John Krasinski) spends his time pining for perpetually engaged receptionist Pam Beesly (Jenna Fischer) and harassing his cubicle mate, Dwight Schrute (Rainn Wilson), whose title is assistant *to* the regional manager, not assistant regional manager, as he likes to believe. Between Michael's attempts at humor and Dwight's attempts to take over the entire company, the staff of Dunder-Mifflin provides a peek into the funny side of office politics.

THE SCENE: Michael, always conscious of the cameras watching him, unwittingly demonstrates the difference between how he *thinks* his employees view him and how they *really* see their boss as Pam starts the scene by giving Michael several messages that he hasn't returned. After one attempted joke falls flat, Michael tries to joke about the downsizing situation in the Dunder-Mifflin office, which results in a snarky remark from Pam. Michael turns on a dime—dropping his joking demeanor to rebuke Pam for her comment. During a later interview with the cameras, Michael displays his complete ignorance by discussing his relationship with his employees and the legacy he thinks he is leaving behind.

START 0:09:52 STOP 0:11:46 (TOTAL CLIP TIME: 2 MINUTES, 54 SECONDS)

START DIALOGUE: *(Pam)* You still have these messages from yesterday.

STOP DIALOGUE: *(Michael)* It's really beyond words; it's really "incalculable."

BY THE BOOK: Matthew 10:24, Luke 12:48, Romans 12:3, Romans 13:7, Colossians 3:23

WHERE TO TAKE IT:

1. Michael tries to make Pam laugh and then negates her words. What makes a person flip emotions so quickly?

2. Do you know someone who tries too hard to be liked? How do you feel about that person?

3. How do you recognize a person who's truly "needy"? What about someone who's "moody"? Have those words ever been used to describe you?

4. What's the best way to deal with a person who makes it difficult to be his or her friend?

5. What's your definition of a healthy relationship? What does it take to create and maintain a healthy relationship?

6. What makes relationships unhealthy? What can be done to heal a relationship that's broken?

7. Michael truly lives in denial about the way others view him. Is there an inconvenient truth in your life that you're avoiding?

8. Who are your heroes? Why are those people important to you and worthy of your admiration?

Visit www.skitguys.com or www.ysunderground.com for additional elements that might add impact to this clip, including the "God's Chisel" video from You Teach Vol. 1.

The Office
(COMEDY)

SEASON 1, EPISODE 4: "THE ALLIANCE"

TAG: CELEBRATION OR HUMILIATION?

THEMES: Blaming Others, Ego, Giving, Humility, Self-Esteem, Significance, Unity, Worth

THE SERIES/SHOW: This "mockumentary" follows a staff of quirky office workers at the Dunder-Mifflin Paper Supply Company. Regional manager Michael Scott (Steve Carell) may think he's the world's best boss, but behind his back his staff disagrees—considering him obnoxious and unfunny. But though most of the office workers roll their eyes at Michael on a regular basis, each of them has their own set of issues and oddities that make the Dunder-Mifflin office an interesting place to work. Jim (John Krasinski) spends his time pining for perpetually engaged receptionist Pam Beesly (Jenna Fischer) and harassing his cubicle mate, Dwight Schrute (Rainn Wilson), whose title is assistant *to* the regional manager, not assistant regional manager, as he likes to believe. Between Michael's attempts at humor and Dwight's attempts to take over the entire company, the staff of Dunder-Mifflin provides a peek into the funny side of office politics.

THE SCENE: When the Dunder-Mifflin staff throws a birthday party for Meredith (Kate Flannery), Michael is determined that his card will be the best and funniest, switching the focus of the party from Meredith to himself. Michael also bites off more than he can chew when Oscar (Oscar Nuñez) comes around seeking pledges to support his nephew's charity walk for Cerebral Palsy. Looking at the pledge sheet, Michael notices what he thinks are small pledges from other employees and commits to a generous sum in order to "beat" everyone else. He is dismayed to learn, however, that what he thought were low pledges were actually commitments for *each mile* of the charity walk, making his pledge even larger than he intended it to be.

START 0:17:04 STOP 0:20:21 (TOTAL CLIP TIME: 3 MINUTES, 17 SECONDS)

START DIALOGUE: *(Pam)* Happy birthday, Meredith!

STOP DIALOGUE: *(Michael)* Don't cash that 'til Friday, okay?

BY THE BOOK: Psalm 119:36, Proverbs 11:2, Philippians 2:3, 1 Thessalonians 4:11, James 3:13-15

WHERE TO TAKE IT:

1. Have you ever been a part of a situation in which someone tried to make everything all about him or herself? How did you feel about that person?

2. Why do some people turn every conversation around to talk about themselves? What does this behavior say about a person's character or self-esteem?

3. What's the difference between *hearing* someone and *listening* to someone? What kind of listener are you?

4. How willing are you to accept responsibility when things go wrong? How do you feel about people who place blame on you when something is their fault?

5. Have you ever done something you couldn't afford to do just to impress everyone? How did that turn out?

6. What does the Bible say in Proverbs 11:2 about pride and humility?

7. What's your definition of the word *discretion*? What about *tact*? *Wisdom*?

8. What would you do if you had to deal with someone like Michael Scott in this scene?

Visit www.skitguys.com or www.ysunderground.com for additional elements that might add impact to this clip, including the "Dirty Rose" script from Skits That Teach.

SATURDAY NIGHT LIVE

(COMEDY)

BEST OF PARODIES: "BABY TOUPEES"

TAG: NICE TOUPEE!

THEMES: Acceptance, Appearance, Body Image, Confidence, Judging Others, Self-Esteem

THE SERIES/SHOW: Since the creation of *Saturday Night Live* in 1975, one of the signatures of the sketch comedy show has been its commercial parodies. From subtle to outrageous, silly to realistic, *SNL* has made it a point to poke fun at commercials, covering subjects from breakfast foods to adult diapers and everything in between. This prime-time TV special hosted by Will Ferrell contains more than 80 minutes of short videos starring several favorite cast members.

THE SCENE: Thanks to the scientists at Nelson Pediatrics, insecure babies will never again have to suffer from "male infantile baldness." This commercial demonstrates the self-esteem boost every baby is looking for—thanks to the development of the "Baby Toupee."

START 0:21:11 STOP 0:22:40 (TOTAL CLIP TIME: 1 MINUTE, 29 SECONDS)

START DIALOGUE: The first months of a child's life are…

STOP DIALOGUE: You gave him life; now give him confidence.

BY THE BOOK: 1 Samuel 16:7, Proverbs 31:30, Matthew 23:27, James 2:2-4, 1 Peter 3:3-4

WHERE TO TAKE IT:

1. Do you believe balding men should wear toupees? Do you believe women should wear makeup? Is there a difference? If so, what is it?

2. Do you have more confidence in yourself when you feel that you look good? Explain.

3. 1 Samuel 16:7 says that God looks at the heart, not at people's physical appearances. Would you say you judge people more on their outward appearances or on their actions and words?

4. Name a time when you decided not to do something because you felt like you didn't look good enough.

5. Describe a time you judged someone on that person's appearance and made a misjudgment.

6. Jesus says in Matthew 23:27 that the Pharisees spent more time working on their outsides than they did on their insides. Which do you spend more time on? Why?

7. What are some ways you can help yourself and others feel better about themselves?

8. Why do we place so much emphasis on our looks?

Visit www.skitguys.com or www.ysunderground.com for additional elements that might add impact to this script, including "The Meaning of Love" dramatic reading from Skits That Teach.

SATURDAY NIGHT LIVE
(COMEDY)
BEST OF PARODIES: "CHEAPKIDS.NET"

TAG: CHILDREN SHOULD *NOT* BE A FINANCIAL BURDEN.

THEMES: Greed, Lifestyle, Money, Parenting, Selfishness

THE SERIES/SHOW: Since the creation of *Saturday Night Live* in 1975, one of the signatures of the sketch comedy show has been its commercial parodies. From subtle to outrageous, silly to realistic, *SNL* has made it a point to poke fun at commercials, covering subjects from breakfast foods to adult diapers and everything in between. This prime-time TV special hosted by Will Ferrell contains more than 80 minutes of short videos starring several favorite cast members.

THE SCENE: Nothing is more important to the wealthy couple played by Seth Meyers and Amy Poehler than maintaining their expensive lifestyle—not even their children. Thank goodness Cheapkids.net spokesperson Gary B. Anthony (Chris Parnell) is on the scene, explaining that spending more than five percent of your disposable income on kids is unnecessary. According to Anthony, money-conscious parents can find great deals at Cheapkids.net, including "semi-flame-retardant" pajamas, factory-second car seats, used pacifiers, and much more.

START 1:14:38 STOP 1:16:08 (TOTAL CLIP TIME: 1 MINUTE, 30 SECONDS)

START DIALOGUE: We're pretty well-off financially.

STOP DIALOGUE: When it comes to your children, why pay more?

BY THE BOOK: Proverbs 15:16, Proverbs 23:4-5, Luke 12:15-21, Colossians 2:8, 2 Timothy 3:1-2

WHERE TO TAKE IT:

1. Would you consider yourself "cheap"? Explain.

2. What's the worst thing you've ever done to save money?

3. If you could pick something to spend less money on, what would it be?

4. If you could save $5,000 by not putting seat belts in the passenger seats of your car, would you? Why or why not?

5. Define the word *greed*.

6. Would you consider yourself a greedy person? Explain.

7. Greed is more about what you want than what you have. Is there anything you want so badly right now that you think about it all the time?

8. Luke 12:15-21 explains that our lives aren't about our "stuff." If that's true, why do we spend so much time trying to get more and more stuff? What can we do to change that in ourselves?

Visit www.skitguys.com or www.ysunderground.com for additional elements that might add impact to this clip, including the "Meet the Stewards" script.

SATURDAY NIGHT LIVE
(COMEDY)
BEST OF PARODIES: "FEAR FACTOR JUNIOR"

TAG: I THINK YOUR KID NEEDS COUNSELING!

THEMES: Abuse, Expectations, Fear, Reality TV

THE SERIES/SHOW: Since the creation of *Saturday Night Live* in 1975, one of the signatures of the sketch comedy show has been its commercial parodies. From subtle to outrageous, silly to realistic, *SNL* has made it a point to poke fun at commercials, covering subjects from breakfast foods to adult diapers and everything in between. This prime-time TV special hosted by Will Ferrell contains more than 80 minutes of short videos starring several favorite cast members.

THE SCENE: A parody of the *Fear Factor* reality show, *Fear Factor Junior* show-cases first- and second-grade children attempting terrifying and disgusting feats in an effort to win money. Host Joe Rogan (Fred Armisen) explains each exploit to the children, along with the dreadful consequences that will occur if they fail.

START 0:30:52 STOP 0:32:22 (TOTAL CLIP TIME: 1 MINUTE, 30 SECONDS)

START DIALOGUE: This month, *Fear Factor* takes it to the next level!

STOP DIALOGUE: Mondays at 8, followed by *Fear Factor Alcoholics*!

BY THE BOOK: Job 18:11, Psalm 111:10, Proverbs 28:1, Proverbs 29:25, John 14:27

WHERE TO TAKE IT:

1. Name the top three things you're afraid of. Why do you have these fears?

2. President Franklin D. Roosevelt said, "The only thing we have to fear is fear itself." What does that mean, and do you agree or disagree with his statement?

3. Can fear be a healthy emotion? Why or why not?

4. What can you do to overcome some of your fears?

5. Name a time you tried to face one of your fears. What was the result of that situation?

6. This parody shows children being forced to overcome "grown-up" fears. How does this parallel real life today?

7. What's a fear many people have that you think is unnecessary? Is there anything you fear that most people don't have a problem with?

8. Psalm 111:10 says the fear of the Lord is the beginning of wisdom. What does this mean to you?

Visit www.skitguys.com or www.ysunderground.com for additional elements that might add impact to this clip, including Faith Conflicts 6.8d from Instant Skits.

SATURDAY NIGHT LIVE
(COMEDY)
BEST OF PARODIES: "HAPPY FUN BALL"

TAG: ARE YOU SURE THAT THING IS SAFE?

THEMES: Choices, Consequences, Danger, Drugs and Alcohol, Perceptions, Sin, Temptation

THE SERIES/SHOW: Since the creation of *Saturday Night Live* in 1975, one of the signatures of the sketch comedy show has been its commercial parodies. From subtle to outrageous, silly to realistic, *SNL* has made it a point to poke fun at commercials, covering subjects from breakfast foods to adult diapers and everything in between. This prime-time TV special hosted by Will Ferrell contains more than 80 minutes of short videos starring several favorite cast members.

THE SCENE: As this commercial opens, three children (Mike Myers, Jan Hooks, and Dana Carvey) are playing with Happy Fun Ball, the "toy sensation that is sweeping the nation." Spokesperson Phil Hartman tells potential buyers that you can get a Happy Fun Ball today for only $14.95, but a disclaimer that follows explains that the Happy Fun Ball is made of an unknown substance that apparently fell to earth from outer space and is not safe at all.

START 0:55:27 STOP 0:57:00 (TOTAL CLIP TIME: 1 MINUTE, 33 SECONDS)

START DIALOGUE: It's happy. It's fun. It's Happy Fun Ball!

STOP DIALOGUE: Happy Fun Ball—accept no substitutes.

BY THE BOOK: Proverbs 5:22, Proverbs 23:29-35, Romans 6:23, Galatians 6:7, Hebrews 11:25

WHERE TO TAKE IT:

1. Name something that looks harmless, but can be deadly.

2. Have you ever played with something that was fun, but it could have really harmed you?

3. Name some ways that Satan works to make harmful things appear harmless.

4. Anyone who would actually buy a Happy Fun Ball would be considered crazy. However, time and time again people choose things that are fun for a little while and yet hurt them in the end. Discuss what some of those things are and why people continue to make those kinds of choices.

5. How does Proverbs 23:29-35 relate to the Happy Fun Ball?

6. Just as the Happy Fun Ball disguises its deadly components, how do people try to disguise their sins?

7. If someone were to throw a Happy Fun Ball at you, what would you do? How does this compare to how we should respond to the temptation of sin?

8. Do you believe sin is fun? Why or why not? How does that relate to Hebrews 11:25?

Visit www.skitguys.com or www.ysunderground.com for additional elements that might add impact to this clip, including the "Fast Food" script.

SATURDAY NIGHT LIVE

TAG: I THINK I'M GONNA HAVE TO SLEEP THIS ONE OFF!

THEMES: Avoidance, Drugs and Alcohol, Healing, Quick Fix, Sickness

THE SERIES/SHOW: Since the creation of *Saturday Night Live* in 1975, one of the signatures of the sketch comedy show has been its commercial parodies. From subtle to outrageous, silly to realistic, *SNL* has made it a point to poke fun at commercials, covering subjects from breakfast foods to adult diapers and everything in between. This prime-time TV special hosted by Will Ferrell contains more than 80 minutes of short videos starring several favorite cast members.

THE SCENE: In this parody, a man with a cold (Chris Farley) talks to his wife (Julia Sweeney) about how difficult this cold and flu season is going to be. Product spokesperson Phil Hartman steps in to explain that all the man needs is HiberNol—a cold medicine that puts you to sleep for the entire cold and flu season. Excited about avoiding an entire season's worth of sickness, the man takes the HiberNol and sleeps for months.

START 0:13:10 STOP 0:14:41 (TOTAL CLIP TIME: 1 MINUTE, 31 SECONDS)

START DIALOGUE: Are you sick again?

STOP DIALOGUE: From the makers of Comadose.

BY THE BOOK: Matthew 9:12, 1 Corinthians 6:12, Galatians 5:1, Galatians 5:13, Ephesians 5:18

WHERE TO TAKE IT:

1. Do you know anyone who abuses over-the-counter drugs?

2. Have you ever been tempted to use illegal drugs or abuse prescription drugs? Explain.

3. Do you believe our society has become "addicted" to medicine? Why or why not?

4. What are some reasons people use drugs (other than for medicinal purposes)?

5. If you could create a drug to overcome something in your life quickly, what would it be?

6. What does 1 Corinthians 6:12 have to do with legal or illegal drug use?

7. In this commercial parody, Chris Farley's character wants to avoid his cold symptoms. If you could go to sleep and avoid something, what would you avoid?

8. What would be a better way to deal with your situation?

Visit www.skitguys.com or www.ysunderground.com for additional elements that might add impact to this clip, including the "Laziness" video from You Teach Vol. 1.

SATURDAY NIGHT LIVE
(COMEDY)
BEST OF PARODIES: "ME-HARMONY"

TAG: IF YOU WERE MORE LIKE ME, YOU'D BE PERFECT!

THEMES: Compatibility, Dating, Relationships, Self-Centeredness

THE SERIES/SHOW: Since the creation of *Saturday Night Live* in 1975, one of the signatures of the sketch comedy show has been its commercial parodies. From subtle to outrageous, silly to realistic, *SNL* has made it a point to poke fun at commercials, covering subjects from breakfast foods to adult diapers and everything in between. This prime-time TV special hosted by Will Ferrell contains more than 80 minutes of short videos starring several favorite cast members.

THE SCENE: Finding that special someone can be so difficult, so thank goodness for online dating services! "Me-Harmony" founder Dr. Terry McQuarren (Will Forte) pledges to ask questions about your favorite person—you—in an effort to find that perfect match for each client. Successful Me-Harmony clients (Horatio Sanz, Maya Rudolph, Kenan Thompson, Rob Riggle, and Seth Meyers) share the stories of how they found the love of their lives—themselves.

START 0:07:41 STOP 0:08:50 (TOTAL CLIP TIME: 1 MINUTE, 9 SECONDS)

START DIALOGUE: I tried online dating, but never found anyone…

STOP DIALOGUE: Thank you, Me-Harmony!

BY THE BOOK: Haggai 1:9, Galatians 6:3, Philippians 2:4, Philippians 2:21, 2 Timothy 3:2-4

WHERE TO TAKE IT:

1. What do you think about online dating?

2. Do you believe that God has someone special for everyone? Why or why not?

3. What qualities do you look for in a boyfriend or girlfriend?

4. Would you be happy dating someone who was just like you? Why or why not?

5. Would you ever consider using an online dating service?

6. Philippians tells us to consider other people's interests. How do you do that in your relationships?

7. Have you ever known a couple who were just "alike"? Describe them.

8. Do you believe that opposites attract or that similar people attract?

Visit www.skitguys.com or www.ysunderground.com for additional elements that might add impact to this clip, including the "Modern Romance" script.

SATURDAY NIGHT LIVE
(COMEDY)
BEST OF PARODIES: "TACO TOWN"

TAG: WOULD YOU LIKE TO SUPER-GIANT-BIGGIE-SIZE THAT?

THEMES: Eating, Food, Gluttony, Taking Care of Your Body

THE SERIES/SHOW: Since the creation of *Saturday Night Live* in 1975, one of the signatures of the sketch comedy show has been its commercial parodies. From subtle to outrageous, silly to realistic, *SNL* has made it a point to poke fun at commercials, covering subjects from breakfast foods to adult diapers and everything in between. This prime-time TV special hosted by Will Ferrell contains more than 80 minutes of short videos starring several favorite cast members.

THE SCENE: Exemplifying the fast-food excesses of today's world, the "Taco Town" commercial begins with three guys (Andy Samburg, Bill Hader, and Jason Sudeikis) sitting at a table at the fictitious fast-food restaurant discussing how much they love tacos. To their delight, the latest, greatest invention of Taco Town proves to be the most complicated, ridiculously unnecessary food creation ever made.

START 0:06:14 STOP 0:07:40 (TOTAL CLIP TIME: 1 MINUTE, 26 SECONDS)

START DIALOGUE: You know what I love about tacos?

STOP DIALOGUE: Only at Taco Town...Taco Town!

BY THE BOOK: Proverbs 23:2, Proverbs 23:20, Luke 12:23, 1 Corinthians 6:20, Philippians 3:19

WHERE TO TAKE IT:

1. When you hear the word *gluttony*, what comes to mind?

2. Do you know anyone you would consider a glutton?

3. Would you consider yourself a glutton? Why or why not?

4. We all eat when we're hungry. What are some other reasons you eat?

5. Proverbs 23:2 gives a very serious statement about gluttony. How serious do you believe most Christians are about this topic?

6. Why has gluttony become an acceptable sin to most Christians?

7. 1 Corinthians 6:20 calls us to honor God with our bodies. How can you honor God in the way you eat?

8. What are some ways you can help yourself overcome gluttony?

Visit www.skitguys.com or www.ysunderground.com for additional elements that might add impact to this clip, including the "Stevie and Danny: Experiment 101 Excessiveness" video.

SEINFELD

SEASON 8, EPISODE 137: "THE BIZARRO JERRY"

TAG: FRIENDS ARE FRIENDS FOREVER?

THEMES: Friendship, Giving to the Poor, Living Differently, Peer Influence, Rejection

THE SERIES/SHOW: Centered around friends Jerry, Elaine Benes (Julia Louis-Dreyfus), George Costanza (Jason Alexander), and Cosmo Kramer (Michael Richards), *Seinfeld* bounced from mundane subject to mundane subject within each episode, putting the main characters in a series of crazy, frustrating, and difficult situations.

THE SCENE: Elaine has met new "bizarro friends" (Tim DeKay, Pat Kilbane, and Kyle T. Hefner) who are the complete opposites of Jerry, George, and Kramer. One night on the street, Elaine is approached by both groups of friends. As Jerry, George, and Kramer start complaining, and the bizarro friends selflessly give money to a homeless man, Elaine makes a choice and leaves with her new bizarro friends.

START 0:17:40 STOP 0:18:48 (TOTAL CLIP TIME: 1 MINUTE, 8 SECONDS)

START DIALOGUE: *(Elaine)* Jerry, George, Kramer…
STOP SCENE: Scene ends.

BY THE BOOK: Psalm 88:18, Proverbs 17:9, Proverbs 17:17, Proverbs 27:10, Luke 6:30-35

WHERE TO TAKE IT:

1. Do you have a small group of friends you hang out with most of the time? Describe them.

2. Have you ever left one group of friends to hang out with another group? How did that work out?

3. Discuss a time when you were with one group of friends, and some of your other friends showed up.

4. Do you have "church friends" and "school friends"? If so, have you ever had the two sets come together?

5. According to Luke 6:30-35, what responsibilities do you and your friends have toward the less fortunate?

6. Would you say your primary group of friends encourages or discourages your relationship with God? Explain.

7. Have friends ever rejected you because you befriended someone they didn't approve of?

8. In your opinion, what's the most important characteristic in a friend?

Visit www.skitguys.com or www.ysunderground.com for additional elements that might add impact to this clip, including the "To Be or Not to Be" script.

SEINFELD

SEASON 8, EPISODE 144: "THE ANDREA DORIA"

TAG: DEPRESSED-DELIVERY-MAN DILEMMA.

THEMES: Choices, Confrontation, Depression, Disappointment, Duty, Responsibility

THE SERIES/SHOW: Centered around friends Jerry, Elaine Benes (Julia Louis-Dreyfus), George Costanza (Jason Alexander), and Cosmo Kramer (Michael Richards), *Seinfeld* bounced from mundane subject to mundane subject within each episode, putting the main characters in a series of crazy, frustrating, and difficult situations.

THE SCENE: Jerry's nemesis Newman (Wayne Knight), who also lives in Jerry's building and works for the United States Postal Service, is stashing full mailbags in Jerry's storage unit. Jerry confronts Newman, telling him to remove the mail because stashing it in Jerry's unit is illegal. Newman tells Jerry that since he was passed over for a transfer to Hawaii, he's too depressed to deliver the mail anymore.

START 0:05:57 STOP 0:06:46 (TOTAL CLIP TIME: 49 SECONDS)

START DIALOGUE: *(Jerry)* Newman?

STOP DIALOGUE: *(Jerry)* Well, a law's a law.

BY THE BOOK: Lamentations 3:18, Psalm 42:5, 2 Corinthians 4:8-9, Galatians 6:1, Titus 3:10

WHERE TO TAKE IT:

1. Can you share a time when you discovered that a friend was doing something wrong? How did you feel? What did you do about it?

2. According to Galatians 6:1, what should we do when we have a friend who's caught up in sin? What are some effective ways to handle a situation like that?

3. Newman made a poor choice because he was depressed. Can you name a time you made a poor choice because you were depressed? How did that situation turn out?

4. How do you generally respond when things don't go the way you want them to?

5. If you knew someone who struggled with depression, what would you counsel that person to do about it?

6. Was Newman justified in choosing not to deliver mail because of his depression? Why or why not?

7. What could be some more effective ways for him to deal with his situation?

8. Do you believe Jerry dealt with Newman effectively? What would you have done differently?

Visit www.skitguys.com or www.ysunderground.com for additional elements that might add impact to this clip, including "Piece of a Peace" from Skits That Teach, *written in the vein of* Seinfeld.

SEINFELD

(COMEDY)

SEASON 8, EPISODE 140: "THE FATIGUES"

TAG: MALICIOUS-MEAT-MISHAP MEMORY.

THEMES: Dealing with the Past, Fear, Helping, Mistakes, Serving

THE SERIES/SHOW: Centered around friends Jerry, Elaine Benes (Julia Louis-Dreyfus), George Costanza (Jason Alexander), and Cosmo Kramer (Michael Richards), *Seinfeld* bounced from mundane subject to mundane subject within each episode, putting the main characters in a series of crazy, frustrating, and difficult situations.

THE SCENE: Kramer needs George's dad Frank Costanza (Jerry Stiller) to help him cook food for a large party he's throwing. After Kramer begs him to help, Frank finally admits that he was a cook during the Korean War, but a terrible mishap occurred during his tour of duty that made Frank vow never to cook again.

START 0:11:36 STOP 0:13:58 (TOTAL CLIP TIME: 2 MINUTES, 22 SECONDS)

START DIALOGUE: *(Kramer)* Come on, Frank, I need you.

STOP SCENE: Scene ends.

BY THE BOOK: 2 Corinthians 5:17, Philippians 3:7-14, Hebrews 8:13, Hebrews 12:1-2

WHERE TO TAKE IT:

1. Name a time when a memory kept you from doing something.

2. Do you have fears because of something that happened in your past?

3. Can you recall your past and see times that you chose not to serve or help others?

4. Can you name a mistake you made that hurt someone else? How does that affect you today?

5. As a group, discuss some of your mistakes and how you can help each other overcome them.

6. Generally speaking, are you anxious to help others or apprehensive about helping others? Explain your answer.

7. In Philippians 3:13, Paul says that he forgets what is behind and strains toward what is ahead. What are some good ways to do that? How can you keep your past from holding you back?

8. How do you handle it when you ask a friend for help and you're turned down?

Visit www.skitguys.com or www.ysunderground.com for additional elements that might add impact to this clip, including "Piece of a Peace" from Skits That Teach, *written in the vein of Seinfeld.*

SEINFELD

(COMEDY)

SEASON 8, EPISODE 135: "THE FOUNDATION"

TAG: I THINK I CAN'T, I THINK I CAN'T, I THINK I CAN'T...

THEMES: Confidence, Doubt, Encouragement, Responsibility, Support

THE SERIES/SHOW: Centered around friends Jerry, Elaine Benes (Julia Louis-Dreyfus), George Costanza (Jason Alexander), and Cosmo Kramer (Michael Richards), *Seinfeld* bounced from mundane subject to mundane subject within each episode, putting the main characters in a series of crazy, frustrating, and difficult situations.

THE SCENE: Elaine's boss J. Peterman (John O'Hurley) has left the country and wants Elaine to take over the catalog his company produces. Elaine has serious doubts about her ability to be in charge, but Kramer comes in and offers encouragement. Thanks to Kramer, Elaine begins to believe that she really can do it.

START 0:07:46 STOP 0:09:44 (TOTAL CLIP TIME: 1 MINUTE, 58 SECONDS)

START DIALOGUE: *(Jerry)* Where?

STOP DIALOGUE: *(Jerry)* No, she's not.

BY THE BOOK: Proverbs 17:17, Philippians 4:13, 1 Thessalonians 4:18, Hebrews 10:25, Jude 22

WHERE TO TAKE IT:

1. Can you name a time when you were asked to do something that you didn't think you could do? How did it turn out?

2. When you feel overwhelmed by something, where do you turn?

3. Would you say that you believe in yourself or doubt your abilities?

4. What are your thoughts on Philippians 4:13? Do you believe that verse is true for you?

5. Can you name a time when you encouraged someone to believe in him or herself?

6. Hebrews 10:25 calls us to "encourage one another" as we await the return of Christ. What does that mean to you?

7. What's one thing you'd like to do but lack the confidence to try?

8. Take time in your small group to encourage one another, having each member list one good quality about each person in the group.

Visit www.skitguys.com or www.ysunderground.com for additional elements that might add impact to this clip, including "The Roller Coaster of Life" script.

SEINFELD
(COMEDY)
SEASON 8, EPISODE 136: "THE SOUL MATE"

TAG: I GUESS I SHOULD HAVE THOUGHT THAT THROUGH A LITTLE MORE.

THEMES: Choices, Decision Making, Impulsive Actions, Mistakes, Plans, Regrets

THE SERIES/SHOW: Centered around friends Jerry, Elaine Benes (Julia Louis-Dreyfus), George Costanza (Jason Alexander), and Cosmo Kramer (Michael Richards), *Seinfeld* bounced from mundane subject to mundane subject within each episode, putting the main characters in a series of crazy, frustrating, and difficult situations.

THE SCENE: Elaine has met a new man, Kevin (Tim DeKay), who overheard her telling George and Jerry that she might not want to have children. After the two begin dating, Elaine is dismayed to discover that Kevin has had a vasectomy. When Elaine questions Kevin about his decision, the two discuss other spontaneous choices they've made that they each ended up regretting.

START 0:16:42 STOP 0:17:40 (TOTAL CLIP TIME: 58 SECONDS)

START DIALOGUE: *(Kevin)* I thought you'd be a little more enthusiastic.

STOP DIALOGUE: *(Elaine)* Yeah!

BY THE BOOK: Genesis 6:6-7, Genesis 25:29-39, Genesis 27:32-24, Proverbs 20:25, Matthew 6:33

WHERE TO TAKE IT:

1. Would you consider yourself an impulsive person? Why or why not?

2. It's been said that the first impulse is the best choice of action. Do you agree or disagree? Why or why not?

3. What's one decision you've made that you regret?

4. What are some ways to avoid making poor decisions?

5. Read Matthew 6:33. How could that verse play a role in your decision-making process?

6. What would "seeking the kingdom of God first" look like in your life?

7. Do you find that you learn from your mistakes easily, or do you tend to fall often?

8. How does God's grace come into play with your decision making?

Visit www.skitguys.com or www.ysunderground.com for additional elements that might add impact to this clip, including the "Acting 101" script.

THE SIMPSONS

TAG: MEN ARE FROM URANUS, AND WOMEN ARE FROM PLUTO.

THEMES: Communication, Family, Marriage, Self-Control

THE SERIES/SHOW: The longest-running animated sitcom on prime-time television, *The Simpsons* is an irreverent view of an American family, led by lovable idiot Homer (voice of Dan Castellaneta) and practical housewife Marge (voice of Julie Kavner), who does her best to maintain order over town troublemaker Bart (voice of Nancy Cartwright), intelligent activist Lisa (voice of Yeardley Smith), and perennial baby Maggie, as well as a host of quirky friends, neighbors, teachers, animals, police officers, bartenders...and one killer clown. Life in Springfield, especially in the Simpson household, is a series of crazy adventures, ill-advised schemes, and the occasional heart-warming moment.

THE SCENE: After spending hours watching a self-help video course, Marge and Homer try to communicate in a healthy way.

START 0:09:18 STOP 0:10:05 (TOTAL CLIP TIME: 47 SECONDS)

START DIALOGUE: *(Marge)* That video really opened my eyes.

STOP SCENE: Bart and Lisa look at each other.

BY THE BOOK: Psalm 19:14, Psalm 55:21, Proverbs 15:21, Proverbs 25:15, James 1:19

WHERE TO TAKE IT:

1. Do you believe you're effective in communicating with others? Why or why not?

2. How well do your family members communicate with each other?

3. What are the biggest obstacles to good communication between your family members?

4. If you were looking to improve something about yourself, what would it be?

5. Would you say that most of the words from your mouth are pleasing to God? Why or why not?

6. What do you think Proverbs 25:15 means?

7. How could your relationships be more effective if you applied James 1:19 to your life every day?

8. Who is the most effective communicator you know and why?

Visit www.skitguys.com or www.ysunderground.com for additional elements that might add impact to this clip, including "DTR: Define the Relationship" from Skits That Teach.

THE SIMPSONS

(COMEDY)

SEASON 5, EPISODE 88: "BART'S INNER CHILD"

TAG: A FIVE-MINUTE REST PERIOD, IF YOU WILL.

THEMES: Anger, Attitude, Nagging, Negativity, Receiving Correction, Stress

THE SERIES/SHOW: The longest-running animated sitcom on prime-time television, *The Simpsons* is an irreverent view of an American family, led by lovable idiot Homer (voice of Dan Castellaneta) and practical housewife Marge (voice of Julie Kavner), who does her best to maintain order over town troublemaker Bart (voice of Nancy Cartwright), intelligent activist Lisa (voice of Yeardley Smith), and perennial baby Maggie, as well as a host of quirky friends, neighbors, teachers, animals, police officers, bartenders...and one killer clown. Life in Springfield, especially in the Simpson household, is a series of crazy adventures, ill-advised schemes, and the occasional heart-warming moment.

THE SCENE: When Homer accuses Marge of being a nag, she denies his claim and asks the kids what they think. After evidence of her nagging habit is demonstrated through a series of "flashback" scenes, Marge becomes very upset and leaves the house. She speeds over to her sisters', where they decide she is close to a nervous breakdown.

START 0:06:15 STOP 0:07:00 (TOTAL CLIP TIME: 45 SECONDS)

START DIALOGUE: *(Marge)* Kids, tell me the truth.

STOP DIALOGUE: *(Selma)* You're headed for a nervous breakdown.

BY THE BOOK: 1 Kings 11:11, Job 7:11, Proverbs 21:9, Ephesians 4:22-23, 1 Peter 4:1

WHERE TO TAKE IT:

1. Would you say you generally have a positive or negative attitude? What would your family say about you?

2. How do you deal with people who aren't doing the things you've asked them to do?

3. According to Ephesians 4:22-23, Christians are to have a "new attitude." How do you believe that is different from the "old" attitude?

4. How can we have the same attitude as Christ?

5. Do you feel like either of your parents nags at you too much? If so, why?

6. How could your parents communicate with you better? Have you ever expressed that idea to them?

7. Who or what do you turn to when you're stressed out?

8. If you could change one thing about yourself, what would it be?

TAG: IF IT FEELS GOOD, THEN...YOU KNOW THE REST...

THEMES: Blaming Others, Doing What You "Feel," Duty, Responsibility, Selfishness

THE SERIES/SHOW: The longest-running animated sitcom on prime-time television, *The Simpsons* is an irreverent view of an American family, led by lovable idiot Homer (voice of Dan Castellaneta) and practical housewife Marge (voice of Julie Kavner), who does her best to maintain order over town troublemaker Bart (voice of Nancy Cartwright), intelligent activist Lisa (voice of Yeardley Smith), and perennial baby Maggie, as well as a host of quirky friends, neighbors, teachers, animals, police officers, bartenders...and one killer clown. Life in Springfield, especially in the Simpson household, is a series of crazy adventures, ill-advised schemes, and the occasional heart-warming moment.

THE SCENE: The residents of Springfield have decided to follow Bart's example of doing what you "feel." To celebrate, Springfield holds a "Do What You Feel" Day. Chaos ensues when people fail to do their jobs in preparation for the festivities. The townspeople start blaming each other for the problems, but no one takes responsibility.

START 0:18:58 STOP 0:19:36 (TOTAL CLIP TIME: 38 SECONDS)

START SCENE: James Brown sings while the bandstand collapses.

STOP SCENE: A loose Ferris wheel bursts through the gate of the zoo.

BY THE BOOK: Psalm 119:36, Romans 1:28, 1 Corinthians 10:23, Philippians 2:3, 1 Thessalonians 4:11

WHERE TO TAKE IT:

1. If there really were a "Do What You Feel" day, what would you do?

2. How would you describe your work ethic?

3. Does God care if we work hard or slack off?

4. What does 1 Corinthians 10:23 mean to you?

5. Do you do work around your house? If not, why not? If so, do you have to be told to do it?

6. Name the hardest-working person you know. How do you feel about that person?

7. What's your definition of the word *lazy*?

8. How does your life compare to 1 Thessalonians 4:11?

Visit www.skitguys.com or www.ysunderground.com for additional elements that might add impact to this clip, including the "Stevie and Danny Experiment 101: Excessiveness" video.

THE SIMPSONS

(COMEDY)

SEASON 5, EPISODE 97: "HOMER LOVES FLANDERS"

TAG: OKILY DOKILY, PLAY BALL!

THEMES: Giving, Kindness, Loving Others, Selflessness, Using People

THE SERIES/SHOW: The longest-running animated sitcom on prime-time television, *The Simpsons* is an irreverent view of an American family, led by lovable idiot Homer (voice of Dan Castellaneta) and practical housewife Marge (voice of Julie Kavner), who does her best to maintain order over town troublemaker Bart (voice of Nancy Cartwright), intelligent activist Lisa (voice of Yeardley Smith), and perennial baby Maggie, as well as a host of quirky friends, neighbors, teachers, animals, police officers, bartenders…and one killer clown. Life in Springfield, especially in the Simpson household, is a series of crazy adventures, ill-advised schemes, and the occasional heartwarming moment.

THE SCENE: Homer's neighbor Ned Flanders (Harry Shearer), who drives Homer crazy with his cheery, pious nature, has won tickets to the big football game between Springfield and Shelbyville. Homer really wants to go to the game but can't get tickets. Flanders offers to take Homer, and during the game the two run into a football player who happens to be a friend of Ned's. When the football player gives Ned the game ball, Ned gives it to Homer in a gesture of friendship.

START 0:07:40 STOP 0:08:37 (TOTAL CLIP TIME: 57 SECONDS)

START DIALOGUE: *(Stan Taylor)* Ned Flanders?

STOP DIALOGUE: *(Homer)* This is Ned Flanders, my friend!

BY THE BOOK: Proverbs 18:1, Philippians 2:3, 1 Thessalonians 2:8, 1 Timothy 6:18, James 2:8

WHERE TO TAKE IT:

1. Have you ever "used" someone you didn't like? Explain.

2. Do you believe Homer was wrong to go to the game with Ned—a person he normally can't stand?

3. What do you think about Ned's actions? What do you think his motivation was for sharing with Homer?

4. Can you name a time you shared something "big" with someone who wasn't really a great friend?

5. God calls us to share with those in need. How well do you answer that call?

6. How do you think God wants us to view and use our possessions? How well are you doing that?

7. Name someone you honestly wouldn't like sharing your stuff with. Why?

8. Name three things you can do this week to become more generous.

Visit www.skitguys.com or www.ysunderground.com for additional elements that might add impact to this clip, including the "Mr. Art Guy" video.

THE SIMPSONS

(COMEDY)

SEASON 5, EPISODE 95: "LISA VERSUS MALIBU STACY"

TAG: I'M TIRED OF LIVING LIKE A MODEL.

THEMES: Following the Crowd, Role Models, Status Quo, Stereotypes, Taking Action

THE SERIES/SHOW: The longest-running animated sitcom on prime-time television, *The Simpsons* is an irreverent view of an American family, led by lovable idiot Homer (voice of Dan Castellaneta) and practical housewife Marge (voice of Julie Kavner), who does her best to maintain order over town troublemaker Bart (voice of Nancy Cartwright), intelligent activist Lisa (voice of Yeardley Smith), and perennial baby Maggie, as well as a host of quirky friends, neighbors, teachers, animals, police officers, bartenders...and one killer clown. Life in Springfield, especially in the Simpson household, is a series of crazy adventures, ill-advised schemes, and the occasional heart-warming moment.

THE SCENE: Lisa is fed up with the trivial, sexist comments made by her Malibu Stacy doll, so she contacts the doll's creator to see what can be done. Together Lisa and doll maker Stacy create a new doll, Lisa Lionheart, a more realistic representation of women, complete with positive, affirming, and empowering sayings. Lisa Lionheart is on the shelves ready to be sold to countless young girls when the Malibu Stacy company sabotages the event by releasing a "new" Malibu Stacy and drawing all the attention.

START 0:20:32 STOP 0:21:40 (TOTAL CLIP TIME: 1 MINUTE, 8 SECONDS)

START DIALOGUE: *(Smithers)* I want it! I want it!

STOP SCENE: Lisa, Marge, and Stacy exit the store.

BY THE BOOK: Exodus 23:2, Matthew 7:13, Ephesians 5:6, 1 Peter 3:14, Revelation 22:11

WHERE TO TAKE IT:

1. What commercial products promote sexist attitudes toward women?

2. Name something you purchased because everyone else had one.

3. Have you ever taken a public stand against anything? Explain.

4. In your opinion, who are the best public role models today?

5. Just as the Malibu Stacy dolls distracted the girls, what distracts you from being the person God created you to be?

6. Exodus 23:2 says, "Do not follow the crowd in doing wrong..." Can you recall a time when you followed the crowd in doing wrong?

7. If you could create a doll for kids, what would you call it, and what would you want it to say?

8. What can you start doing tomorrow to become a better role model for those who look to you?

Visit www.skitguys.com or www.ysunderground.com for additional elements that might add impact to this clip, including Friendship Conflicts 6.6 from Instant Skits.

SURVIVOR: THE AUSTRALIAN OUTBACK

(REALITY)

SEASON 2, EPISODE 12: "NO LONGER JUST A GAME"

TAG: BROTHER, CAN YOU SPARE SOME RICE?

THEMES: Adversity, Destruction, Loss, Natural Disaster, Perseverance, Risk, Trials, Worry

THE SERIES/SHOW: *Survivor* is an extreme reality-based game show consisting of 16 American contestants who are dropped off in a remote location and left to survive on their own. The second season of *Survivor* takes place in the Australian Outback, pitting the Ogakor tribe of Kel Gleason, Maralyn Hershey, Mitchell Olson, Jerri Manthey, Amber Brkich, Keith Famie, Colby Donaldson, and Tina Wesson against the Kucha tribe of Debb Eaton, Kimmi Kappenberg, Michael Skupin, Jeff Varner, Nick Brown, Alicia Calaway, Rodger Bingham, and Elisabeth Hasselbeck. Each competitor must work with his or her tribe under brutal conditions to create shelter, make a fire, cook food, and survive the natural elements. After competing in games to win rewards or immunity, the participants gather at a tribal council to vote one person off the island. The last two people remaining on the island must face a jury of their former competitors, hoping that those votes will win them $1 million and the title of "Sole Survivor."

THE SCENE: After a reward challenge, a major storm tears through the Outback. On the way back to camp, the recently merged Barramundi tribe finds water rising over the path, forcing them to wait several hours to cross the water that has risen from the creek. The tribe members begin to worry about the location of the camp since they have placed it in a dry creek bed. When they finally get back to their camp, they're dismayed to see that most of the camp has been flooded. The rice, matches, and other important supplies have been swept away with the rolling current, leaving the tribe in awe of how quickly they could lose everything they had built.

START: 00:20:17 STOP: 00:23:49 (TOTAL CLIP TIME: 3 MINUTES, 32 SECONDS)

START DIALOGUE: *(Rodger)* Wow, how fast did that come?

STOP DIALOGUE: *(Elisabeth)* We have no food. We can't even fish with our new fishing rods. We haven't eaten all day.

BY THE BOOK: Genesis 7:19, Proverbs 11:4, Matthew 6:19-21, Romans 5:3-4, James 1:2-4

WHERE TO TAKE IT:

1. When hard times come, are you able to persevere, or do you give up easily?

2. If you were in the same position as the Barramundi tribe, would you have kept trying to get the rice, or would you have given up?

3. Have you ever been so determined to accomplish something that you put your life at risk to complete it? If so, what did you do?

4. In respect to your spiritual life, are you as determined to live righteously as you should be? Do you go after God and learn about God, no matter what ridicule you may endure?

5. How do you suppose the apostle Paul found his resolve to keep persevering? How could he keep preaching after being rebuked by so many people, being imprisoned time after time, and even being stoned almost to death?

6. What's the most difficult situation you've ever had to deal with?

7. If you lost everything you own, how do you think you would cope with it?

8. Discuss the following statement: "You never know God is all you need until he is all you have."

Visit www.skitguys.com or www.ysunderground.com for additional elements that might add impact to this script, including the "Here I Am, Lord, Send Me" reading.

SURVIVOR: THE AUSTRALIAN OUTBACK
(REALITY)

SEASON 2, EPISODE 2: "SUSPICION"

TAG: I'M TELLING YOU, I DIDN'T DO IT!

THEMES: Apologizing, Condemnation, Confrontation, False Accusations, Forgiveness, Judging Others

THE SERIES/SHOW: *Survivor* is an extreme reality-based game show consisting of 16 American contestants who are dropped off in a remote location and left to survive on their own. The second season of *Survivor* takes place in the Australian Outback, pitting the Ogakor tribe of Kel Gleason, Maralyn Hershey, Mitchell Olson, Jerri Manthey, Amber Brkich, Keith Famie, Colby Donaldson, and Tina Wesson against the Kucha tribe of Debb Eaton, Kimmi Kappenberg, Michael Skupin, Jeff Varner, Nick Brown, Alicia Calaway, Rodger Bingham, and Elisabeth Hasselbeck. Each competitor must work with his or her tribe under brutal conditions to create shelter, make a fire, cook food, and survive the natural elements. After competing in games to win rewards or immunity, the participants gather at a tribal council to vote one person off the island. The last two people remaining on the island must face a jury of their former competitors, hoping that those votes will win them $1 million and the title of "Sole Survivor."

THE SCENE: At the Ogakor camp, Jerri accuses Kel of smuggling in beef jerky and secretly eating it without sharing with the other tribe members. After getting everyone all worked up over the accusation, Jerri and Tina decide to look through Kel's backpack to see if they can find any evidence to back up Jerri's claim, but they aren't successful. As Kel is walking back to camp, he overhears the tribe members talking about him, so he confronts them. He denies Jerri's accusation that he was eating contraband beef jerky and even tries to prove his innocence and commitment to the tribe by offering to give the other tribe members two of the three razors he had brought as his "personal item." As it becomes obvious that Kel is innocent, the tribe turns to Jerri for the apology they feel Kel deserves.

START: 0:19:08 STOP: 0:23:56 (TOTAL CLIP TIME: 4 MINUTES, 48 SECONDS)

START DIALOGUE: *(Maralyn)* I am very disappointed at what happened five minutes ago. Jerri reported to the rest of us that she had seen Kel chewing a brown substance—what she thought was beef jerky.

STOP DIALOGUE: *(Maralyn)* Gee whiz, it's been four days, and things are heating up at our encampment.

BY THE BOOK: Psalm 34:13, Proverbs 4:24, Proverbs 12:17, Romans 8:1, 1 Peter 3:16

WHERE TO TAKE IT:

1. What would you do if you were accused of doing something you didn't do?

2. How would you feel about the person who accused you?

3. Could you forgive the person who accused you, even if he or she wasn't remorseful and wouldn't apologize?

4. Why do you think the tribe was so quick to believe Jerri without any proof to back up her claim?

5. Do you agree with Jerri that Kel's offer of the razors really proved his guilt, or do you suppose he was just trying to prove how much he wanted to be a part of the tribe?

6. If you know for a fact that someone has done something wrong, when should you share it with others?

7. Is it ever "okay" to search through someone else's things? If so, when?

8. How would you deal with someone who has hurt you, if that person doesn't feel he or she has done anything wrong?

Visit www.skitguys.com or www.ysunderground.com for additional elements that might add impact to this clip, including the "Blair, Which Project?" video.

SURVIVOR: THE AUSTRALIAN OUTBACK
(REALITY)
SEASON 2, EPISODE 2: "SUSPICION"

TAG: WHY DON'T YOU GO JUMP OFF A CLIFF?!

THEMES: Apprehension, Challenges, Conquering Fear, Peer Influence, Respect

THE SERIES/SHOW: *Survivor* is an extreme reality-based game show consisting of 16 American contestants who are dropped off in a remote location and left to survive on their own. The second season of *Survivor* takes place in the Australian Outback, pitting the Ogakor tribe of Kel Gleason, Maralyn Hershey, Mitchell Olson, Jerri Manthey, Amber Brkich, Keith Famie, Colby Donaldson, and Tina Wesson against the Kucha tribe of Debb Eaton, Kimmi Kappenberg, Michael Skupin, Jeff Varner, Nick Brown, Alicia Calaway, Rodger Bingham, and Elisabeth Hasselbeck. Each competitor must work with his or her tribe under brutal conditions to create shelter, make a fire, cook food, and survive the natural elements. After competing in games to win rewards or immunity, the participants gather at a tribal council to vote one person off the island. The last two people remaining on the island must face a jury of their former competitors, hoping that those votes will win them $1 million and the title of "Sole Survivor."

THE SCENE: The tribes retrieve their tree mail, which explains that their next reward challenge will require each person to jump from a very high cliff into the water. At the Ogakor camp, Rodger is apprehensive since he doesn't know how to swim well and isn't all that fond of heights. Rodger confesses that the challenge makes him nervous, but he will do his best to complete the challenge for his tribe members. When the tribes get to the cliff and look over the edge to see how far they're going to have to jump, they all feel somewhat nervous, but once the challenge begins, they all jump off. When it's Rodger's turn, he keeps his word and jumps, but has difficulty swimming and slows his team down. Rodger doesn't give up, however, and by giving the challenge his best effort, finds that he has gained the respect of his team.

START: 00:07:37 STOP: 00:13:34 (TOTAL CLIP TIME: 5 MINUTES, 57 SECONDS)

START DIALOGUE: *(Jeff and Alicia)* This is big time—it's a reward. *(Reading)* "A leap of faith is not for the skilled, just jump off the edge and try not to get killed. Like Sundance and Butch jump from a cliff, count on your friends while you're set adrift."

STOP DIALOGUE: *(Rodger)* I'm glad that's over.

BY THE BOOK: Psalm 27:14, Isaiah 41:10, 1 Corinthians 16:13, Philippians 2:3, 2 Timothy 1:7

WHERE TO TAKE IT:

1. Even though Rodger was afraid to jump off the cliff, what do you think helped him to finally do it?

2. Why do you think his tribe mates respected him for trying even though his lack of swimming ability caused them to lose the challenge? What do you think they would have done if he had refused to jump?

3. Why do you think we give in to our fears and miss out on many great experiences?

4. What would help you achieve something difficult, something you feared but knew you needed to do?

5. Share some times when you've found the courage to do something that was difficult for you.

6. What are some "cliffs" you need to jump off in your life?

7. In this situation the fact that Rodger gave in to peer pressure seemed to be a good thing. When is following the crowd the right thing to do?

8. How do you think Rodger would have responded if he had been injured jumping off the cliff?

Visit www.skitguys.com or www.ysunderground.com for additional elements that might add impact to this clip, including the "Comfort Zone" video from You Teach Vol. 1.

SURVIVOR: THE AUSTRALIAN OUTBACK

(REALITY)

SEASON 2, EPISODE 6: "TRIAL BY FIRE"

TAG: I'LL TAKE MY TRIALS MEDIUM RARE, PLEASE.

THEMES: Accidents, Compassion, Pain, Prayer, Trials

THE SERIES/SHOW: *Survivor* is an extreme reality-based game show consisting of 16 American contestants who are dropped off in a remote location and left to survive on their own. The second season of *Survivor* takes place in the Australian Outback, pitting the Ogakor tribe of Kel Gleason, Maralyn Hershey, Mitchell Olson, Jerri Manthey, Amber Brkich, Keith Famie, Colby Donaldson, and Tina Wesson against the Kucha tribe of Debb Eaton, Kimmi Kappenberg, Michael Skupin, Jeff Varner, Nick Brown, Alicia Calaway, Rodger Bingham, and Elisabeth Hasselbeck. Each competitor must work with his or her tribe under brutal conditions to create shelter, make a fire, cook food, and survive the natural elements. After competing in games to win rewards or immunity, the participants gather at a tribal council to vote one person off the island. The last two people remaining on the island must face a jury of their former competitors, hoping that those votes will win them $1 million and the title of "Sole Survivor."

THE SCENE: One morning while tending the Kucha tribe's fire, Michael is overcome by smoke and passes out right into the flames. He returns to consciousness almost immediately, but only after being badly burned. Show medics arrive quickly to dress Michael's wounds as his shocked tribe looks on. As the medics take Michael to the MedEvac helicopter to leave the camp for more treatment, the tribe encourages him with kind words of hope and friendship. Once the helicopter takes off, everyone breaks down emotionally, trying to make sense of the accident that just took place.

START: 00:28:23 STOP: 00:42:10 (TOTAL CLIP TIME: 13 MINUTES, 47 SECONDS)

START DIALOGUE: Michael screams in pain. *(Nick)* Are you okay?

STOP DIALOGUE: *(Tribe prays together.)* Amen.

BY THE BOOK: Psalm 106:4, Psalm 107:28-31, Romans 8:28, James 1:2-3, 1 Peter 1:6-7

WHERE TO TAKE IT:

1. Have you ever seen or been involved in a serious accident? How bad were the injuries of those involved?

2. What were your emotions during or after the accident? How did you feel watching the situation with Michael and the effect his accident had on his tribe?

3. Instead of just feeling bad for the people who got hurt in an accident, what could you do to help them?

4. Why is it that we eventually turn to God during situations over which we have no control?

5. Pain can cause us to be angry with God or to cling to God with all of our might. What do you think your reaction to God would be if an unexpected accident happened to you or your loved ones? Why do you think you would react this way?

6. Do you trust God and believe that no matter what kind of accident may come your way, God can bring good from it?

7. Why do you think God allows bad things to happen to people?

8. Discuss a time something "bad" happened to you and God turned it into something good.

BONUS CLIP: START 0:26:14 STOP 0:28:50 (TOTAL CLIP TIME: 2 MINUTES, 36 SECONDS)

SCENE 2: Season 2, Episode 17—"Back from the Outback"
After returning from Australia, Michael explains in an interview the impact his accident has had on his life, his family, and his relationship with God.

Visit www.skitguys.com or www.ysunderground.com for additional elements that might add impact to this clip, including "Psalm 139" from Best of the Skit Guys Vol. 1.

UGLY BETTY
(COMEDY)
SEASON 1, EPISODE 8: "FOUR THANKSGIVINGS AND A FUNERAL"

TAG: WHO NEEDS A FAMILY, ANYWAY?

THEMES: Dependence, Family, Generational Sin, Legacy, Taking Care of Each Other

THE SERIES/SHOW: There's nothing that Queens native Betty Suarez (America Ferrera) wants more than to land a job in the field of publishing. Her dream comes true when New York City fashion magazine publisher Bradford Meade (Alan Dale) catches sight of the plump, unstylish young lady applying for a job as an assistant. Not knowing what a kind, hardworking, honest person Betty is, Bradford chooses her for the job in order to curb the impulses of his playboy son Daniel (Eric Mabius), the new editor of *Mode*. It isn't long before Betty finds herself immersed in Daniel's life, all while withstanding the jokes and criticism of the stylish but shallow people around her, including sharp-tongued receptionist Amanda (Becki Newton), viciously jealous style editor Wilhelmina (Vanessa Williams), and catty assistant Marc (Michael Urie). Supporting Betty at home in Queens are her father Ignacio (Tony Plana), older sister Hilda (Ana Ortiz), and nephew Justin (Mark Indelicato).

THE SCENE: Betty and Hilda have learned that their father is an illegal immigrant who has been living in the U.S. for 30 years. Since his illegal status has thrown a wrench in the family dynamics, Betty and Hilda take it upon themselves to find a lawyer to help their father avoid deportation. While selling Herbalux at the gym, Hilda meets a lawyer named Leah (Debi Mazar) and recruits her to help Ignacio with his case. Before Hilda gives Leah a deposit, however, Betty discovers from a former client that Leah is a fraud, and warns Hilda not to give Leah the money. Believing that Betty is jealous because Hilda was the one to find a lawyer first, Hilda overrules her sister, and Leah predictably takes off with the Suarez family's money. At the end of the day, Betty and Hilda put aside their differences and remember what makes them a true family.

START 0:37:11 STOP 0:38:33 (TOTAL CLIP TIME: 1 MINUTE, 22 SECONDS)

START DIALOGUE: *(Hilda)* What are you doing?

STOP DIALOGUE: *(Hilda)* Maybe we're stronger than we think.

BY THE BOOK: Deuteronomy 5:16, Psalm 127:3, Proverbs 11:29, Jeremiah 32:18, 1 Timothy 3:4-5

WHERE TO TAKE IT:

1. What kind of family situation did your parents have as children?

2. How do you think their experiences affected the way you've been raised?

3. What kind of legacy are your parents passing on to you? What kind of legacy do you want to leave through your future family?

4. How much support do you get from your family? Could you make it without them?

5. Is there anyone in your world who absolutely depends on you? How does that dependence make you feel?

6. How far would you go to rescue a member of your family?

7. Have you ever needed to be rescued by your family?

8. Why is it so easy to argue with family members?

Visit www.skitguys.com or www.ysunderground.com for additional elements that might add impact to this clip, including "The Answering Machine" from Skits That Teach.

UGLY BETTY
(COMEDY)
SEASON 1, EPISODE 1: "PILOT"

TAG: ARE YOU SURE YOU BELONG HERE?

THEMES: Appearance, Character, Embarrassment, First Impressions, Judging Others

THE SERIES/SHOW: There's nothing that Queens native Betty Suarez (America Ferrera) wants more than to land a job in the field of publishing. Her dream comes true when New York City fashion magazine publisher Bradford Meade (Alan Dale) catches sight of the plump, unstylish young lady applying for a job as an assistant. Not knowing what a kind, hardworking, honest person Betty is, Bradford chooses her for the job in order to curb the impulses of his playboy son Daniel (Eric Mabius), the new editor of *Mode*. It isn't long before Betty finds herself immersed in Daniel's life, all while withstanding the jokes and criticism of the stylish but shallow people around her, including sharp-tongued receptionist Amanda (Becki Newton), viciously jealous style editor Wilhelmina (Vanessa Williams), and catty assistant Marc (Michael Urie). Supporting Betty at home in Queens are her father Ignacio (Tony Plana), older sister Hilda (Ana Ortiz), and nephew Justin (Mark Indelicato).

THE SCENE: Betty's first day at *Mode* is approaching, and her fashion-conscious nephew Justin wonders if she has anything appropriate to wear. Betty comes up with just the thing—a bright poncho with the word *Guadalajara* across the front. When the day arrives, Betty's poncho ensures a grand entrance into the *Mode* office, where she stuns sleek receptionist Amanda with her bright, frumpy appearance. Shocked but amused at the new employee, Amanda takes Betty to the conference room where a meeting is already in progress. Betty's attempt to enter the room unnoticed goes terribly wrong, to the delight of her new coworkers.

START 0:07:49 STOP 0:09:30 (TOTAL CLIP TIME: 1 MINUTE, 41 SECONDS)

START DIALOGUE: *(Amanda)* Hi, you the "before"?

STOP DIALOGUE: *(Daniel)* ...how excited I am to be working with a talented, dedicated staff.

BY THE BOOK: 1 Samuel 16:7, Proverbs 4:23, Proverbs 15:13, Galatians 2:6, Ephesians 4:32

WHERE TO TAKE IT:

1. Have you ever judged someone based on his or her looks? What did you learn from that experience?

2. Why does our society accept only those whose appearance fits a certain profile?

3. Have you ever been judged by what you wear? How did that make you feel?

4. What have you noticed about the cliques or groups at your school? Which group would you say you're a part of?

5. In Proverbs 4:23, it states that we should guard our hearts, for they are the wellspring of life. What do you think this Scripture means?

6. When it comes to the "heart," why do we judge people on what they look like instead of who they are?

7. Do you think your outer appearance matches who you are as a person?

8. What would people be missing if they didn't get to know the real you?

Visit www.skitguys.com or www.ysunderground.com for additional elements that might add impact to this clip, including the "World Versus Christian: Meet the King" video.

UGLY BETTY
(COMEDY)
SEASON 1, EPISODE 12: "SOFIA'S CHOICE"

TAG: SHE LOVES ME, SHE'S USING ME...

THEMES: Deception, Exploitation, Humiliation, Lies, Love, Using People

THE SERIES/SHOW: There's nothing that Queens native Betty Suarez (America Ferrera) wants more than to land a job in the field of publishing. Her dream comes true when New York City fashion magazine publisher Bradford Meade (Alan Dale) catches sight of the plump, unstylish young lady applying for a job as an assistant. Not knowing what a kind, hardworking, honest person Betty is, Bradford chooses her for the job in order to curb the impulses of his playboy son Daniel (Eric Mabius), the new editor of *Mode*. It isn't long before Betty finds herself immersed in Daniel's life, all while withstanding the jokes and criticism of the stylish but shallow people around her, including sharp-tongued receptionist Amanda (Becki Newton), viciously jealous style editor Wilhelmina (Vanessa Williams), and catty assistant Marc (Michael Urie). Supporting Betty at home in Queens are her father Ignacio (Tony Plana), older sister Hilda (Ana Ortiz), and nephew Justin (Mark Indelicato).

THE SCENE: Womanizer Daniel has fallen hard for the lovely, exotic Sofia (Salma Hayek), editor of the new magazine, *MYW*. Enjoying the fact that Sofia is unlike any woman he has ever dated, Daniel finally considers settling down and getting married. When he offers Sofia a ring, she accepts, but Betty makes the shocking discovery that Sofia's entire relationship with Daniel was research for her new magazine's cover story—"From Fling to Ring in 60 Days." During a TV appearance to discuss their engagement, Sofia unveils her article as well as her deception, returning Daniel's ring and humiliating him in front of millions of viewers.

START 0:33:57 STOP 0:35:58 (TOTAL CLIP TIME: 2 MINUTES, 1 SECOND)

START SCENE: Betty bursts through the studio doors.

STOP SCENE: Close-up of Daniel on the monitor.

BY THE BOOK: Psalm 12:2, Psalm 34:13, Ecclesiastes 7:26, 1 Corinthians 13:4-8, Colossians 3:9

WHERE TO TAKE IT:

1. Have you ever been humiliated in front of others?

2. When you look back at this memory, how does it make you feel?

3. What makes people do selfish and cruel things like Sofia did to Daniel?

4. Have you ever liked someone and realized you were being used? How did that experience affect you?

5. Why is it hard to turn away from watching the terrible things people do to each other on TV?

6. Have you ever had your heart completely broken? What made the experience so powerful?

7. Have you ever had someone turn out to be exactly the opposite of who you thought he or she was?

8. Why is it so dangerous to open your heart to someone? How is it possible to protect yourself from having your heart broken?

Visit www.skitguys.com or www.ysunderground.com for additional elements that might add impact to this clip, including "The Apple Skit" script.

UGLY BETTY
(COMEDY)

SEASON 1, EPISODE 5: "THE LYIN', THE WATCH, AND THE WARDROBE"

TAG: THE PRICE OF BEAUTY KEEPS GETTING HIGHER...

THEMES: Aging, Beauty, Body Image, Comparisons, Identity, Self-Esteem

THE SERIES/SHOW: There's nothing that Queens native Betty Suarez (America Ferrera) wants more than to land a job in the field of publishing. Her dream comes true when New York City fashion magazine publisher Bradford Meade (Alan Dale) catches sight of the plump, unstylish young lady applying for a job as an assistant. Not knowing what a kind, hardworking, honest person Betty is, Bradford chooses her for the job in order to curb the impulses of his playboy son Daniel (Eric Mabius), the new editor of *Mode*. It isn't long before Betty finds herself immersed in Daniel's life, all while withstanding the jokes and criticism of the stylish but shallow people around her, including sharp-tongued receptionist Amanda (Becki Newton), viciously jealous style editor Wilhelmina (Vanessa Williams), and catty assistant Marc (Michael Urie). Supporting Betty at home in Queens are her father Ignacio (Tony Plana), older sister Hilda (Ana Ortiz), and nephew Justin (Mark Indelicato).

THE SCENE: Desperate to find a special gown for an event, Wilhelmina commands *Mode* seamstress Christina (Ashley Jensen) to find her something fabulous to wear. Knowing Wilhelmina's measurements better than she does her own, Christina doctors a size-four gown so that Wilhelmina will think she can still wear her typical size two. When Wilhelmina demands the truth, Christina admits that the dress is a size four, and Wilhelmina begins to realize that the strict standards of beauty that she helped create have now turned against her.

START 0:30:59 STOP 0:31:54 (TOTAL CLIP TIME: 55 SECONDS)

START DIALOGUE: *(Wilhelmina)* Is this a size four?

STOP DIALOGUE: *(Wilhelmina)* I set the standards!

BY THE BOOK: Psalm 139:14, Proverbs 31:10, Proverbs 31:30, 2 Corinthians 10:12, 1 Peter 3:3-4

WHERE TO TAKE IT:

1. What is your idea of "beautiful"? How would you explain the concept to someone?

2. How close are you to the world's idea of beauty? How much do you worry about meeting that standard?

3. Do you judge others by a certain standard? How does that affect the way you treat people?

4. What do you think the word *beautiful* means to a guy? How are guys' and girls' opinions of beauty different?

5. Would you like it if others judged you as harshly as you judge yourself?

6. How do you think others see you? How much do you care about what others think?

7. Whose opinion matters most to you—God's, your friends', the media's, or your own?

8. How far are you willing to go to reach the standard of beauty you've set for yourself? What does the Bible say about beauty in 1 Peter 3:3-4? Do you agree with this statement?

Visit www.skitguys.com or www.ysunderground.com for additional elements that might add impact to this clip, including "Dennis" on You Teach Vol. 1.

TAG: MOM, NOTICE ME...OR ELSE!

THEMES: Acting Out for Attention, Communication, Parenting, Selfishness, Values

THE SERIES/SHOW: There's nothing that Queens native Betty Suarez (America Ferrera) wants more than to land a job in the field of publishing. Her dream comes true when New York City fashion magazine publisher Bradford Meade (Alan Dale) catches sight of the plump, unstylish young lady applying for a job as an assistant. Not knowing what a kind, hardworking, honest person Betty is, Bradford chooses her for the job in order to curb the impulses of his playboy son Daniel (Eric Mabius), the new editor of *Mode*. It isn't long before Betty finds herself immersed in Daniel's life, all while withstanding the jokes and criticism of the stylish but shallow people around her, including sharp-tongued receptionist Amanda (Becki Newton), viciously jealous style editor Wilhelmina (Vanessa Williams), and catty assistant Marc (Michael Urie). Supporting Betty at home in Queens are her father Ignacio (Tony Plana), older sister Hilda (Ana Ortiz), and nephew Justin (Mark Indelicato).

THE SCENE: After being kicked out of several boarding schools, Wilhelmina's daughter, Nico (Jowharah Jones), is in town and desperate for her mom's attention. In order to get it, Nico plots and stages a public protest to embarrass Wilhelmina, but it backfires when Wil plays right along and uses the publicity stunt to draw attention to an upcoming issue of *Mode* magazine.

START 0:34:01 STOP 0:36:23 (TOTAL CLIP TIME: 2 MINUTES, 22 SECONDS)

START DIALOGUE: *(Amanda) Wilhelmina!*

STOP SCENE: Scene fades to black.

BY THE BOOK: Exodus 20:12, Ezekiel 16:44, Micah 7:6, Colossians 3:20, 1 Timothy 3:4

WHERE TO TAKE IT:

1. Have you ever acted out in order to get attention from your parents? What did you do?

2. Why are some parents more attentive to their children than others?

3. What type of parent do you think you'll be? What values do you want to instill in your future kids?

4. In today's society, why is it that some adults act like children themselves?

5. What do you need the most from your parents?

6. In what area do you wish they'd give you more freedom?

7. Does money change the dynamic of a household and how a family communicates? Is it better for the family?

8. What's a good way to express your needs to your parents?

Visit www.skitguys.com or www.ysunderground.com for additional elements that might add impact to this clip, including the "What's It Going to Take, Dad?" script.

Hollywood would like to help you

Your students love movies, so why not utilize the movies they're watching to teach them valuable lessons. *Videos That Teach* products are for junior high, high school, college, and adult teachers and leaders. Each book contains 75 movie clip ideas from popular Hollywood films that illustrate a point or can be the point of an entire talk. *Videos That Teach* products are written by veteran youth workers Doug Fields and Eddie James and have been field tested by the authors.

Videos That Teach

RETAIL $12.99
ISBN 0-310-23115-9

Videos That Teach 2

RETAIL $12.99
ISBN 0-310-23818-8

Videos That Teach 3

RETAIL $12.99
ISBN 0-310-25107-9

Videos That Teach 4

RETAIL $12.99
ISBN 0-310-25662-3

visit www.youthspecialties.com/store
or your local Christian bookstore

 youth specialties